First Nations Peoples

SECOND EDITION

Pamela William

2004
EMOND MONTGOMERY PUBLICATIONS LIMITED
TORONTO, CANADA

Printed in Canada.

Edited, designed, and typeset by WordsWorth Communications, Toronto.
Cover design by Susan Darrach, Darrach Design.

We acknowledge the financial support of the Government of Canada through the Book Publishing Industry Development Program (BPIDP) for our publishing activities.

Library and Archives Canada Cataloguing in Publication

Williamson, Pamela, 1959–
First Nations peoples / Pamela Williamson and John Roberts. — 2nd ed.

Includes bibliographical references and index.
ISBN 1-55239-144-2

1. Native peoples—Canada—History. 2. Native peoples—Canada—Politics and government. 3. Native peoples—Legal status, laws, etc.—Canada. 4. Native peoples—Canada—Social conditions. I. Roberts, John A., 1944– II. Title.

E78.C2W495 2004 971.004′97 C2004-904002-2

Contents

Address by Chief Dan George in 1967

How long have I known you — Oh Canada? A hundred years? Yes — a hundred years — and many many years more. Today, when you celebrate your hundred years, Oh Canada — I am sad for all the Indian people throughout the land. For I have known you when your forests were mine. When they gave me food and my clothing. I have known you — in your brooks and rivers — where your fish splashed and danced in the sun, and whose waters said "Come and eat of my abundance." I have known you in the freedom of your winds and my spirit like your winds — once roamed this good land. But in the long hundred years since — the white man came — I have seen my spirit disappear — just like the salmon as they mysteriously go out to sea. The white man's strange ways and customs — I could not understand — thrust down upon me until I could no longer breathe. When I fought to protect my home and my land — I was called a savage. When I neither understood nor welcomed this new way of life — I was called lazy. When I tried to rule my people — I was stripped of my authority. My nation was ignored in your history text books. We were less important in the history of Canada than the buffalo that roamed the plains. I was ridiculed in your plays and motion picture — and when I drank your firewater — I got drunk — very, very drunk — and I forgot. Oh Canada — how can I celebrate with you this Centennial Year — this hundred years? Shall I thank you for the reserves that are left me of my beautiful forests? Shall I thank you for the canned fish of my river? Shall I thank you for the loss of my pride and authority — even amongst my own people? For the lack of my will to fight back? Shall I thank you for my defeat? NO — I must forget what is past and gone. On God in Heaven — give me the courage of the olden chief. Let me wrestle with my surroundings. Let me once again as in the days of old — dominate my environment. Let me humbly accept this new culture and through it rise up and go on. Oh God — like the Thunderbird of old — we shall rise again out of the sea — we shall grasp the instruments of the white man's success — his education — his skill — and with these new tools, I shall spirit my race into the proudest segment of your society: and before I follow the great chiefs that have gone before us — I shall see these things come to pass. I shall see our young braves and our chiefs sitting in the house of Law and Government — ruling and being ruled by the knowledge and freedom of our great land. So shall we shatter the barriers of our isolation. So shall the next hundred years be the greatest in the proud history of our tribes and nations.

Preface

Until 25 to 30 years ago, any history taught within the elementary and secondary educational system in Canada regarding the Americas began when Christopher Columbus landed in the New World in 1492. A cartoon expresses the irony of the term "New World": a little Native boy peers out from some trees at the three ships of Christopher Columbus — the *Niña*, the *Pinta*, and the *Santa Maria*. He says to his mother standing behind him, "Look, Mom, we've been discovered!"

Little history was presented about the numerous cultures that had roamed and survived as powerful groups or nations in the two continents that we now know as North America and South America before Columbus's landing. For the most part, information was imparted about Native ways of living before contact with Europeans in an abridged version that lumped Native groups together as one or a few homogeneous groups. The images written about Natives before and even after contact with "whites" tended to be romanticized — for example, "noble savage," "Indian princess" — or denigrating — for example, "bloodthirsty savages." As Daniel Francis notes in his book *The Imaginary Indian: The Image of the Indian in Canadian Culture*, too often the information given about Native peoples in the past was and even today continues to be stereotypical and often subtly or overtly demeaning. Have the stories written or told about Native peoples been accurate and/or objective? Given human nature and our propensity to see others, situations, and events from our personal cultural perspective, the view of indigenous people has often been presented in a biased manner, much to the detriment of the Native peoples whom the stories and descriptions claim to represent. James Frideres, author of *Native Peoples in Canada: Contemporary Conflicts*, said, "our historians have largely been Euro-Canadians: as a result, they have largely based their inferences on the same primary assumptions and therefore have presented similar views of social reality." He also wrote that "history is humanity's way of recording the past behaviour; historians are extremely susceptible to the political and social forces that govern while their histories are actually being written." Another example that reinforces the concept that the information passed down by European people regarding the indigenous populations is biased is contained in a quotation by the Shawnee Chief Chiksika, "When a white army battles Indians and wins, it is called a great victory, but if they lose, it is called a massacre" (Maynard, 1996).

To be fair, data and information about Native peoples have become more prevalent and available to the larger public within recent years. Native studies courses and programs are available at both the college and university level. So, has the availability of information regarding indigenous peoples of Canada led to a greater awareness of them and contributed to constructive changes to their situations? The response might be that while the quality of life has improved (longer life spans, lower infant mortality rates, etc.), conditions in which Natives live continue to be critical in socioeconomical, political, and legal areas. This book is intended to create a greater awareness of Native cultures and their issues. If one asks, "Why?" the counter question might be, "How can one develop a better understanding of Native peoples if one is unfamiliar with the diversity of their cultures and their issues?"

It is from this perspective that this book was created – to provide students with a greater awareness of and further sensitivity to Native cultures, their history, and the issues that they face. It was written as a resource for participants who will be or are working with Native populations. The book will provide the reader with links and references to other resources that provide descriptive and statistical information regarding Native peoples and issues. It is intended to provide a link connecting what is known about Native people historically and culturally, with their responses to the situations and issues confronting them today.

To achieve this, it is imperative that the reader be provided with an understanding of the foundation of all Native cultures – primarily, the underlying traditional belief in the importance of spirituality. Through acculturation and assimilation, many Native peoples have lost a number of their traditional ways and the question may be asked, "Why is it important to learn about Native spirituality if it is no longer accepted or practised by many Native peoples?" The response might be that, first, Native history cannot be discussed in any other context because spirituality is the basis upon which Native cultures exist. Second, the tenets followed by many Native organizations, many First Nation communities, and many Native peoples today are based on traditional concepts and practices. In 1997, the Union of Ontario Indians, a provincial Native organization, elected their leader in the traditional manner. Replacing the system of a secret ballot, the candidates were nominated for specific positions. Then each First Nations chief or representative clearly identified whom he or she supported by standing directly behind his or her candidate. The candidate with whom the representatives selected to identify themselves became their spokesperson. In turn, the candidate then had the right to negotiate and align himself or herself with other potential candidates until the person with the most representation was identified as the next leader. Many Native organizations also open their meetings with a smudge (a ceremonial cleansing) or a prayer.

To offer further insights into Native peoples and Native issues, this book will provide students with a basic introduction to Native "ways of being" in an effort to better understand the challenges that face Native peoples today.

The support of the Native Education Department at Sault College is acknowledged in the preparation of the first edition of this book.

Preface to the Second Edition

The second edition of *First Nations Peoples* updates the information found in the first edition and focuses on issues that have affected First Nations peoples at the turn of the millennium. The main source of new information is the 2001 census of Canada.

In 2001, 1.3 million people, or 4.4 percent of the population, identified themselves as aboriginal. This was an increase of 200 000 or 3.8 percent from 1996. Aboriginal peoples in Canada have been experiencing a steady increase in the rate of population growth. Since 1951, the Canadian population has doubled, while the aboriginal population has grown by seven times. About one-third of the reported aboriginal population is under the age of 14, and the median age is approximately 10 years younger than the non-aboriginal population. This suggests that the aboriginal population will continue to increase steadily in the forseeable future. We will examine the statistics relating to First Nations peoples specifically in chapter 6.

First Nations peoples continue to be overwhelmed by the larger society. There are, however, signs that aboriginal cultures are making a resurgence. As an example, approximately 25 percent of all First Nations peoples report that they can carry on a conversation in a Native language. While this is down from the 1996 figures, 8 of the 14 Native languages that have been documented show an increase. The issue of language will be discussed in chapter 2. Since culture is largely transmitted and sustained through language, the survival of Native languages suggests a survival of Native cultures.

January 2004

Introduction

CULTURE, SUBCULTURE, AND SYMBOLISM

The definition of culture is as varied as the number of sources. The *Longman Dictionary of Contemporary English* defines culture as "the customs, beliefs, art, music, and all the other products of human thought made by a particular group of people at a particular time." An extended definition is proposed by Laura Curley (2003):

> Culture is social and intellectual formation. It is the totality of socially transmitted behaviour patterns, arts, beliefs, institutions, and all other products of human work and thought characteristic of a community or population. It is a style of social and artistic expression peculiar to a society or class. Subculture, on the other hand, is a cultural subgroup, especially of a nation, differentiated by status, ethnic background, residence, religion, or other factors that functionally unify the group and act collectively on each other ... .
>
> There is another aspect of the word "culture" that warrants consideration; that is, the concept of indigenous culture. Many people can identify themselves with the terms Native North American, Native Canadian, First Nations, Aboriginal, and so on. These are rather generic terms that refer more to cultural groupings; that is, the whole group of smaller groups ... .
>
> To consider aboriginality in terms of diversity, we might consider the various differences between Algonquin, Cree, Ojibway, and the many other aboriginal Nations indigenous to Canada. The most important differences ... are language, territory, and customs. There are also cultural differences as whether a Nation is matrilineal or patrilineal. There are also subcultural differences within the larger indigenous cultural frameworks.

Aboriginal cultures have had an oral tradition for centuries which has preserved histories, legends, and traditions. Since the oral tradition is characterized by myth ("an unproved collective belief that is accepted uncritically") and symbolism, written history of aboriginal culture has to reconcile the differences between the written and the spoken word, making it difficult for anyone outside of the culture to understand the world view of that culture.

An understanding of symbolism is also important in understanding the aboriginal world view. Symbols dominate aboriginal culture, as they do the cultures of all human groups. The *Longman Dictionary of Contemporary English* defines a symbol as "something which represents or suggests something else, such as an idea or quality." To expand upon this definition, Tom Harpur (2004) explains:

> The truth is that symbols ... have everything to do with reality. To dismiss them as mere fiction or ... "the equivalent of lies" is sheer ignorance or lack of thought. Think about it. A wedding ring is of itself merely a circle of precious metal, but it's a symbol of a mighty reality. It is not of itself love, commitment, fidelity, marriage or family, but it can powerfully represent all of these and more. Its potency is far beyond all proportion to its commercial value or beauty.
>
> Life is surrounded by and only made possible by symbols and symbolism, from the world of advertising to quantum physics to the various grades of mathematics. More obvious even still is the fact of human language. All words are symbols. It's

> what they stand for and the power they represent and convey that's so important. Life is virtually impossible without them ... .
>
> American educator John Dewey, in *The Quest for Certainty*, writes: "The invention or discovery of symbols is doubtless by far the greatest single event in the history of man. Without them no advance is possible; with them there is no limit to intellectual development except inherent stupidity."

Aboriginal cultures cannot be understood without an understanding of the symbolism inherent in these cultures. Look at the creation stories in the first chapter of this book and note the rich symbolism there that helps to explain the origins of aboriginal peoples. Look at the non-scientific discussions about the origins of aboriginal peoples in the Americas, and try to get beyond the theories to the symbolism of the beliefs. It is only through symbolism that the aboriginal world view can be understood.

PART I

Native Cultures Prior to European Contact

CHAPTER 1

Origins of Native Peoples

Chapter Objectives

After completing this chapter, you should be able to:

- Recognize differences in oral creation stories among specific Native cultures.
- Explain the significance of oral traditions versus written methods of historical maintenance of Native cultures.
- Identify and compare scientific theories and myths concerning origins of Native peoples in the New World.
- Recognize the significance of the land to Native peoples based on the oral stories and Native traditional teachings.

INTRODUCTION

Many **Native** cultures have existed and, while a number have disappeared either partially or completely, most continue to thrive in contemporary North America. To develop a greater sensitivity to Native issues and Native peoples, it is imperative to examine both the common and the distinctive traits of Native groups. Collectively, Native **cultures** share a number of common traits and characteristics but, when you consider the six distinct Native cultural categories that can be identified in Canada alone, and that each group consists of many **subcultures**, the differences within each group represent a great diversity of cultures and subcultures. To examine each culture and subculture in Canada in this book would be too time consuming. Therefore, we will closely examine the three predominant Native cultures in Ontario — the Ojibwe, the Iroquois, and the Cree. We will study each group's traditions, cultures, and issues as a basis from which to develop a better understanding of the more general Native population.

Native
a term for First Nations peoples

culture
abstract values, beliefs, and perceptions of the world that are shared by a society and reflected in the behaviour of the people in a society

subculture
a group that has the general characteristics of a culture but also has distinctive features in their values, norms, and lifestyles

ORAL TRADITIONS

origins
the place or source from which things come; their beginning

To understand Native cultures, it is essential to begin studying them from their **origins**. As you go through this book, you will begin to understand why any discussion on Native origins is and will continue to be a contentious and lively debate.

Throughout time, we, as part of humanity, have attempted to answer questions about the mystery of our existence and to answer things that are beyond our control: "Where did we as a people come from? Who am I? Where will I go when I die?" These questions are part of our quest to understand ourselves, not only as people in a specific culture but as individuals. Understanding our past is usually an attempt to make greater sense of our future. Each culture has often responded with its own explanations — stories that are unique to that culture.

GROUP DISCUSSION

Given your personal background, provide a response to the following questions and discuss your answers with the group:

1. Based on what you have been told, where did humanity come from originally?
2. How do we as humans fit into the greater scheme of things — that is, nature, the universe?
3. What happens to us when we die?
4. From your discussions on origins, identify the influences that your culture, community, or family has had on your perceptions of human origins. How does your situation differ from the influences faced by Native peoples from their families, communities, and environment prior to European contact?

Discussion Note

You should be able to observe different responses in the class (these responses will be either religious, cultural, or scientific in nature). Prior to European contact, families and communities exerted tremendous influence on Natives' lives and perceptions. Similarly, our personal beliefs today often are heavily influenced by our parents, school, peers, teachers, media, etc. — a melding of all environmental influences.

Storytelling

oral tradition
information that is passed from one person to another by word of mouth

Storytelling, for example, is an **oral tradition** that is used by many cultures to pass down their knowledge of themselves to future generations. The question "Where did we come from?" has been answered by each culture in its own way. Storytellers are considered unique in that they have the power to mesmerize their audiences with their eloquence and their ability to spark the imagination. Because few Native tribes devised a written method of communication to keep records of their history, culture, and traditions, the oral tradition was vital, linking the past with the present and the future.

Native myths and stories possess some general characteristics. First, the stories reflect the culture and the area from which they came. Native peoples living near the ocean included components of the ocean in their stories of origin — for example, water, conch shells, and seaweed — while Native groups living on the plains described the prairie grass, the buffalo, and so on.

Second, the stories contribute answers to the meaning and order about the world in which the Native person lives. The Inuit, for example, tell a story about the meaning behind the Aurora Borealis (Northern lights). They believe that the Aurora Borealis are giants who are great hunters and fishermen who cannot be seen and are perceived to be friendly. Whenever they hunt animals or spear fish, they use their torches, which are seen as the Northern lights.

Third, the stories often include places that each culture deems to be sacred and describe how these places came to have **spiritual** significance. "Dreamer's Rock" on Birch Island, near Manitoulin Island, is considered a sacred place where Natives go to **fast** and receive a vision. Traditionally, it was believed that the vision received provided direction and a life purpose to the vision seeker.

spiritual
for Natives, to be spiritual is to respect and believe that all things in the world are alive and have a role in the land or "Mother Earth"

fast
from a traditional Native perspective, to fast is to abstain from food and, in some cultural practices, water; the intent of a fast is to purify one's self to connect with the spiritual world

Fourth, the stories are seen by Natives to be about living and real spirits — beings that are as alive as humans. *Webster's Ninth New Collegiate Dictionary* defines living as "to remain in human memory or record." Essentially, many of the stories are alive and have lived longer than any of us. In the oral tradition, the stories have been passed down from one generation to the next and have provided a legacy to each Native group.

Finally, the season in which the stories are told is important. For example, the Cree would only tell certain stories at specific times of the year. If stories based on fiction were told in the summer, the person risked having his or her life destroyed by lizards, which would come to suck his or her blood. If a person told such stories before the first snowfall of winter, toads or snakes would creep into his or her bed. The rationale for such punishments was that the spirits — that is, animal, human, plant, or other things in the natural environment — were offended by having the stories told at forbidden times and would take revenge on the storyteller. The Cree believed that Wisakecahk, a supernatural being and a trickster himself, had devised these punishments.

CREATION STORIES

As a predominant theme in Native stories of origin, the people either came in some fashion from the land in which they historically lived or the people moved from another territory — mythical or otherwise — to live within their historical territory. In both situations, the stories depict Native peoples dwelling in their traditional lands from the beginning.

While creation stories often overlap and possess many similarities, some are quite different. Look at the three creation stories in the appendixes to this chapter and compare them with the creation story of the Haida on the Queen Charlotte Islands of British Columbia. The Haida believe that a god named Quantz came upon a crying woman who was startled by his appearance. She sneezed, and sneezed out a small man. This man was housed in clam shells until fully grown and became the progenitor of the Native race.

The creation stories of the Ojibwe and Iroquois (Mohawk) describe their origins as being from their traditional lands. Many Natives in Canada believe they originated from "Turtle Island" or, as we know it, North America. Many Native elders claim that Native peoples were created and were intended to live in the Americas by the "Creator." The stories are philosophically true: Natives have been here for a long time. Coming from the land is part of Native heritage and involves a "belief in origin" rather than a "theory of origin."

GROUP DISCUSSION

Read the three creation stories of the Ojibwe, the Iroquois (Mohawk), and the Cree nations in appendixes 1.1, 1.2, and 1.3 at the end of this chapter. After you have finished, answer the following questions:

1. What values, beliefs, and other things are important to each culture based on what you have read in their creation story? Explain the reasons for your responses.
2. What role does the environment play in each story?
3. What role do the humans play in the stories (heroes? initiators? victims? subservients? etc.)

RELIABILITY OF ORAL STORIES

Most Native stories and myths have been passed down through the generations in the oral tradition. Native communities were thus able to establish continuity and stability among their people. How consistent and reliable are the oral stories?

The problem with oral tradition is that it *is* oral; without a written reference, the message may be forgotten, misunderstood, misinterpreted, or embellished. Educators believe that only about 12 percent of what is spoken during a lecture is remembered in a month's time, and this may apply to oral traditions as well.

In addition, oral traditions that were recorded raise the question, who did the writing? If the writer was not Native, misunderstanding could be expected. Morrison and Wilson (1988) give an example of a linguist analyzing an unwritten Native language who spent hundreds of hours listening to and recording stories from someone who had a speech impediment. It is unlikely that someone from a European cultural background could interpret Native cultural stories properly, when that culture is completely foreign to the interpreter; moreover, the story would likely go through a translator and would therefore be acquired third hand. An exception is the writings of the Jesuits, which appear to be faithful to the oral traditions.

Another problem is whether or not the stories should be interpreted as factual, mythological, or symbolic. The discussion in the introduction to this book points out the dangers in interpreting oral tradition from these perspectives.

Finally, Europeans question whether any of these creation stories really happened at all, or were merely superstitions devised by an uneducated (in Western terms) and unsophisticated culture looking for answers to phenomena in the natural world. Anthropologists and archeologists certainly look for the "truth" in scientific evidence rather than in unproveable oral tradition. For instance, some Native people believe in the theory of American genesis illustrated in the next section; however, the lack of scientific "evidence" to support this theory relegates it to the area of the superstitious for a person trained in Western science.

Native people might have reason to be cynical about the Western dissection of the oral tradition. Is the Christian tradition not based on symbol and allegory? Can anything be scientifically proven? Much is based on faith. Why, then, can Western scientists not accept the Native oral traditions that are also based on faith?

Despite what has been written here, there are many good reasons to accept the Native creation stories at face value. The Ojibwe refer to the stories as "gardens to the past" and the stories are believed to be very old. Stories told by Ojibwe, Cree, and Iroquois storytellers can be found in records and journals of the first European settlers, government officials, coureurs de bois, and others. The stories remain virtually unchanged. How can this happen?

Have you ever participated in a game called "Start a Rumour"? The premise is to initiate gossip that each member of the group is required to repeat, based on what the previous participant shared with him or her. When the last person repeats the tale out loud, significant differences from the original rumour can usually be heard.

Traditional Native stories were not passed down in such a spontaneous manner. Over the course of an individual's life, the stories were told and retold in teaching circles and other formal ceremonies. Often, it was the responsibility of a particular family to be the storytellers and to pass down the stories to the next generation. This responsibility was highly honoured and respected because the stories were important as both a historical and a cultural account of each Native group. To forget an element of a particular story would be similar to the medicine man's forgetting an important ingredient in a medicine that he was making for an ailing community member. Consequently, oral records were vital to the maintenance and continuity of each Native culture.

GROUP DISCUSSION

Read the following quotation and then respond to the questions:

> When I was young, my grandfather and I, almost every evening we would sit on the west side of the summer house and watch the sun set or we would sit on the east side and watch the colors cover the mountains. My grandmother would join us. Then they would tell me about the mountain, about the evening sounds, my grandfather would sing a particular song and tell me "remember it." I would try. Sometimes I would ask my grandmother to help me remember. She would only tell me that that was between my grandfather and me. She would not interfere and it was the same with what my grandmother was teaching — my grandfather did not interfere. And these things they were advising me, their thoughts were the same. (Beck, Walters, & Francisco, 1992)

1. Based on the quotation, in what manner did the child learn from his grandparents?
2. What were the differences of roles, if any, between the grandparents?
3. Can you provide similar examples of this method of learning from your own experience? Discuss with the class.

RECORDED HISTORY

Prior to European contact, few Native groups maintained permanent documents of historical information. One example of written communication can be found in

South American Native groups who created hieroglyphics (words depicted by pictures and symbols). In addition, the Iroquois created laws, provided teachings, and described historical events — for example, treaty signings — on wampum (shells placed in designs to depict meanings). The Ojibwe and Cree people wrote symbols and, later, script on birch bark to record their historical events, teachings, etc. As well, many different Native cultures created pictographs (ancient drawings or paintings on rock walls) or petroglyphs (a carving or inscription on a rock). Both of these methods were used to represent spiritual experiences — for example, dreams, visions, and prophecies — that were experienced by the medicine men and spiritual leaders. These are just a few examples of the recording methods used by the various North and South American Native groups. For the most part, however, the oral tradition was the means by which events, stories, and other cultural teachings and knowledge were handed down.

Most of what we know about Native peoples today was recorded by the Europeans — for example, explorers, government officials, soldiers, fur traders, coureurs de bois, settlers, and missionaries — who first came into contact with them. Their accounts have become the written history of the Native nations. Interestingly, in the 1600s, Jesuit priests recorded descriptive accounts about their contacts with the Native peoples whom they came to convert to Christianity. Stories told to them by the Natives during that time period, which they recorded, are consistent with stories that are told by elders and other Native storytellers today. The Jesuits' journals reinforce the premise that the stories are timeless or, at the least, very old.

GROUP DISCUSSION

Identify another culture that is unlike your own and with which you have some familiarity. Pretend that you are meeting people from that culture for the first time.

1. List what you consider to be strange about the mannerisms, behaviour, clothes, foods, and practices of this culture.
2. Consider the difficulties you would encounter while writing about a totally different culture. How would your views affect your ability to accurately interpret or describe the people about whom you are writing?

SCIENTIFIC EXPLANATIONS OF ORIGINS OF NATIVE PEOPLES

Science has developed a number of different theories to explain the presence of Native peoples within the Americas. The most commonly accepted theory today is that Native peoples populated the Americas by coming across on Beringia (see figure 1.1), a land bridge that was created between Alaska and Asia during the last ice age, about 10 000 to 25 000 years ago (*Canadian Geographic*, 1992). The dates are the most widely debated aspect of this theory. Vast ice sheets are believed to have frozen 5 percent of ocean waters about 12 000 years ago, uncovering the land bridge (*Discover*, 1993). For a period during this ice age, the glaciers melted, exposing a dry terrain that eventually became re-forested. During this time, the first Americans purportedly travelled to the Americas. From this entry point, the Amerindians travelled down the only passable route along the present border of Alberta and British Columbia. These first peoples were identified as land-based hunters who followed big game from Asia to North America.

Other research suggests that this corridor was impassable during the period identified, based on examination of glacial deposits, ancient pollen, and other organic materials located there. The period or periods in which this migration took place continues to be debated.

The Beringia land mass theory has been questioned further with recent discoveries. In 1996, items identified as primitive stone tools found in the Bow River Valley in Calgary suggest that prehistoric people may have lived in that area of Canada before the last glaciation (*Sault Star*, 1996). From the perspective of discovering life in the Americas, humans are recognized as latecomers to the North and South American continents.

A number of archeologists theorize that aboriginal peoples crossed over at repeated intervals, as opposed to a single mass migration, between 40 000 and 13 000 years ago. Again, the Bering land bridge appears to have the most support about how Native peoples came to live in the Americas. Many clues to this puzzle are speculated to lie under water in the Bering Strait. As evidence, coastal Siberia and coastal Alaska share a number of similarities in the types of animals, plant life, and peoples. Similar animal species include the wolf, brown bear, and sandhill crane (National Park Service, 1995). Similar languages, dental patterns, spiritual practices, and implements for hunting and daily living of the peoples on both sides of the strait are some examples of human similarities cited by ethnologists.

Recent archeological discoveries appear to support the Bering Strait theory. An article in *The Hamilton Spectator* in January 2004 ("America's Ancestors?," 2004) announced a significant discovery in Siberia:

> People who may have been ancestors of the first Americans lived in Arctic Siberia, enduring one of the most unforgiving environments on earth at the height of the Ice Age, said Russian researchers who discovered the oldest evidence yet of humans living near the frigid gateway to the New World.
>
> Scientists uncovered a 30,000-year-old site where ancient hunters lived on the Yana River in Siberia, some 500 kilometres north of the Arctic Circle and not far from the Bering land bridge that then connected Asia with North America … .
>
> Finding evidence of human habitation at the Yana site "makes it plausible that the first peopling of the Americas occurred prior to the last glacial maximum … ." The last glacial maximum was 20,000 to 25,000 years ago.

Another theory posits that early migrants may have come to the Americas by sea following the Pacific coast from Asia down the Americas. Some of the more persuasive evidence comes from South America. An early coastal entry may be argued from artifacts discovered in southern Chile and northeastern Brazil (*Canadian Geographic*, 1992). Although there are debates over whether the "tools" were made by humans or naturally created, the stones' flakes and shaped pieces of wood may suggest that an earlier occupation of the Americas occurred than was estimated.

In yet another theory, prehistoric groups with mariner backgrounds may have crossed the Pacific from Southeast Asia and settled in the Americas. Dr. D.C. Wallace, a geneticist, has been studying the mtDNA of Native Americans in an effort to identify when Native American groups entered the Americas. DNA can be used to trace

FIGURE 1.1 Beringia Theory of Migration

Migration began between 12 000 and 40 000 years ago at the retreat of the last ice age. The shaded area represents the Beringia land bridge between Siberia and Alaska.

the ancestry of groups or individuals. Wallace studied DNA located uniquely outside of the cell nucleus that is referred to as mitochondrion, hence the term mtDNA. From his findings, the results suggest that each continent has a different pattern of mtDNA mutations. American Natives have distinct mtDNA variations or mutations that native Siberians (found near the Bering Strait) appear to lack. However, this particular mutation pattern is also found in aboriginal populations in Southeast Asia and in the islands of Melanesia and Polynesia (Bishop, 1993), suggesting that Amerinds (original Americans) came by sea across the Pacific and not across the Bering Strait.

The theories regarding the origins of Native peoples are divergent. Nonetheless, they all suggest that Native peoples came from elsewhere. The verdict is still out on how Native people came to the Americas. The stories told by Native groups are equally dissimilar, although they also suggest a common theme: that they came from the Americas as the original inhabitants.

GROUP DISCUSSION

Contrast the essential differences between a "belief in origin" and a "theory of origin."

MYTHS CONCERNING ORIGINS OF NATIVE PEOPLES

A myth, according to *Webster's Encyclopedic Unabridged Dictionary*, is "a traditional or legendary story, usually concerning some superhuman being or some alleged person or event, with or without a determinable basis of fact or natural explanation." A myth is also "an unproved collective belief that is accepted uncritically."

Myth is common in the study of the origins of **aboriginal** people. While the Bering Strait theory is the most commonly accepted archeological theory, there are a number of myths that have their adherents.

aboriginal
original people of an area; may include First Nations, Métis, and Inuit

Theory of American Genesis

Archeologist Jeffrey Goodman proposed the theory of American genesis in 1981. While this theory is not scientifically popular, it does illustrate a belief system held by some North American aboriginal peoples.

Goodman's theory states that there was an evolutionary line that occurred in the Americas separate from that in either Asia or Africa, and that line developed into today's aboriginal peoples. In fact, Goodman argues that, rather than a Mongoloid people who came to the Americas by way of the Bering Strait, aboriginal people evolved here and migrated to Asia, displacing Neanderthal man in the evolutionary scale. Figure 1.2 outlines this possibility.

Goodman's theory is based on archeological evidence, which seems to indicate that humans were hunting on the North American continent as long as 100 000 years ago, far longer than the 35 000–40 000 years ago indicated in classical theories. Goodman also believes that certain cultural features, such as cave art, developed in North America before being transported to Europe.

Most archeologists don't accept Goodman's theories, even though the Theory of American Genesis is accepted by many **First Nations** people in North America, according to Harvey Longboat of the Brantford, Ontario, Six Nations. However, according to Brizinski (1993):

First Nations
refers to Indians as opposed to other aboriginal groups such as Inuit or Métis

> Many of Goodman's arguments are intriguing; they suggest new realms of possibility. If some of his interpretations are ever firmly supported by new evidence, certainly any arguments that Aboriginal people are relative newcomers can be set aside. Goodman does not reject the importance of the Bering Land Bridge, but he reverses the direction of the current; certainly ... his model is more credible than some of the other proposed alternative theories.

FIGURE 1.2 Theory of American Genesis: Evolutionary Scale

Dates	Events	Genesis theory
2.5 million BP[a]	Beginning of Pleistocene Era	
1.6 million BP	*Homo erectus* evolved from earlier forms, possibly in Africa	
1 million BP	Beginning of Ice Ages	
200 000–300 000 BP	Neanderthal Man (*Homo sapiens*) evolved and appeared in Africa, Europe, and Asia	
70 000 BP	Beginning of last Ice Age	
	Beginning of period when modern humans may have evolved, either once in a single location or more than once in Africa, Europe, and Asia	Evolution of modern humans in North America
	Bering Strait accessible for human migration	
35 000–40 000 BP	Spread of modern humans through inhabited world	Migration of humans from North America to Asia
10 000–12 000 BP	Distinctive fluted points appear in North America, signifying the adaptation of humans to a Paleo-Indian, big-game hunting way of life; spread of humans throughout the Americas	
	Ancestors of Athapaskan-speaking peoples may have entered North America	Distinctive adaptations arising in North America
	End of Ice Age; climatic changes	
5000–7000 BP	Domestication of plants for food in central and south Americas	
4500 BP	Egyptian civilization	
4000 BP	Paleo-Eskimo people spread across the Arctic	
3500 BP	Indigenous states (Inca, Maya, etc.) develop in Mexico, central and south Americas	
3000 BP	Woodland cultures, with agriculture and pottery, found in what is now the eastern United States	
2500 BP	Golden Age of Greece	
2200 BP	Rise of the Roman Empire	
2000 BP	Beginning of Christianity	
1000 BP	Thule people, ancestors of modern Inuit, come from Alaska and spread across northern Canada and Greenland	

[a] Before the present.

Source: Adapted from Brizinski (1993, p. 29).

External Migration

Some myths revolve around the theory that aboriginal people in North America came here from somewhere, other than across the Bering Strait. One myth holds that aboriginals were ancestors of the 12 Lost Tribes of Israel, who were banished from the Middle East in pre-Christian days and made their way to the New World. The Mormon religion maintains that there were two Israelite migrations to the Americas. Mormons believe the second migration, which took place 600 years before Christ, split the Israelites into two groups, one founding the ancient civilizations of Mexico and South America, the other establishing the aboriginal civilizations in North America. Another theory is that aboriginals are survivors of the lost continent of Atlantis. Yet another has aboriginals coming to the Americas from a lost continent in the Pacific Ocean called Lemuria or Mu.

Regardless of attempts to apply scientific "proofs" to these myths, it is generally accepted in scientific circles that aboriginal people in the Americas came from somewhere else. This does not, however, negate the importance of using myth to teach the origin and significance of culture and to help outsiders understand the nature of aboriginal beliefs.

NATIVE CONNECTION TO THE LAND

Native cultures share both a strong and tangible bond to "Mother Earth." To reiterate this idea in another way, Native cultures and their "ways of being" are strongly linked to the land. It is impossible to separate the basic premise of Native spirituality (the foundation of Native cultures) from its connection to the land. Understanding this point is essential, because in later chapters we examine a number of past and current issues relating to Native people and look at the role that land has played in these controversies.

The Medicine Wheel

How and why is the land so important to Native cultures? To explain the significance of the land, let's look at the teachings of the Medicine Wheel, shared by the Anishnaabe people (Ojibwe, Potowatomi, and Odawa). Teachings of the Medicine Wheel are orally passed down and provide the listeners with a means to understand and improve themselves and their world from a spiritual perspective. All the teachings — and there are many — given with the Medicine Wheel begin with the drawing of a circle. In the past, the teachings would be given on natural surfaces, such as the sand or a rock. Figure 1.3 depicts aspects of the Medicine Wheel.

The circle of the Medicine Wheel is cut into four segments of teachings. The belief that the Anishnaabe share with many other Native cultures is that the number four is an important number; many things and events occur in fours — for example, the four seasons (fall, winter, spring, and summer), four directions (north, south, east, and west), four elements (earth, wind, fire, and water), four aspects of the individual (emotional, physical, spiritual, and mental), four stages of life (childhood, teen, adult, and elder), four sacred medicines (sage, tobacco, sweetgrass, and cedar), and the four colours of humans (red, yellow, black, and white).

Each segment of the wheel relates to something in the environment. Another important aspect of the Medicine Wheel teachings is that all of the four aspects are interconnected. Therefore, each aspect is affected by what happens within all the other

FIGURE 1.3 Medicine Wheel

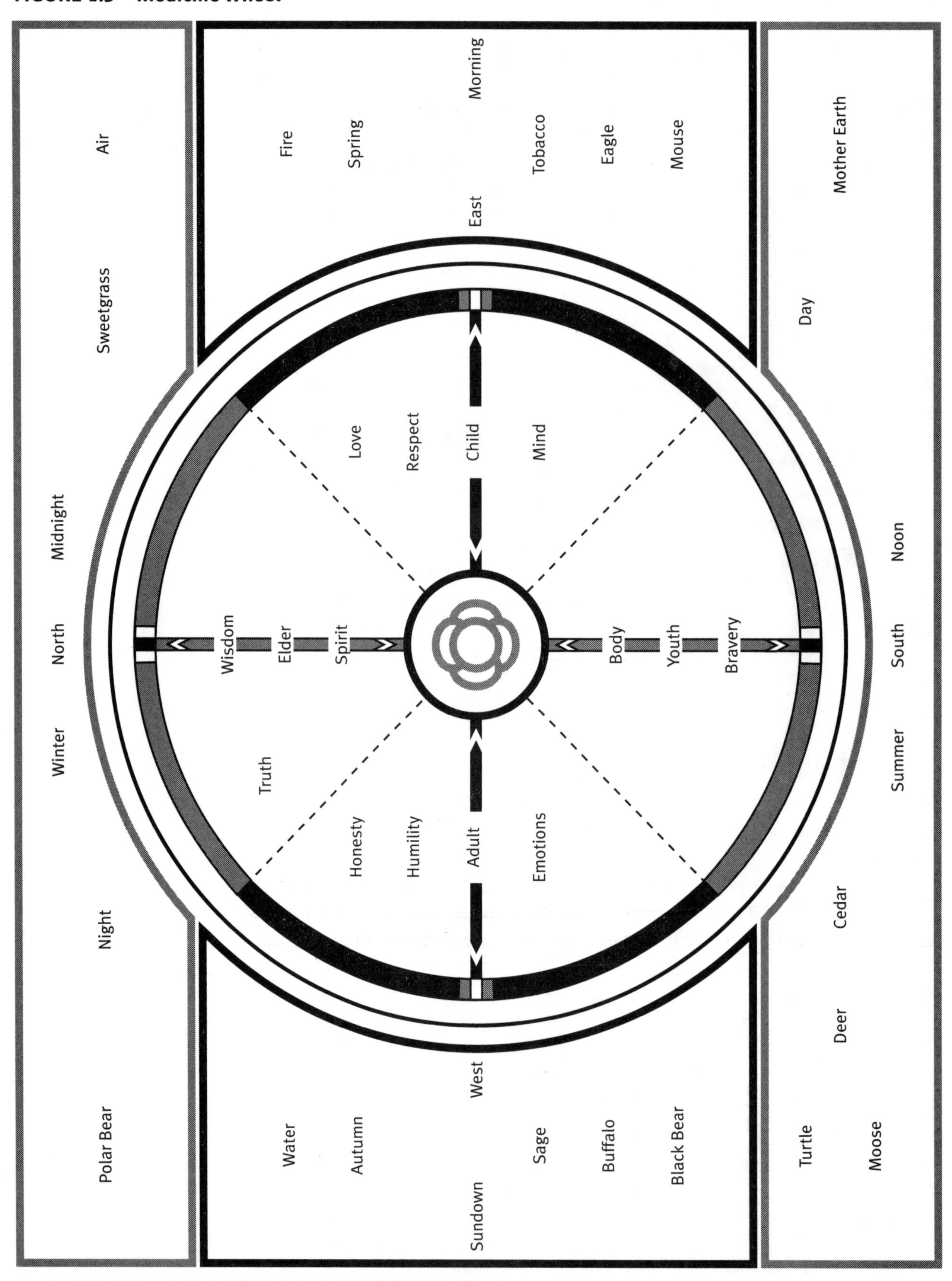

Source: Based on a drawing by Henry Angeconeb, 1998.

segments, and one aspect can influence all the others. For example, if the spring of a particular year is dry, then the summer and the food growing at that time may be affected. Without the spring rains, the crops would not have a chance to grow roots, thereby causing the plants to wither and die in the summer or the crops to be small in the fall. This explains the concept of **interdependence**. Keeping all four aspects in balance enables Mother Earth to be healthy and strong.

interdependence
being influenced or determined by another

As another example of the Medicine Wheel teachings, the earth comprises four main elements: earth, wind, fire, and water. If one of these elements is abused, then the other three suffer. For instance, when all of the trees are cut from an area, that site is at risk for a number of problems. Erosion may occur because the water washes away the nutrient-laden topsoil. The wind may blow down small trees, which no longer have the protection of a standing and mature forest. Fires also start easily in a bush that is dry, has a ground of dead foliage and branches from the trees that were cut, and has dry soil because of sun overexposure caused by the absence of larger trees. This teaching shows that interdependence and balance of the ecosystem is critical to the health of our natural environment. In chapter 2, we will discuss in more detail the interdependence of community members.

The significance of the land can also be noted in another Native teaching expressed in a number of Native creation stories. Humans, according to these stories, were the last to be created. As the final creation, they were given the roles of servants and caretakers for the rest of the creation, not lords or masters. This view directly contrasts to the Judaeo-Christian belief that humans have "dominion over the fish of the sea, and over the fowl of the air, and over the cattle, and over all the earth" (Genesis 1:25, King James Version). Another belief of Native peoples is in animate and inanimate spiritualism — that everything organic and alive or inorganic and inert has a spirit. The land is considered to be alive; it is Mother Earth and she speaks to humans in many ways. The attributes of the land are meant to be used and enjoyed with respect.

The Medicine Wheel provides another teaching that demonstrates the Native connection to the land. In the teaching of the four colours of humans, each group was given by the Creator different elements of Mother Earth for which to be responsible. The white people were given the task of taking care of the air. The black races were endowed with responsibility for the water. Yellow people were responsible for fire and, finally, the red race was given the obligation of taking care of the earth. As we will see in chapter 4, the land has become a preoccupation with Native peoples.

CONCLUSION

To end this chapter, it is important to remember that one of the main goals of this book is to help readers understand Native issues and see them from a new perspective. To quote James Dumont (1976):

> If we choose to try to understand and sensibly appreciate Native Culture, way of life and spirituality, we must be willing, first to accept that there is involved here a very special way of "seeing the world." Secondly, and a necessary further step, we must make an attempt to "participate" in this way of seeing. The implications are very serious. Quite simply, if we are not willing to consider another way of "seeing the world" and take it seriously, we limit ourselves critically or eliminate entirely our chances of ever really appreciating North American Native mythology and legend.

WORKSHEET

1. In point form, identify five terms that you have heard being used to describe Native or Indian peoples. Describe the labels you have identified as being either more positive or negative. In sentence form, based on the material covered in the book, explain factors that may have led to the images that have been perpetuated about Native peoples now and in the past. Identify two strategies that could be aimed at eliminating these negative stereotypes. (4 marks)
2. Explain what two factors substantiate the longevity of the stories told by Native peoples. (2 marks)
3. Based on the creation stories about the Ojibwe, the Mohawk, and the Cree in the appendixes to this chapter, answer the following:
   a. Identify three common themes shared by the three Native creation stories. (3 marks)
   b. Identify three distinct differences among the stories. (3 marks)
4. Outline the most commonly accepted theory of Native origins. Provide two cited sources to support this theory — for example, the Internet, books, and journals. (5 marks)
5. Explain the connection that Native peoples hold to the land and briefly describe a teaching in your own words that reflects this link. (3 marks)

TOTAL — 20 MARKS

KEY TERMS

aboriginal

culture

fast

First Nations

interdependence

Native

oral tradition

origins

spiritual

subculture

APPENDIX 1.1

The Ojibwe Creation Story

The Creation Story of the Anishinabe is told as the Seven Fires of Creation, each fire being an era of time. How long each one of these are, we don't know. But in the time that the universe knows, they are seen as eons of time: from the place before time even was, when there was only silence and emptiness and darkness and cold, to the time when earth was finally created and life was placed upon its surface.

Creation unfolded in seven stages. At first we are told that there, in the vast unknown, was only darkness, emptiness, silence and cold: forever and without boundaries. And that somewhere in that darkness a sound was heard. It was a sound like the rumbling of the thunder far in the distance. Then there was silence again. And after a long unimaginable silence, the sound was heard again, only this time it seemed closer. This is the way that the very beginning stage of creation is talked about: this sound that rumbled in the distance, which after each long period of silence would be heard again. Each time it would seem closer and closer, until, finally, after an incredible time of emptiness, a blinding flash of light and a deafening sound of thunder broke the long silence. What we are given to understand is that there must have been "Someone" listening in the darkness to that sound; that what was taking place was the first spark of creation, the first explosion of creative activity outward.

And then, it is said, there was a shaking and shimmering sound: a sound like the shaking of seeds in a gourd, that was heard everywhere in the darkness, without end. "What was that sound?" we are given to ask. What was shimmering and shaking? What were the seeds? Were they the thoughts in the Creator's mind? But, it is said, there was another sound. It was a different sound, a "feeling sound." That sound was before the shimmering shaking sound; it was before the rumbling sound that came from the distance. It was before all else. It was the First Thought that ever was. There in the centre of the darkness, that sound, that thought went out into the vast reaches of the unknown. Myriads of thoughts emerged from that first thought. They went on forever in the darkness, there being nothing out there for them to bounce back from. It was known, now, that a "place" had to be created to send the thoughts to.

In the centre there was also a rhythm that was generated from the very heart, the very centre where the Thought first emerged. That heart throb was at the centre of all that was to be. It moved out from the centre in great rhythmic circles, filling the whole empty void. And so it was that even in the beginning, creation could not take place by Thought alone, but by the Heart also. The rhythm of the heartbeat permeated the vastness. The thoughts, touching on the darkness, left a star; the star world was born. By that First Heartbeat and by that First Thought, the universe was created. The First Thought is the first fire of creation.

In the second fire of creation, he created a light. He built, in the darkness, a fire: the first fire, the Creator's fire which is the Sun. He did this to light up a place in the darkness, in order to create. Around that fire, he traced out a great circle and assigned the four directions.

Then he created another light: the Moon whom we know as grandmother, universal woman, the Grand Woman of the sky world. In completing this, he had created

Sun and Moon, the twinness of all reality. Without this twinness, nothing else could unfold; so in all things, there must be a twin in order for life to evolve to completion in the created reality. All of wholeness is composed of twinness. In all things we see the twin. Sunrise and sunset, day and night, the two sides of being — even in you there is the twin. The unfolding of twinness is the third stage of creation, and is thus known as the third fire.

Then, in the fourth stage of creation — having created the star world with his thoughts, having built the first fire in the universe (the Sun), and having created the twin (Grandmother Moon) — the whole of the universe was established and he caused the universe to move according to the four directions. This was the fourth fire: the First Movement. And so we know that at the fourth stage in the development of all things, in the unfolding of all life, is the beginning of movement, measured by the principles of the four directions. When you have four, then you can have movement, complete in itself and moving upon itself.

Then he gathered all of what he had created and encapsulated it in a shape and form. It contained the inspiration and the motivation to be. It was possessed of intention and it held in its blueprint the two sides of the whole (the twinness that makes up life itself), and the four quarters of the whole which is the cause of movement. By taking those things and shaping them into a form, he created a Seed, the germ of life. For every form, every shape, every being that would be given life, he shaped a seed, within which was the potential to be. And this was the fifth fire of creation: the First Seed. The Creator took his seed-thoughts and shaped them into the kernels of life essence, to be reflected back to him as creation's every possibility when planted in fertile ground.

Having completed this, he began to make a place to send the seeds of life. And so he created this Earth. Four times he tried, and the fourth time he completed this world, as we know it today. When he had completed the Earth and caused the waters to flow in and around the Earth (being her veins and arteries to carry the force of life itself), then all the birds carried the seeds to spread them over the ground. Then he saw the beauty of the one that he created: the Earth. In this Earth was absolute perfection, absolute wholeness, harmony and balance. All was complete in her, the First Earth, the First Woman. And in having created her, his creation was complete. Then he took from his first fire, the Sun, and placed a heart at the very centre of that first woman, making her first mother: the Mother Earth. She was a mother with a heart, who gave birth to all the seeds of life, her children. This is the sixth fire of creation: the Creation of Earth. Out of his desire to create, to bring into actuality his seed-thoughts, to make them real, to cause his thoughts to bounce back to himself, he therefore created this world. Out of love he created her. Out of his desire to create the most beautiful place to give the finest expression to his thoughts, so he created the Earth. And so it was that out of kindness he created all of creation; that this Earth was made as a place for the highest expression of the Grandfather's desire to manifest and embody his dream: to give shape and form, intention, purpose and meaning to the spirit of life itself.

In the seventh fire of creation, he wished to create "one in his own image." And so he took of the very created world itself: he took four parts of the Earth and he shaped those four parts together, and formed a physical being. Then of his own thoughts, as many as the stars in the universe, he placed within that first being. With this was given the ability and the capacity to hold the very thoughts of the Creator himself. The Creator gave to the first human being his own thoughts. Then he caused to beat in his breast that same heart-throb, that same rhythm that was there is the beginning at the centre of the universe. And so it is said that he caused to beat in the heart of Anishinabe the very rhythm, the very heartbeat, of the creator himself. Then he breathed into him his first breath, the spirit of life itself. And so, being made of this earth, the physical vessel, and being vested with mind, heart and spirit, he was lowered to the Earth: the First Human Being, made of Earth and Sky.

Though knowing that he was formed outside of the created realm, he could see that he belonged to the Earth, being made of the very stuff of the earth. He desired to be a part of this creation, as all other beings of creation were already seen and felt to be, as he saw them moving about on the earth. It was his every desire to be at home in this world, part of that same great harmony and great balance of life.

He wanted to be a part of the great beauty of this creation, seeing how everyone of this creation was kind and was true to the ways that they were created, and shared in the harmony of life. Seeing the strength and the beauty of all that was created on this earth, he too desired to be as this earth and as the creation. And so it is said that, as he approached the earth, he pointed his toes so that somehow, if at all possible, when he touched down on this earth, he would not stamp out or crush even the smallest blade of grass, the tiniest flower, the smallest living creature that crawled upon the earth. Rather, he would come down in and amidst the creation and be a living and loving, harmonious part of all that is.

This is how Original Human Being touched down upon the Earth. That is how the First Human Being, Anishinabe: the red colour of man, met his Mother the Earth for the first time. And from that time, Anishinabe has always known his Mother and has always felt his relationship to the family of creation. Being vested of spirit, the human being comes from the Creator from whom he receives his purpose and intention to be. Through him flows, always, his life force that comes directly from the Creator. But with him also comes his desire to be a part of this life and to give the finest and highest expression to his being in this world. He has within him this desire to reflect back to the Creator the Creator's very intention in making him in his image and lowering him to this earth.

And so, in these seven stages of creation, we see how all things began for Anishinabe, the red colour of the human being. From the first thought, to the final image, the creation unfolded. In the same way, all of creative activity continues to evolve, through those seven stages of unfoldment. It is still reflected in all life activity, even to this day. Everywhere we should be able to see this. From the first thought of bringing new life into this world by couples who come together, bringing about conception itself; to the first division of that first cell, the twinness of life — of man and woman coming together inside the womb; to the first movement within the womb; to the development of that seed to its fullest potential as a human being; so life unfolds according to the original blueprint of creation. It follows that a good and kind and caring place to be in this world is fashioned — the family, the earth-home, and it is completed by the emergence of the first image — the actual human being emerging from the womb to place footsteps for the first time upon the earth. In this natural creative process itself we can see the seven stages of unfoldment. And so it is with all of life.

Even from the first thought in the darkness of our confusion and of our unknowing, to the conception of an idea, we put together the darkness with the light and we create the twinness of our reality. In our thoughts, in our mind, we can cause the idea to move within ourselves and then introduce that idea to others so that they too can be a part of the movement and inspiration it causes. From there we create a seed of change within ourselves and around ourselves. We then make a way; make a place to plant that seed within ourselves and within others, for all to benefit from. The final result is a new being, a realized dream, that is created from this first thought that emerged in the darkness of our own mind. From the idea to the reality is again reflected the process of creation.

And so, Anishinabe can see that if he knows his creation story, if she knows her creation story, they know also how all of life moves. They can know how life comes to be. All of life is a creative process that began in this original way and continues in the same way in all aspects of our life. In all places and all facets of creation, and creative activity, these seven stages are reflected.

Source: Based on the Teaching of the Seven Fires of Creation by Edward Benton-Banai, rendered as a poem entitled "The Seven Fires of the Ojibway Nation" and published in *The Sounding Voice*, Indian Country Press, 1978.

APPENDIX 1.2

The Mohawk Creation Story

In the beginning, Onkweshona, or man-like beings lived in the regions above. They knew not what it was to weep or to cry; sorrow and death were thus unknown to them. And the lodges of the man beings were long, each one belonging to a large family of one clan. In one of these lodges there was a woman who had been born with strong power. People such as this were called down-fended, because they slept on beds of soft down. They were always kept separated from the other people of the lodge, and were cared for in their childhood by an older aunt or uncle.

One day, when the people were out from the lodge, a young man entered and went up to this down-fended woman. She reached out and touched the man, and he died. The woman later became pregnant. She gave birth to a daughter called Aientsik meaning Fertile Earth. Aientsik was a beautiful girl. She grew up in the lodge of her mother, and became a healthy young woman. One day, however, she became ill. Sickness was not known to the man beings, and they did not know what to do.

Aientsik went out one night and sought the spirit of her father, who told her to do the following: "*You must travel, my daughter, to the village of Tharonhiawakon, or, He Who Holds Up The Sky. In his village that is lit by the Tree of the Standing Light, you will become his bride. On your way to the village of the Tree of the Standing Light, you must be careful not to touch any man or animal that comes along. When you come to the stream between our village and that of Tharonhiawakon, you will find a maple log. Cross the stream on this log, and accept help from none.*"

Aientsik left the village of her people and traveled to the east. When she arrived at the stream she found the log, but before she could push the log out into the water, Kahahserine appeared. Kahahserine is the White Dragon of the Fire Body; he sometimes appears in the sky as a falling star or meteor. Kahahserine asked Aientsik if she would like some help. She became frightened and ran back to the village of her people. Just as she left the stream, however, Kahahserine reached out and barely touched her on the shoulder.

When Aientskik arrived back in her village she sought the spirit of her father. He asked if Kahahserine had touched her, and she replied no. He then advised his daughter to return to the stream and to make way for the village of the tree of the Standing Light. Aientsik arrived at the stream's shoreline again, and finding the maple log where she had left it, crossed over to the other side.

When Aientsik arrived at the village of the Tree of Standing Light, she sought out Tharonhiawakon, the chief of the upper world.

She said, "*I have come to be your bride.*"

He said, "*Good, make me some supper.*"

When night time came, Aientsik slept on one side of the lodge, and her new husband slept on the other. They did not really know each other that well, and they did not think that it was such a good idea to start having children right away. Even so, Aientsik became pregnant.

This disturbed the mind of Tharonhiawakon and he had a dream. Tharonhiawakon brought the people of his village together to try to guess the meaning of his dream. None of the people could correctly guess the dream of the Sky Holder.

Finally the White Dragon of the Fire Body stepped forward and said, "*Tharonhiawakon, surely your dream means this, that your new wife is pregnant, and you are upset. Therefore, you will take the Tree of the Standing Light by the trunk, you will uproot this tree and place your wife by the abyss. Once done, you will push her through the hole, and cause her to leave the upper world forever.*"

When Kahahserine had finished speaking, the chief of the upper world said, "*Yes, what you have said is true, and by correctly guessing the meaning of my dream, it is as if you have made it come true.*"

Tharonhiawakon then uplifted the Tree of the Standing Light, he placed his pregnant wife at the edge of the hole, and he pushed her through into the space below.

Aientsik fell. Below her, all of the universe was water. The animals of the water saw her falling, but because the sky was blue, as well as the water, they did not know if she was falling from the sky, or coming up from the bottom of the lake. All of the water animals had an argument about this. The otter said that she was coming up from the bottom of the lake. The beaver agreed, as did the muskrat. The geese and the ducks, however, said that she was falling from the sky. They flew up, and breaking the fall of Aientsik, let her rest upon their backs, and brought her gently down to the surface of the water.

In the meanwhile, a great turtle came up out of the water and volunteered to be a resting place for Aientsik, or Fertile Earth. The beaver, otter and muskrat each dove to the bottom of the lake to try to bring up a mouthful of earth to place on the back of the turtle. The beaver failed and died. The otter failed and also died. But the muskrat was successful. He placed the mud on the back of the turtle and Aientsik was laid down to rest.

When she woke, there was a fire next to her and a pot of corn soup. The back of the turtle had grown in size and it was visibly continuing to grow with every passing minute. Aientsik stood up on the earth, and walked about it, helping in the process of its creation. Every day when she returned to her resting place, there was a fire and a supply of corn, or some beans or squash for her to eat. Corn, beans and squash have been known ever since as the three sister-providers of the Mohawk people.

Aientsik was pregnant and she soon gave birth to a daughter, Tekawerahkhwa, or Gusts of Wind. This daughter grew to maturity, and she soon was a beautiful young woman. One day when Tekawerahkhwa was sleeping in the forest, a man being came up to her and passed two arrows over her stomach. One arrow was tipped with flint, the other was a maple shaft. Tekawerahkhwa became pregnant with twins.

After about nine months, these twins inside the womb of Tekawerahkhwa had an argument. One of the twins, called Thawiskaron, or Flint, said that the best way to leave their mother was by way of the armpit. The other twin, called Okwiraseh, or Young Tree, said that the best way to leave was by between the legs. Before the argument was over, Thawiskaron pierced through his mother's armpit and killed her. Okwiraseh followed, but was blamed for killing his mother by Thawiskaron and his grandmother, Aientsik.

Aientsik asked, "*Who is it that killed my daughter?*"

Thawiskaron replied, "*It was Okwiraseh, my brother.*"

Okwiraseh was then thrown into the forest by his grandmother and left to die. This was not to be his fate, however. Tharonhiawakon came down from the upper world and taught his grandson how to live in the forest. He taught him how to hunt and to make foods from the things that grew about the earth. He taught him to make the lodges of the Onkweshona and the method of preparing the bark.

Finally, Tharonhiawakon told Okwiraseh to prepare the earth for the coming of man. He told him to make the earth beautiful and to provide growing space for the three sister-providers, corn, beans and squash. Okwiraseh made the Indian corn to grow tall and strong. His brother Thawiskaron took the corn, however, and threw it into the fire, burning the ends and ruining that part of the ear. Okwiraseh rushed to take the corn out from the fire, however and saved the rest of the ear. Notice today how the end of the corn cob cannot be eaten. Okwiraseh made all of the rivers to run in two directions. This way, men would be able to travel in any direction without having to paddle against the current. Thawiskaron changed the course of the rivers and made them all go just one way. He then threw large boulders in the river in order to prevent river travel. Fortunately, Okwiraseh caught Thawiskaron in time and stopped him, but many of the rivers were made difficult to travel on.

Okwiraseh asked the various animals how they would avoid man in the hunt. When the animals responded, Okwiraseh changed that part of the animal that was going to have a special advantage over man. One day, as Okwiraseh was going about the earth, he noticed that there were no animals about. The animals had all been captured by Thawiskaron and locked into a cave. The season began to grow cold and there was no game. Okwiraseh located the cave where the animals had been confined and he moved back the rock holding them in and freed them.

After this last confrontation with his brother Thawiskaron, Okwiraseh decided to challenge his brother to one last contest of strength. He asked his brother to meet him on top of a mountain deep within the Adirondacks and play a game of dice. The winner was to rule the day, the loser the night.

When Thawiskaron showed up for this contest he brought his own dice. Okwiraseh agreed to use the bowl of Thawiskaron, but not his dice. He called to the sparrows and asked them to give their small heads for dice. The sparrows agreed.

Okwiraseh then called out to all of creation and said, "*All you things that are alive, send me your power now so that I may be victorious, and so that all of you may live!*"

The animals and the plants, the very earth itself sent power to Okwiraseh and he proved victorious over his brother.

Thawiskaron was banished to the lower world, below the turtle and the earth, only to come out at night when it is dark and cold. Okwiraseh assumed preeminence on the earth during the day, and continued to carry out his grandfather's command to continue the work of making the earth a better place for the coming of man.

One day while traveling about the earth, reviewing all of his work, Okwiraseh came across a man being, Hatowi, blocking the path through the forest.

Hatowi said, "*What are you doing here, walking about my creation, as if you had made it?*"

Okwiraseh responded that he, Okwiraseh, had done all of this work of creation, and not Hatowi. The two men agreed to a contest of strength. Whoever could make the mountains to move was the agreed upon maker of the earth, and the loser was to serve the winner for all the rest of time. Hatowi went first. He commanded the mountain to move, but of course the mountain stayed in its place.

Then Okwiraseh said, "*See, you are not the maker of the earth and all here present that it contains.*"

Hatowi said, "*But you too must try to make the mountain to move.*"

Okwiraseh replied, "*Yes, but first you must turn around and close your eyes.*"

Then Okwiraseh ordered the mountain to move right up behind Hatowi. The mountain moved, and when Hatowi turned around, he slammed his face right into the side of the mountain. This twisted his face and bent his nose all out of shape.

Hatowi was so surprised that he asked Okwiraseh not to hurt him. Hatowi promised to help mankind for all times. Hatowi said that if men would address him as Grandfather, burn tobacco to him and carve his image in the trunk of a living tree, he would cure men of their sicknesses. Okwiraseh agreed to this and the great curing ceremony of the False Face was born, dedicated to Hatowi, the Great Twisted Face.

Now the earth was ready for the habitation of man. Okwiraseh went to the shore of a great lake and he scooped up a handful of deep red earth.

He said, "*Now I make what shall be called Onkwehonwe, or human beings. They will dwell here on this floating island.*"

So as soon as he had stopped talking he began to make them, and he made the body of the human being. He took up the earth and he said, "*This earth that I take up is really alive. It is alive, just as the earth is alive. So too, the body of the human being that I make shall also be alive.*"

Then at that time he made the flesh of the human being.

As soon as he had completed it he thought for a while then he said, "*This will result in a good thing that I have done, and these human beings will continue to have life, just as I myself am alive.*"

Now at this time he took a portion of his own life and he gave it to the human being; so also he took a portion of his own mind and he enclosed it in the head of the human being; so also he took a portion of his own blood and enclosed it in his flesh; so also did he take a portion of his power to see and enclosed it in the eyes of the human being. Now at the time too, he placed his breath in the body of the human being and man rose and stood on the earth.

Then Okwiraseh said, "*Truthfully I have made your body and you now walk on the earth. Look now and see what the earth contains.*"

At this time, as if by magic, Okwiraseh showed all of the earth to man. He showed him the valleys nestled in between tall gracious mountains. He showed man the clear waters of Iroquoia and the waterways of all the various territories. Okwiraseh showed man the beauty and wealth of the forest, the numerous medicines and foods. Fields of the three sisters growing to maturity were pointed out to man. Large trees bearing nuts and fruits, bushes of berries and the large bounty of game were shown to man. Likewise, the spots where flint could be found, calimite for making pipes and bowls, deposits of clay and sand for pottery, and smooth pebbles for beadwork. All of these things were shown to the first man and he was made very glad.

Then Okwiraseh said, "*I have given you all of this that the earth contains. It will continue to give comfort to your mind. I have planted human beings on the earth for the purpose that they shall continue my work of creation by beautifying the earth, cultivating it and making it more pleasing for the habitation of man.*" Now then man saw his elder brother the Sun come up and cause the daylight on the earth to be warm. And man saw that the earth was beautiful, that the sky was beautiful and he was glad.

Okwiraseh told man that all of this was for man, and all that man had to do was to feel good and to be thankful for all of the gifts of creation. Man must never take the good things of the earth for granted, he was told, or else they would be taken away. Man must always be thankful.

But men forgot these words of the Creator, and they lost respect for the earth and for each other. Because of this the Creator returned to earth, and instituted the four ceremonies of thanksgiving. These four thanksgiving ceremonies would bring the people together at harvests, mid-winter, when the maple runs from the trees, and at the time of green corn. Human beings were told that they had forgotten to be thankful, and so they were ruining the earth. These four ceremonies helped them to remember.

Even with the four ceremonies, however, there was fighting amongst the people. And so the Creator returned to earth again, this time to inspire the formation of the Great Law of Peace and the founding of the Five Nations Confederacy.

Source: http://www.schoolnet.ca/aboriginal/7gen/creation-e.html.

APPENDIX 1.3

The Cree Creation Story

So then, I shall tell another legend. I'll tell a story, the legend about ourselves, the people, as we are called. Also I shall tell the legend about where we came from and why we came ... , why we who are living now came to inhabit this land.

Now then, first I shall begin.

The other land was above, it is said. It was like this land which we dwell in, except that the life seems different; also it is different on account of its being cold and mild [here]. So then, this land where we are invariably tends to be cold.

So that is the land above which is talked about from which there came two people, one woman and one man, ... they dwelt in that land which was above. But it was certainly known that this world where we live was there.

Now then at one time someone spoke to them, while they were in that land of theirs where they were brought up. He said to them, "Do you want to go see yonder land which is below?"

The very one about which they were spoken to is this one where we dwell.

"Yes," they said, "we will go there."

"That land," they were told, "is different, appears different from this one which we dwell in, which you dwell in now during your lifetime. But you will find it different there, should you go to see that land. It is cold yonder. And sometimes it is hot."

"It fluctuates considerably. If you wish to go there, however, you must go see the spider at the end of this land where you are. That is where he lives."

The spider, as he is called, that is the one who is the net-maker, who never exhausts his twine, — so they went to see him, who is called the spider. So they reached him.

Then he asked them, "Where do you want to go? Do you want to go and see yonder land, the other one which is below?"

"Yes," they said.

"Very well," said the spider. "I shall make a line so that I may lower you."

So then, he made a line up to, — working it around up to, up to the top.

"Not yet, not yet even half done," he said.

Then he spoke to them telling them, better for him to let them down even before he finished it the length it should be.

Then he told them, "That land which you want to go and see is cold and sometimes mild. But there will certainly be someone there who will teach you, where you will find a living once you have reached it. He, he will tell you every thing so you will get along well."

So he made a place for them to sit as he lowered them, the man and the woman.

They got in together, into that thing which looked like a bag.

Then he instructed them what to do during their trip. "Only one must look," he said to them. "But one must not look until you have made contact with the earth. You may both look then."

So, meanwhile as they went along, one looked. At last he caught sight of the land.

The one told the other, "Now the land is in sight."

Again the first told the other, "Now the rivers are in sight."

They had been told however, that "if one, ... if they both look together, before they come to the land, they will go into the great eagle-nest and they will never be able to get out and climb down from there."

That's where they will be. That's what they were told.

Then the one told the other, "Now the lakes are in sight. Now the grass."

Then they both looked before they arrived, as they were right at the top of the trees. Then they went sideways for a short while; then they went into the great eagle-nest. That's where they went in, having violated their instructions.

Now then, "Look down!"

They saw all the creatures which live there on earth: the bear, the caribou, the beaver, the otter, the fisher, the mink, the wolverine, the lynx.

Then at one point the caribou walked there right across [from them].

They said to him, "Come and help us. We cannot get down."

The caribou said to them, "No. I never climb up."

He showed them what his hooves looked like.

Then the lynx came by.

So once more they said to him, "Come and help us."

"Never, ... not effer am I climbing," said the lynx.

He was not telling the truth. He was deceiving them. Then away he went again past them.

Then the bear arrived.

So he said to them, ... they said to him, "Come and help us."

The bear didn't listen for long; but then he started to get up on his hind legs to go and see them. Also another one, the wolverine as he is called. They made one trip each as they brought them down.

But the bear was followed by those people.

That was the very thing which had been said to them, "You will have someone there who will teach you to survive."

This bear, he taught them everything about how to keep alive there.

It was there that these people began to multiply from one couple, the persons who had come from another land. They lived giving birth to their children generation after generation. That is us right up until today. That is why we are in this country.

And by-and-by the White People began to arrive as they began to reach us people, who live in this country.

That is as much as I shall tell.

Source: Ellis (1995).

CHAPTER 2

Native Cultures Prior to European Contact

Chapter Objectives

After completing this chapter, you should be able to:

- Understand the role of archeology in Native history.
- Identify common cultural characteristics among Natives in Canada.
- Identify the six Native cultural groups in Canada.
- Compare and contrast the six Native cultural groups based on their geographic location in Canada.
- Identify and note differences among the 11 Native linguistic groups in Canada.
- Identify the similarities and differences between specific subcultures among the Woodland Indians.

INTRODUCTION

In this chapter, we examine Native prehistory from c. 70 000 years ago to the arrival of Europeans. This examination is conducted by looking at the role archeology played in the study of Native prehistory. Following this, the ways of Native cultures prior to European contact are discussed. By the end of the chapter, the reader should be able to understand that there were many Native cultures and languages, some of which no longer exist. Despite their differences, Native cultures share many similarities. This chapter should give you a better understanding of the Native world view and why it became the basis for many future clashes with European cultures.

DEMOGRAPHICS

Natives did not keep census records, and those who study Native populations have been able to make only rough estimates of early Native populations. Modern census figures estimate there were only about 100 000 Natives in all of Canada at the beginning of the 20th century. Since these numbers were recorded after the arrival of the Europeans, it has been estimated that the Native population could have been as many as 300 000 persons before contact. The population of the Hurons of central Ontario, for instance, was reduced by one-third to one-half by European diseases during the 1630s and 1640s. It is estimated that the mortality rate for Natives stood at 90–95 percent between contact and the 20th century. Scientific evidence puts new estimates of the Native population at as many as 3 million persons before contact.

BIOLOGICAL TRAITS

In general, First Nations peoples share some common biological traits. Most have straight, black hair, type O blood, adult lactose deficiency, distinctive dental patterns, and sparse body hair. In recent years, it has been thought that Native people also have a high incidence of diabetes, as compared with non-aboriginal populations. However, these distinguishing biological traits are of considerably less importance than cultural characteristics that distinguish the various Native groups from each other.

THE ROLE OF ARCHEOLOGY IN NATIVE STUDIES

Natives used legends, songs, and personal example to pass on their culture from generation to generation. They did not write history books or keep diaries or official records. As Native people before 500 CE were without a system of reading and writing, except for pictographs, the main source of information about these people comes from archeological studies.

Archeology can be defined as the science of what humans have left behind, according to C.W. Ceram (1971). Archeology provides clues to the understanding of ancient cultures. Archeologists have provided time periods for each Native culture, from the earliest, known as Paleo-Indian, to the Terminal Woodland, which existed at the time of the arrival of Europeans (see figure 2.1).

The Archaic Period (7000–3000 Years Ago)

The Paleo-Indian cultures were followed by those of the Archaic peoples, who were divided into two groups, the Laurentian and the Shield cultures.

The *Laurentian Culture*, a distinctive Indian culture, emerged in southern Ontario, probably as a result of nomadic migrations from the United States. This culture was to last almost 3000 years, until the introduction of agriculture. The people were mainly big-game hunters, but they supplemented their diets with smaller game, fish, berries, and wild plants.

Religious beliefs included sprinkling their dead with red ochre, and placing tools and ornaments of stone, bone, and native copper, and sometimes shells from the Gulf of Mexico and the Atlantic coast, in their graves to indicate trading contacts with these areas.

The *Shield Culture*, found in central and northern Ontario, shared some cultural traits with the Laurentian Culture, while developing others that were quite distinct. Caribou and fish were the staple diet, probably supplemented by smaller game and waterfowl. The Shield people likely used birchbark canoes and may have used snowshoes.

FIGURE 2.1 Native Cultures Time Periods

Years ago	Period	The environment	The people
70 000	Wisconsin Glaciation	Cold Glacial ice covers most of Canada and Northern United States	People migrate from Siberia to Alaska across the Bering land bridge (Several waves beginning 40 000 years ago?) Populate most of the New World
12 000	Paleo–Indian	Cool Glaciers begin to melt Tundra-spruce parkland	People enter Ontario as the glaciers melt Big-game hunters and gatherers
7000	Archaic	Warmer White pine and oak Many big-game animals become extinct	Less nomadic (seasonal camps) Hunting and gathering (smaller game, fish, edible plants) Many new tools (i.e., woodworking)
3000	Initial Woodland	Similar conditions to Archaic	Pottery, bow and arrow introduced from the south Extensive trade networks Burial mounds (east-central United States and southern Ontario)
		2000 years ago	A Point Peninsula band begins to occupy Serpent Mounds circa 200 BCE Serpent Mounds abandoned as regular camp circa 400 CE
1000	Terminal Woodland	Similar conditions to Archaic	Ontario Iroquois cultures Corn agriculture Population explosion Warfare, large palisaded villages and longhouses Mass graves (in pits) Only intermittent occupation of Serpent Mounds Arrival of Europeans

Source: Ceram (1971), in Ontario Ministry of Education (n.d., p. 17).

The Woodland Period (3000 Years Ago to Contact)

The culture of the Woodland period was similar to that of the Archaic period, except that the Woodland people developed the use of pottery. Since this is the closest prehistorical period to contact, and since the population was expanding, more artifacts were preserved than from the Archaic period, making modern-day knowledge of this period more complete than for previous periods.

The *Initial Woodland period* lasted from 3000 to 1000 years ago. Five different pottery types have been discovered, aiding archeologists in the study of the period. Five corresponding cultures have been identified:

1. *Laurel* culture in the forests of northern Ontario.
2. *Point Peninsula* culture in eastern Ontario.

3. *Saugeen* culture in southern Ontario.
4. *Princess Point* culture in southwestern Ontario.
5. *Hopewell* and *Meadowood* cultures in southwestern Ontario and midwestern United States. One characteristic of the Hopewell culture was the use of burial mounds, one of which, the Serpent Mound, is near Rice Lake, southeast of Peterborough, Ontario.

The *Terminal Woodland period* lasted from 1000 years ago to the time of contact and marked the emergence of the Algonquian-speaking people of northern Ontario and the Iroquoian-speaking people of southern Ontario.

COMMON CHARACTERISTICS OF NATIVE CULTURES IN CANADA

Historically, the Native peoples living on the land now known as Canada were diverse populations characterized by many distinct ways of living and being within their traditional territories. Conversely, they also shared and continue to share many characteristics. Among these are their strong connection to the land and a respect for the animals upon the land, their interdependence as community members, their respect for all community and family members (from the children to the elders), the importance of symbols, and their spirituality. These distinctions and similarities are part of what has been defined as "culture" and "subculture" in the introduction to this book.

Natives all shared the ability to adapt to their environments. The eastern Woodlands people adopted agriculture as well as hunting and fishing. The Iroquois, for instance, harvested the Three Sisters (corn, beans, squash) as staples of their diet. In the Maritimes, the Beothuk and Mi'kmaq fished in the ocean and engaged in seasonal rounds of hunting. North of Lake Superior, the Cree and Ojibwe engaged in seasonal movement to follow the beaver, moose, and fish.

Connection to Land and Animals

As discussed in chapter 1 and illustrated in the teachings of the Medicine Wheel, many Native peoples have maintained a strong connection to the land, which represents their way of life and spirituality. Mother Earth, Turtle Island, or whatever culturally specific term that they use to identify the land is more than a geographic territory; it is considered a sacred, living entity with its rhythms and cycles tied to the destiny of humankind. As also mentioned in chapter 1, Natives have their sacred places where it is believed that power, wisdom, or the meaning to one's life can be accessed from the spiritual world. In Ontario, many sites are seen by Native peoples as sacred — for example, the petroglyphs near Peterborough, the Sleeping Giant island in Thunder Bay, and Manitoulin Island (home of G'chi Manitoo).

GROUP DISCUSSION

Identify sites in your area that are considered sacred or special to Native people and explain why.

Traditionally, Native peoples have had great respect for the land, which kept them strong as nations. They were highly sensitive to the rhythms of their environment, and necessity or survival dictated that they heed the signs in their natural surroundings. This view has formed the basis for many of the present-day land claims, as well as the hunting, fishing, and logging disputes.

Native peoples have also maintained a strong connection to the animals in their environment. Each animate and inanimate thing in the physical world is believed to have a spirit and therefore must be treated with respect. Aboriginal people shared a view of humans and their place in the world called animism. All of creation is alive. Offerings of tobacco were made to ensure safe passage, and rituals were performed before hunting to guarantee a successful hunt. Traditionally, when a deer is killed for food, the hunter lays down tobacco at the site of the killing as a sign of respect and to thank the spirit of the deer for giving up its life to nurture the man, his family, and, possibly, his community. It is believed that if the hunter offended the deer spirit, he could potentially face great difficulty in obtaining meat or food in the future or face other trials. This is done in reverence to the **Seven Grandfathers**' teachings about respect and humility. This was in direct contrast to the European world view. Today, many Natives across Canada continue to rely on wild game and fish for their food and their livelihoods. The incorporation of traditional spiritual practices in hunting and fishing varies with each Native culture or individual.

Seven Grandfathers
traditional Native teachings describing the qualities of wisdom, love, respect, bravery, honesty, humility, and truth by which a person's life should be guided

Interdependence of Community Members

As seen in the last chapter, traditional Native peoples believed that everything on Mother Earth was interdependent. This notion also extended to the relationship between humans. In the traditional Native society, people lived together cooperatively, relying on each member of the community and his or her skills for basic survival. Consequently, the roles played by each member were valued and respected. Such a society is referred to as an **egalitarian society**.

egalitarian society
the belief in human equality, especially with respect to social, political, and economic rights and privileges

Understanding the concept of interdependence requires further familiarity with the environment in which the people lived. The area we know as Canada was and is essentially in a northern climate. The growing and gathering seasons are short and, for the Natives living here, most of the spring, summer, and fall were spent gathering roots and berries, drying fish and/or meat, sewing clothes from hides, mending or making tools, etc., to prepare for the winter. The Native groups that survived and thrived in this climate were hardy people. Since Native people could be found in all regions of the North, they developed amazing abilities and skills to survive in this portion of the continent.

The necessity of relying on others for basic survival created Native societies that believed in the intrinsic worth of all its community members. Each member of the community was given the same respect. An individual's age, gender, or position did not give him or her any greater importance than another person. Everyone in the community shared the responsibilities of daily living. The women were responsible for managing activities related to food gathering and preparation, home activities, and child rearing. Men primarily managed activities that related to fishing, hunting, politics, and warfare. The children helped the women gather food and run errands for elders, and they slowly began to assume their gender roles. Often, these gender roles were taught to the children by the elders and other community members. The elders performed gender-related tasks for as long as they could. In addition, they were seen as the community mediators, storytellers, teachers of children, and community advisers.

Further evidence that egalitarian values were important can be observed in the decision-making process in which all decisions were reached by consensus. As well, the community shared meat and food. When a hunter returned with meat, it was distributed within the community. This practice still exists in many Native communities, where they hunt and depend upon wild game for sustenance.

With the exceptions of certain seasons and milder climate regions, the people of the North were predominantly hunters of game who lived a few meals away from starvation, especially in the winter. Living in a world where survival might have depended on the cooperation of all community members, it was critical that each member performed his or her roles and responsibilities – from the youngest to the oldest. Everyone had responsibilities for obtaining food and shelter, for ensuring protection from the environment and, sometimes, from other tribes and cultures, and for maintaining the emotional, mental, physical, and spiritual balance that promoted strong and thriving communities. As mentioned earlier, each member of the community – from the children to the elders – had clearly defined duties and roles to play. With the exception of the Inuit and a few other Native cultures (and only under severe conditions), Native peoples did not intentionally eliminate their elders, the infirm, or the handicapped.

Because each member was integral to the survival of the community, the harshest punishment that could be imposed on an individual was banishment, which was rarely enforced and used only as a last resort. Inevitably, being expelled from the community meant death for the individual. Each member of the community was clearly aware of the consequences of any unacceptable behaviour and, as a result, communities experienced relatively few contraventions of community norms and taboos by their members.

Since every person was important, respect was given to all community and family members. No one role was seen as any less important than another. As mentioned, children had vital responsibilities and were considered as important as any adult or elder. Seen as the future of the community, they had more autonomy than European children of this era. During the 1600s to 1800s, when contact between Europeans and Natives steadily increased, European children were often deemed chattels. Men were the heads of households, and children and wives were under the dictates of the "master of the home." Men could beat their wives and children to death with little or no legal consequences. The notion "spare the rod and spoil the child" was common.

Native children, during this same period, were given specific duties such as gathering food, running errands for elders, hunting for small game, and other gender-related duties. They received respect for their roles and were expected to carry out their responsibilities. However, they did not "belong" to their parents but were part of a bigger collective of extended family members and/or community members. It was common for children to live with a grandparent or an aunt or uncle for a period, perhaps when their parents were unable to meet the needs of the child or when their grandparents were in need of help. At the end of this time, the children would return to the home of their parents or choose to remain where they were.

As well, each member of the community assumed responsibility for children's care and learning. When the Europeans first observed the relationship between Native children and their families, they wrote about Native children being spoiled and given excessive freedom. The differences in parenting styles were no more apparent than when the government and the churches set up residential schools for Natives. The intent was to "civilize" them and to teach Native children discipline (implying perhaps that they did not have any).

Trade

Natives were heavily involved in trade. Different groups produced a variety of products and traded their surplus to other tribes. The Iroquois, for instance, were able to establish themselves as intermediaries to facilitate the transfer of goods from one area to another. Figure 2.2 indicates the extent of Native trade patterns before contact.

GROUP DISCUSSION

1. Discuss the positive and negative effects on Native children of having to assume community responsibilities at an early age.
2. Note the similarities and differences between Native and North American children today.

Spirituality

Native spirituality is an integral and central component of Native cultures. As discussed in chapter 1, to be spiritual is to be connected to all life and things on earth and to recognize and nurture such connectedness. As the Medicine Wheel in chapter 1 teaches, each person is composed of four components: physical, emotional, mental, and spiritual. These four qualities are interrelated and interconnected, which means that if one aspect is not addressed, then the other aspects are adversely affected, creating imbalance or ill health. For example, if a person does not get enough sleep (physical), he or she cannot function mentally, emotionally, or spiritually in an effective manner. The person becomes irritable (emotional), unable to concentrate in class (mental), and unable to respect and/or care for his or her surroundings or for other people (spiritual). One cannot enjoy life to the fullest when one omits nurturing all life areas. In order to become a **holistic**, healthy person, the individual must ensure that each of these areas of his or her life is worked upon and cared for equitably. This teaching merely provides an understanding of the integral role that spirituality plays in Native cultures.

holistic
balance in all aspects of life — emotional, physical, mental, and spiritual

GROUP DISCUSSION

1. Examine yourself from a holistic perspective. Which area of your life do you think needs work and care to maintain a healthy balance?
2. At a societal level, would you say that our society values all four aspects equally? Cite examples to support your answers.

FIGURE 2.2 Trade Patterns Prior to European Contact

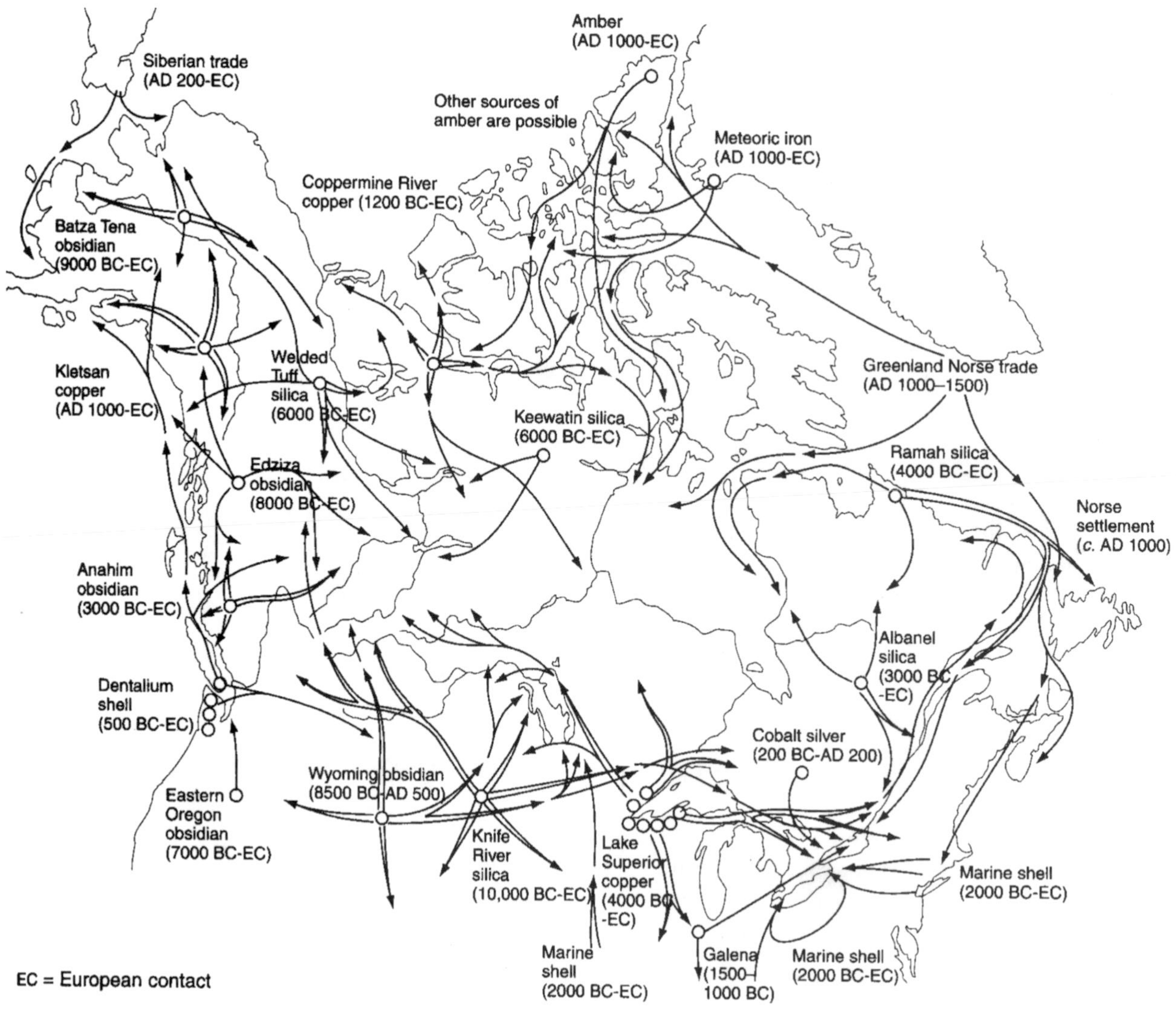

EC = European contact

Source: Adapted from Harris (1987, plate 14).

Traditionally, Native spirituality played such an integral role in the lives of Native peoples that anything and everything surrounding the people had spiritual significance. Dreams and visions were sacred and seen as windows to the future. Interpreting dreams was used as a means to provide answers to the individual and/or the community.

Every event and occurrence had spiritual significance — the means by which the spirit world connected with the everyday world, a conduit that was used to provide guidance in the lives of Native peoples. The weather, the seasons, and the movements and cycles of all things were some of the forces of nature that had a direct impact on the lives of Native peoples. Native peoples sought direction and power from natural sources to understand themselves and their world. For example, encountering an animal in the bush or a bird flying in the air would have been seen as spiritually significant. The individual was required to be alert and to heed these messages. As a further understanding into Native spirituality, each rock, tree, and animal was considered to be a spirit — that is, each animate and inanimate thing was alive, playing a significant role in the Native person's daily world. As mentioned in chapter 1, offending one of these spirits could cause problems for the person, his or her family, and community. When Native hunters offered tobacco or other sacred medicines to an animal that they had killed for food, it was to show respect for its spirit, to thank the animal for giving up its life to sustain the hunters, and to avoid offending the animal's spirit. Famine, sickness, death, poor hunting, etc., were blamed on offending a spirit.

Most Native groups also shared a common code of ethics that was strongly connected to their spirituality. This code provides the communities with strong guidelines that each member was expected to incorporate into his or her life. The following is a summary of these ethics:

1. When rising each morning and before retiring each evening, give thanks to the Creator for the life within you and for all life. Be thankful for the good things that you experience from the sight of a child playing to the worm that travels its own path. Thoughtfully consider your actions and words and in all things seek the courage and the strength to be a better person.
2. In all things, show respect to yourself, to others, and to the world around you. Showing respect is a basic law of life.
3. Respect and listen to the wisdom of the people who make decisions about your world. When you share an idea with others, the idea belongs to all people. Respect the words and decisions made by the council in unity.
4. Be truthful at all times and in all situations.
5. Treat your guests with honour and consideration. Give the best that you have in food, accommodations, and other comforts to your guests.
6. The hurt of one is the hurt of all; the honour of one is the honour of all.
7. Welcome strangers and outsiders with kindness and a loving heart. We are all members of the human family.
8. All races are like the different coloured flowers in a meadow; each is beautiful and each plays an important role. The Creator made each for a special reason and, as such, we must respect each other's gifts.
9. Serve others because this is the primary reason why humans were created. The secret of true happiness comes to those who dedicate their lives to the service of others.
10. At all times and in all things, observe moderation and balance.
11. Be wise and know what things and actions will lead to your health and well-being and those things that will lead to your destruction. Know your heart.
12. Listen and follow the guidance given in your heart. Expect guidance to come in many forms: in prayer, in dreams, in quiet reflection, and in the actions and deeds of elders and other wise people (children or adults).

GROUP DISCUSSION

Consider the code of ethics shared by Native cultures and that of the society in which you live.

- What similarities and differences exist? Are any of the values outlined in the Native code of ethics different from or similar to ethics that are advocated in your culture or are they universal? Provide examples to support your answer.

GENERAL DISTINCTIONS BETWEEN CULTURAL GROUPS

About six primary Native cultural groups have been identified in the area of Canada. To understand the cultural distinctions among the groups that we will be studying, it is important to understand the artificial nature of their borders. First, the Canadian–American border is a boundary that was created in 1867 with the Confederation of Canada. The territories and the areas where Native cultures lived before Confederation extend beyond this border on either side. As an example, Iroquois territory — particularly the Mohawk — extended from southern Ontario and Quebec into Michigan and Ohio (to name a small portion of their original territory). The Six Nations Confederacy, of which the Mohawk are a part, continues to exist on both sides of the border and played a significant role in the Oka crisis in the early 1990s. The Oka crisis will be discussed from this territorial perspective in greater detail in chapter 7.

Second, the cultural boundaries created to identify the various Native groups are artificial by their nature. While there are specific characteristics that set apart cultural groups — for example, tools, type of dress, and mode of transportation — not all the subgroups within the larger cultural group share all these qualities. As defined in chapter 1, subgroups that share some of the collective characteristics but maintain their own distinct qualities are called subcultures. Moreover, "blending" occurs among cultural groups, especially those that are closer to a cultural border. For example, as a northern Woodland cultural group, the Ojibwe were known to be primarily a nomadic people who followed game, such as moose and deer. However, the Ojibwe people who coexisted near the southern Woodland people, the Iroquois, adopted some of their ways — for example, growing crops. The borders, though artificial, provide a means of understanding the similarities and differences among the Native groups in Canada.

To understand the distinctive nature of the Native cultural groups in Canada, it is important to recognize the significant role that the physical environment played in creating these distinctions within each group as they existed before contact with Europeans. The climate, the terrain, and the plant and animal groups heavily influenced the cultural development of each Native group. We will briefly examine the six cultural groups from this context (see figure 2.3).

Woodlands

The Woodlands area extends southwest to Illinois and east to coastal North Carolina. The deciduous forests of southern Ontario, the St. Lawrence Lowlands, and the coastal Atlantic provinces were all part of the Woodlands, as were the southern part of the Canadian Shield and the Appalachians in the east.

FIGURE 2.3 Native Cultural Groups in Canada

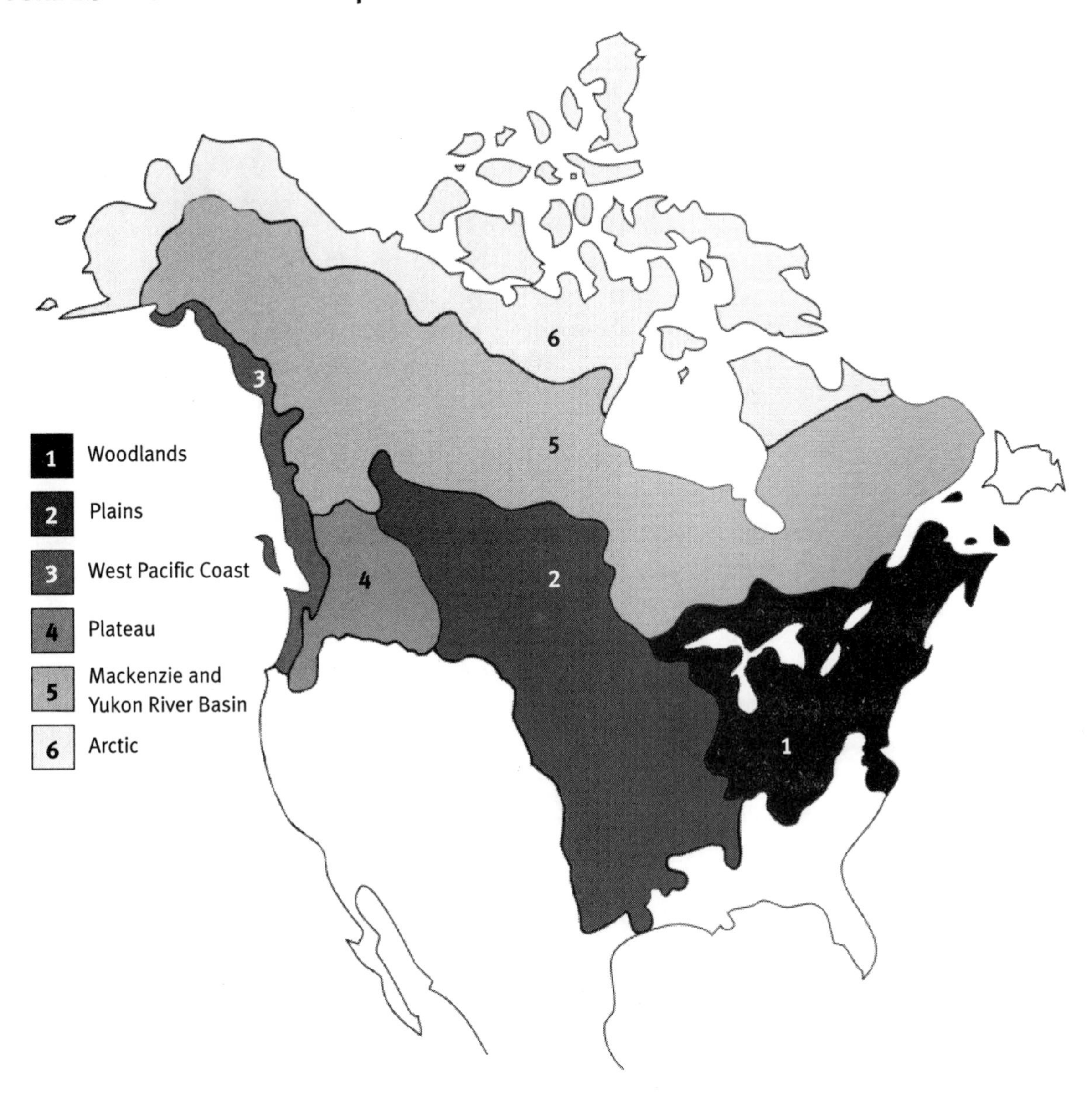

The eastern Woodland Natives comprised two categories: the migratory tribes and the agricultural tribes. The migratory tribes lived in an environment that, among other things, consisted of extensive tree cover, mountainous or rocky terrain, numerous lakes and rivers, and a short growing season. Some examples of the people that could be found in this area are the Ojibwe, Odawa, Potowatomi (found more in the northern United States), and Cree. Their primary food sources included wild game — for example, deer, moose, and beaver; fish — for example, perch, pickerel, pike, and sturgeon; wild fruits — for example, blueberries, strawberries, and chokecherries; and vegetation — for example, roots and wild rice. Because of long, severe winters, the Woodlands people primarily ate meat for most of the year. They also possessed highly developed modes of transportation — canoes, snowshoes, and toboggans — that enabled them to survive successfully within their environment. Their primary dwellings, wigwams or tipis, were transportable and easy to dismantle in their quest to follow the game.

Eastern Woodlands peoples spoke languages belonging to two unrelated families, Iroquoian and Algonquian. Iroquoian speakers occupied much of southern Ontario, northern Ohio, Pennsylvania, New York, and the St. Lawrence Valley. Algonquian groups extended from Lake Superior, north of Lake Huron to the Ottawa Valley, and through New England and the Atlantic provinces.

The southern Woodland peoples consisted primarily of the Iroquois of the Five Nations and, later, the Six Nations Confederacy, as well as other Iroquoian people — for example, Tobacco, Hurons, and Neutrals. The fertile land upon which they lived was conducive to growing food and had the added advantage of a longer growing season. As a result, the southern Woodland peoples were primarily an agricultural-based society with semi-permanent-based communities. They lived in rectangular longhouses (see figure 2.4) that were homes for up to 10 families (or even more). They also built wooden palisades, which surrounded the community. Essentially, they would live in one area for up to 10 years and when the nutrients in the soil were depleted, the community would move to another suitable location. Their crops consisted of corn, beans, squash, and tobacco. (The Three Sisters, from their folklore, were corn, beans, and squash.) Similar in many respects to the eastern Woodland peoples, they also hunted for game, which was an important part of their diet. They had a highly developed political system that was due in part to the permanency of their home base. In addition, they were proficient at pottery making, a result of the abundance of clay found in their territories. They made most of their garments and foot coverings from animal skins but also wove some of their clothing — for example, cloaks and sandals — and other household products — for example, mats — from grasses.

Plains

The Plains Indians culture extended from southern Manitoba and the Mississippi River westward to the Rocky Mountains, and from the North Saskatchewan River south into Texas. The languages spoken by the various Plains tribes belong to six linguistic families, of which three were represented on the Canadian Plains. Algonquian languages were spoken by the Blackfoot, Gros Ventre, Plains Cree, and Plains Ojibwe. Siouan languages were spoken by the Assiniboine, Stoney, and Dakota Sioux. Athapaskan was spoken by the Sarcee.

The Plains cultural groups consisted of the Blackfoot, the Crow, the Cheyenne, and the Comanche, to name a few. They too were a product of their environment, which consisted of great, open expanses of long grasses with few trees and few lakes. One of their predominant food sources was the buffalo. Their dependence on the buffalo was so strong that when the animal became almost extinct in the 1800s because of overkilling by sport hunters and others, many people starved to death.

The Plains peoples had a highly mobile existence and required the use of moveable tipis for their dwellings, which were made of hides (see figure 2.4). Initially, they used the dog and travois for transportation. Later, when horses were introduced by the Europeans, the Plains peoples readily adapted to them, becoming proficient riders. Similar to most Native cultures, the Plains peoples made their clothes from animal skins. Within the Plains cultures was an absence of fishing and agricultural skills, and a limited use of roots and berries.

FIGURE 2.4 Dwellings of Native Cultural Groups

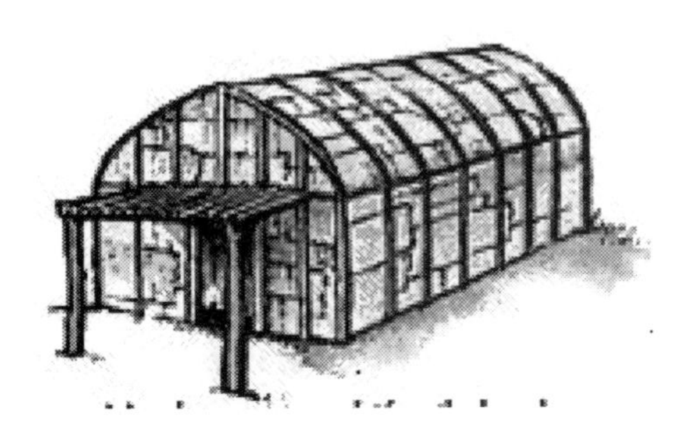

Woodlands forest longhouse

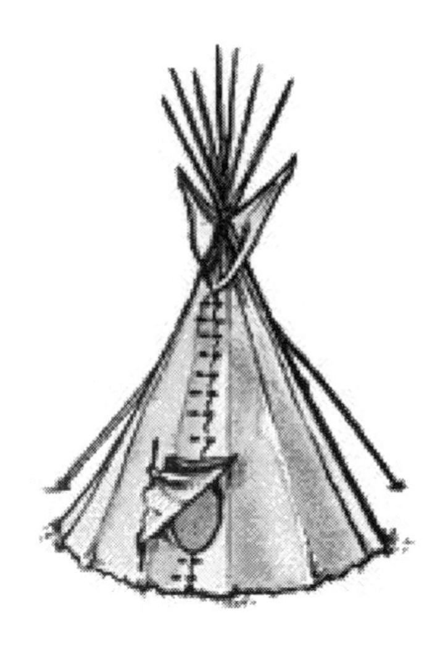

Plains buffalo-hide tipi

Plains earth-covered lodge

West Pacific Coast plank house

Plateau ladder-entrance pithouse

Mackenzie and Yukon River Basin lean-to

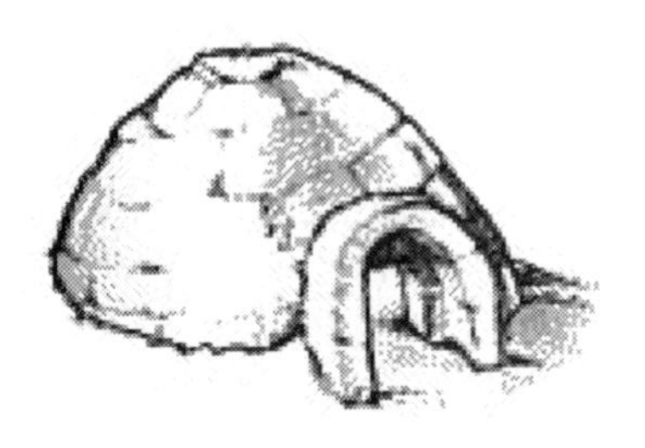

Arctic igloo

West Pacific Coast

Natives of the Pacific Coast occupied coastal areas from southern British Columbia to Alaska. These people had a diversity of languages. Tlingit was spoken on the northern end of British Columbia and the southwest Yukon, Haida on the Queen Charlotte Islands, and three dialects of the Tsimshian language were spoken along the Nass and Skeena rivers and adjacent coast. The Wakashan language family and the Salish language family were also found along the Pacific Coast.

Among the West Pacific Coast Native groups were the Tlingit, Haida, Tsimshian, Bella Coola, and Nootka. Complex and highly individualized groups, the West Pacific Coast Natives lived in a region of imposing mountains and lush vegetation, with most land access only via the ocean and rivers. These Natives were characterized by their great dependence on seafood, which they ate fresh, smoked, and dried. They also hunted wild game. As a secondary food source, they picked and dried berries. They made extensive use of cedar trees for large dugout canoes, upright cedar plank houses, bark clothing, wooden trays, and boxes. (When the Europeans first came into contact with these Native groups, they felt a great familiarity with this group's means of housing construction — that is, square, wooden buildings. See figure 2.4.) In addition, west coast Natives created elaborate totem pole carvings that were both ceremonial and spiritual in nature; they also had highly developed trading relationships with interior Indians and with other coastal bands.

Plateau

The Plateau area covers the Columbia Plateau, the area between the British Columbia coastal range and the Rocky Mountains. The linguistic families represented here are the Athapaskan, Salishan, and Kutenai.

The Plateau Native groups are more difficult to characterize than other groups because the Natives in these groups lived in a land of extremes: in the south, the climate is extremely dry and the land a desert; in the north, the climate is moist and the land is fertile. The Plateau region is flanked on the west by the west coast cultures, whose terrain is mountainous and well treed. On the east is the Plains region, which is predominantly open, treeless, and dry. The Plateau groups included the Shuswap, Nez Perce, Salish, and Shoshone. Traits common to this cultural group included their use of salmon, deer, roots, and berries. As a group, they had similarities in foods, art, clothing, utensils, and methods of cooking and food preparation. For example, they cooked their food with hot stones in holes or baskets. The Plateau peoples had highly developed basket-weaving methods and their baskets were uniquely coiled and rectangular. They developed only very crude dugouts and canoes. Their clothing was either woven from bark fibre or made from animal skins. They had a variety of dwellings, including skin and rush tents, semi-subterranean houses, also known as pithouses, and rectangular log and bark huts (see figure 2.4).

Mackenzie and Yukon River Basin

The Mackenzie and Yukon River Basin cultural groups lived in a region that includes the greater northern interior of Canada, also known as the subarctic. This area is characterized by many trees that thin out in the northern regions to become the tundra, by lakes and rivers, and by long winters. Most people of the eastern subarctic spoke Algonquian languages, while those of the western subarctic spoke Athapaskan languages. Northern subarctic Algonquians spoke dialects of the Cree language, and Algonquians to the south of them spoke dialects of Ojibwe. Some of the tribes that once populated this area include the Dene, Montagnais, the Naskai, Chipewyan, Slavey, Cree, and Dogrib. Predominantly meat and fish eaters, they were characterized as nomadic hunters (large and small game) and fishers. Their traditional economy was based on caribou, moose, hares, fish, and berries. They wore clothing made from animal hides. Their dwellings tended to be made of hides (portable in the summer) or rectangular huts of bark or logs in the winter or lean-tos made of logs and hides or of bark (see figure 2.4). They also made and used canoes and snowshoes.

Arctic

The Arctic or Inuit peoples were said to live on the fringe of the inhabitable world, which included the western subarctic from the interior of Alaska to Hudson Bay. Their environment consisted of treeless tundra, mountains, sparse vegetation, frozen lakes and seas, and periods of 24 hours of darkness. Common cultural traits included hunting for land and sea mammals, such as caribou, seals, walrus, smaller whales, musk-oxen, and polar bears, as well as fishing. The sea provided most of their food and resources. They used hides for clothing, boots, tents, harpoon lines, dog harnesses, and coverings for boats. They lived in snow igloos (see figure 2.4) in the winter and hide-covered dwellings in the summer. Their diet consisted of blubber, raw meat and organs, and eyeballs. Meat was cooked by boiling. They relied heavily on dogs for carrying things. This group spoke largely Inuktitut, a language that is currently going through a revival (see the Linguistic Groups section of this chapter).

GROUP DISCUSSION

1. Identify all of the cultural groups that exist within your community.
2. Describe any diversities that exist within each group. Which groups have become homogeneous despite different cultural backgrounds?

Three Groups of the Woodlands

OJIBWE

The Ojibwe, Odawa (Ottawa), and the Potowatomi were part of the Three Fires Council, a loosely formed coalition of nations within similar cultures that united for political and military purposes. Some evidence exists that all three tribes had migrated from either the east coast or near Hudson Bay in earlier times. At the time of European contact, the Ojibwe were settled in the area of the Great Lakes, primarily on the east side of Lake Huron and farther west around Lake Superior. After contact with Europeans, the Ojibwe expanded their territory substantially. Through fur trade, settling of new arrivals, and various wars (with the Iroquois and as allies with the European powers), the Ojibwe began to move down both sides of Lake Huron, controlling most of lower Michigan and southern Ontario. They also moved beyond Lake Superior, and into northern Minnesota and Wisconsin, as well as North Dakota and Manitoba, Saskatchewan, Illinois, Indiana, and Ohio. They assumed much of the new territories in battles with the Dakota (Sioux). Today, of approximately 600 First Nations recognized by the Canadian government, more than 130 of them are Ojibwe.

Traditionally, the Ojibwe were nomadic tribes who lived on land with poor soil, hilly terrain, and a short growing season. The majority of Ojibwe tribes were found in the Woodlands or Great Lakes area and were skilled hunters and fishers. They used snowshoes and toboggans in the winter, similar to the ones used by the Cree. They also harvested wild rice and maple sugar. Compared with their more western neighbours, the Ojibwe's use of horses prior to the 1800s was more limited. They used domestic dogs for carrying and also for food. Most of their utensils, containers, wigwams (dome-shaped or peaked), and canoes were made of birch bark. Given their nomadic existence, their homes could quickly be dismantled by rolling up the birchbark exterior, leaving behind only the framework of poles (or they took them as well).

The people gathered into larger communities each summer, returning to the same favoured spots known for their access to water, fish, game, and berries or wild rice. In the winter, they would break into smaller bands, often from the same extended family groups or clans, in order to follow the game. The small group size often meant that, collectively, they had a better chance of surviving the harsh winters. Leaders of each small band were selected for their specific skills for specific times. Hereditary chiefs existed as well. However, most bands' moving as autonomous communities during the long winter months made situational leadership necessary.

Ojibwe clothing was made primarily of animal skins, buckskin (fur is removed from skin) in the summer, and fur outer garments in the winter. Men wore breechcloths (longer pieces of buckskin covering both the front and back of the person) and both genders wore leggings. Moccasins were distinct with the lower part of the moccasin overlapping the top of the foot to form a puffed seam. The women spent the long winter nights decorating their utensils with dyed porcupine quills, animal hair, and sweetgrass. Both men and women wore their hair long and braided.

During war, the men were known to take scalps but did not practise torture as a rule. They also practised ritual cannibalism on dead enemies, eating the heart or organs of the enemy to symbolically acquire the others' strength. Ojibwe society was based on a patrilineal system, as well as a strong clan system (further discussion of this system is found in chapter 3), where children assumed the clan of their fathers. Approximately 15 to 20 clans extended across the Ojibwe nation, uniting the Ojibwe into a greater tribal community with loyalties extending beyond their smaller communities. Tribal councils became increasingly important as the fur trade and the wars with other tribes became more prevalent, and the Three Fires Council also became more influential during this time. The council comprised the Ojibwe, the Potowatomi, and the Odawa (Ottawa); they worked together to maintain order and military strength against other combative tribes.

CREE

The Cree were a large group of Natives whose territory stretched across most of northern Canada. Today, they are broken into two categories: the Plains Cree, who live on the prairies, and the Woodland Cree, also known as the Swampy Cree, who live in the north of the eastern Woodland culture area. We will examine the latter group, based on their similarities with other Woodland cultures.

The Cree were nomads, who were known to tattoo themselves. In the southern parts of their territory, the Woodland Cree dwelt in birchbark wigwams, either dome-shaped like the Ojibwe wigwam or conical. This portable structure could be packed up quickly in emergencies or when locating game. The Cree in the more southerly areas used birchbark vessels for cooking, but the bands farther north emulated the Inuit and used soapstone pots for cooking. Their clothing was similar to what the Ojibwe wore — furs and, more predominantly in the north, coats and blankets of woven hare skin or caribou fur. They also wore leggings, an assian (longer cloth hanging in front and in back tied together with a belt), moccasins, a robe that extended below the knees, and perhaps a cloak, cap, and mittens (Jenness, 1932).

The Cree ate mostly meat, living on caribou, moose, beaver, and bear. In the spring and autumn, the men secured ducks and geese to supplement the meat of the larger game and left the fishing to the women. In the winter, they used snowshoes and toboggans to transport their goods.

The Cree shared many customs with the Ojibwe. They had many taboos and hunting customs that regulated how they hunted, gutted, and cleaned the animal, and ate it. Specific rituals were carried out to prevent offending any spirit.

IROQUOIS

The Iroquois were primarily an agrarian society, moving only when the soil no longer produced premium crops, which was approximately every six to eight years. They lived primarily in the southern Woodland region that was conducive to cultivation. The Iroquois comprise a number of nations with similar dialects. The group that we will be addressing in this chapter is the Six Nations Confederacy — the tribes of Mohawk, Oneida, Onondaga, Cayuga, Seneca, and Tuscarora (which joined later). These tribes resembled each other, as well as other Iroquoian tribes that the Six Nations had warred with and that later became extinct or nearly extinct — namely, the Huron, the Tobacco, and the Neutral tribes.

The Iroquois people lived in what Champlain described in his journals as "long houses" (Jenness, 1932). He described the houses as a kind of "arbour" that was covered with bark, approximately 50 or 60 yards (45 or 55 metres) long by 12 yards (11 metres) wide. Down the middle of the house was a passage, and on each side of this hallway was a bench where the people would sleep or store their food and clothing. The houses could accommodate up to two dozen families, making them a communal living society. It is obvious from the permanent nature of their dwellings that the homes of the Iroquoian tribes were not intended to be moved quickly. The coverings of the dwellings were bark (usually cedar bark), skin, or rush mats. The villages were surrounded by palisades erected from logs, indicating that armed hostilities were a reality that the Iroquoian tribes faced.

All Iroquoian tribes were matrilineal social structures, where the women owned all property and determined kinship. Similar to the Ojibwe, they possessed a strong clan system that was headed by a clan leader — in this case a clan mother. The Iroquois were essentially warrior farmers whose leaders were chosen by their women. The eldest women of the clans decided which man became leader and they also had the authority to remove him if he failed to perform his role adequately. Men could choose their own wives, subject to the approval of the mothers. The fathers were not usually consulted in this matter. After marriage, the couple would move into the wife's longhouse and the children would take the clan of the mother.

Though the men hunted for game, the Iroquoian tribes relied more heavily on the food they grew. They subsisted largely on maize (a type of corn), beans, and squash, which were known as the Three Sisters or "the life supporters." They also grew sunflowers for oil and tobacco for ceremonial or trade purposes. Their feasts were associated with the cultivation of the soil and the ripening and harvest of the various domestic and wild fruit and vegetables.

Because of the power of their Six Nations Confederacy, the Iroquois were an aggressive and warmongering people during the 17th century. They sent war parties into Ontario and Quebec, as far as James Bay, and were known to torture their prisoners and eat their organs in a ceremonial manner known as ritualistic cannibalism. Captives were sometimes adopted by community members — for example, a parent who had lost a child — and were accepted as family members. The Iroquoian were very respectful to their own people and did not make it a practice to kill or abandon their ill, infirm, or handicapped.

LINGUISTIC GROUPS

linguistics
the study of general categories of human speech

language
the words, their pronunciations, and the methods of combining them used and understood by a community

Linguistics is a method of identifying the various groups of Native peoples based on similarities within their **languages**. Eleven Native linguistic groups, including the Inuit languages, which are composed of related languages and dialects, can be identified in Canada. It must be noted that none of the indigenous language groups falls exclusively within Canadian borders. The categories are the Tlingit, Tsimshian, Haida, Wakashan, Salishan, Kutenai, Siouan, Algonquin, Eskimo-Aleut, Iroquoian, and Athapaskan. The map of the linguistic areas in Canada (figure 2.5) shows that the majority of the Native languages are contained within a few linguistic families, while the remaining linguistic groups represent a handful of language groups within specific regions.

The environment has played a role in shaping the languages. Groups from the mountainous regions of the west coast were isolated and experienced little contact with other linguistic groups. Thus, their languages were able to develop with minimal influences from outside language families and have retained highly distinctive patterns of speech until today.

The language possessed by each Native culture shapes the thoughts and identity of the speakers and is an important element in the survival of each group as a distinct culture. Native cultures have relied heavily on their ability to pass their stories, songs, history, traditions, etc., to succeeding generations. We will examine the 11 linguistic groups briefly at this point.

1. *Tlingit* The Tlingit is another isolated linguistic group that can be found in the northwestern corner of British Columbia, the Yukon, and Alaska. As with a few other Native linguistic groups, it includes only one language in its family.

2. *Tsimshian* The Tsimshian consists of three language groups and is located along the coastal inlets of northern British Columbia, the Alaskan Panhandle, and the inland areas of British Columbia along the Nass and

FIGURE 2.5 Native Linguistic Groups in Canada

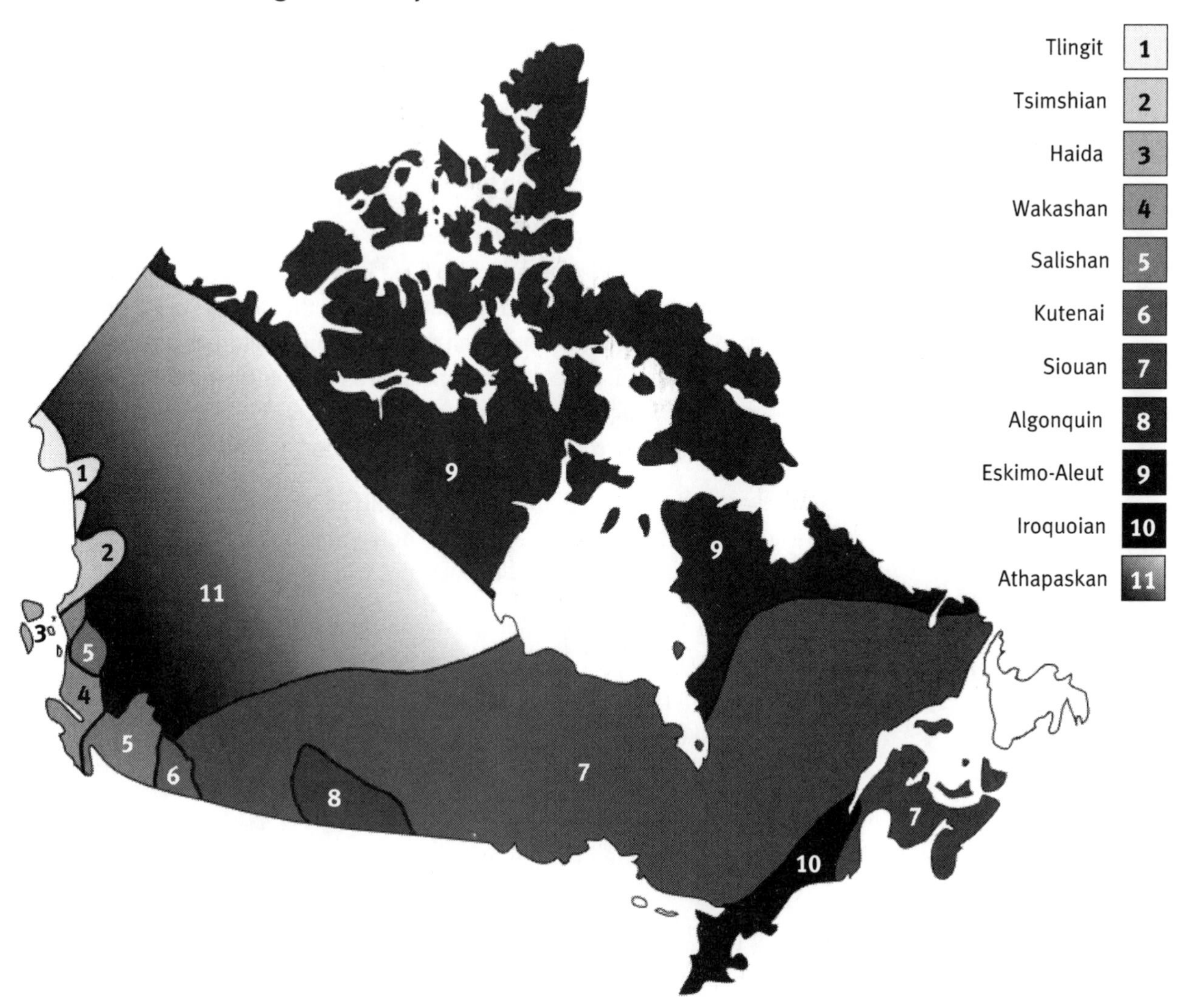

Skeena rivers. Comparatively, Tsimshian is another British Columbia linguistic family that has maintained its distinctiveness as a result of its geographical location. Like all west coast Native languages, the Tsimshian languages are highly complex and distinct.

3. *Haida* The Haida is a unique linguistic family found on the west coast. Currently, the people who speak this language number only a few hundred, all over the age of 50.

4. *Wakashan* This linguistic family can be found on the western and northeastern sides of Vancouver Island and on the adjacent British Columbia coastline. Six languages are within this group; five of them are in Canada.

5. *Salishan* The Salishan linguistic group is also located on the west coast along the eastern and southern coastlines of Vancouver Island and in inlets along the adjacent mainland. Pockets of this linguistic family can also be found along the Fraser and Okanagan rivers.

6. *Kutenai* The Kutenai linguistic family is represented by a single language group. Belonging to a west coast Native culture, its distinct forms of speech

have not been connected to any other language groups within North America. This distinction strongly indicates that this group of Natives spent countless years in isolation.

7. *Siouan* The Siouan is a large linguistic group that is spread out over a large portion of the prairies. As a linguistic group, it can be linked to the Iroquoian linguistic family in the east.
8. *Algonquin* The term Algonquin is somewhat confusing and refers to a specific tribe of Native people who lived in the eastern Woodlands cultural region. As well, the word Algonquin identifies the largest Native linguistic group in North America, of which the Algonquin culture is a part. From this point, any reference to Algonquin will be as a linguistic group. Algonquin comprises 20 languages and subsequent dialects. This family is spread out and has speakers from the Rockies to Labrador.
9. *Eskimo-Aleut* The Eskimo-Aleut is found all across northern Canada from one coast to the other. It is the only indigenous linguistic family in North America that has probable linguistic ties with Siberia.
10. *Iroquoian* The Iroquoian linguistic group is one of the first Native groups to develop contacts with Europeans for purposes of political and trade relations. In particular, they became allies of the French and, later, the British. Some of the group's languages are extinct today — for example, Hurons. Members of the Six Nations Confederacy continue to maintain their languages in healthy numbers.
11. *Athapaskan* The Athapaskan languages are found primarily mid-Canada to the edge of the Rockies. Fifteen of the 24 languages in this family are spoken in Canada.

The number of Native language speakers across Canada has significantly declined, and although some Native languages are recovering, according to the 2001 Census, the situation remains critical. It is generally believed that 1000 speakers are necessary to predict the future usage and maintenance of a language. Currently in Canada, there are only three Native or Inuit languages that can be assured future survival — the Ojibwe, Cree, and Inuktitut-Inupik languages and their dialects. A number of dialects within these three groups are also in decline. The potential for long-term survival of Native languages in Canada rests on very few, such as the Ojibwe and Cree. Native educators, leaders, and other concerned Native groups are racing against time to save their languages; the loss of Native languages has become a real concern. The reason is that the average age of a Native language speaker is over 50 years. If this trend continues, it is predicted that the majority of Native languages will be lost early in the 21st century, and the disappearance of the languages could signal the incipient demise of unique Native cultures.

Co-author Pam Williamson has first-hand experience of this decline in language usage. The use of the Ojibwe and/or Potowatomi languages has dramatically decreased within her own band (Moose Deer Point, Ontario) in the past three generations. Within her father's generation, the majority of the community members spoke Ojibwe and/or Potowatomi fluently; the majority of the elders spoke Potowatomi more fluently than her father's age group. One factor that helped maintain the language – even though her father, cousins, and other community children went to an English school and received their academic instructions in English from a community-built school – was that the children were able to return home each night to parents who spoke Ojibwe and/or Potowatomi almost exclusively. If a census had been taken then, the majority of her father's age group would have identified their first language as Ojibwe and/or Potowatomi, despite acquiring English-speaking skills. Of the author's generation, the children of these fluent Native language speakers, about half acquired varying degrees of fluency in the Ojibwe language and little or no Potowatomi. By this time, many members of the community, including her father, had moved from the **reserve** to seek employment in the city and to raise their families. The children, both those who remained on-reserve and those who lived off-reserve, attended English-speaking schools only. As a result, the author's generation became fluent speakers of English. Finally, within that generation's children, none has become fluent speakers of Ojibwe or Potowatomi. Within three generations, the use of the Ojibwe language has been reduced dramatically and the use of Potowatomi has disappeared, with the exception of a few words. Traditional languages have become endangered within this one community.

reserve
the land base with which Indian status is integrally connected that was set aside for Indians and held in trust by the government through the Department of Indian Affairs

Similar scenarios are currently being played out in Native communities all across Canada: in 1941, less than 10 percent of Natives claimed English as their first language; in 1971, about 54 percent of Canadian Natives claimed English as their primary language; in 1991, 60.4 percent claimed English as their mother tongue. In 1996, only one-quarter of the aboriginal population said that their primary language was their aboriginal tongue.

The 2001 census of Canada illustrates the precarious position of aboriginal languages. Table 2.1, which illustrates the percentages of aboriginal speakers who know an aboriginal language and use it regularly at home, looks promising at first glance. For example, the Cree language appears to be the most widely spoken, with 92 630 persons who have some knowledge of the language, and 69 210, or 74.7 percent, who use the language regularly at home.

However, when comparing this information with the data in table 2.2, it can be seen that the use of the Cree language is actually declining. In 1996, 95 555 people had some knowledge of the language, showing a net loss of 3.1 percent of speakers in 2001. In addition, 82 420 persons claimed Cree as their mother tongue in 1996, while only 77 285 did so in 2001, a net loss of 6.2 percent.

To examine the statistics even further, while 77 285 persons claimed Cree as their mother tongue in 2001, only 69 210 persons claimed to use Cree regularly at home. It would appear, then, that 8075 people claim Cree as their mother tongue but don't use it regularly at home.

Other aboriginal languages are in danger of disappearing. While 21 980 persons claimed Ojibwe as their mother tongue in 2001, a decline of 10.1 percent since 1996, only 17 140 use the language regularly. Blackfoot has suffered a 27.1 percent loss in speakers who claim the language as their mother tongue, Algonquin has lost 12.6 percent, and Carrier 34.8 percent; only 1490 persons in Canada use Algonquin at home, and only 950 use Carrier. It can be assumed that both languages will disappear within 50 years.

On the other side of the scale, aboriginal language usage has shown improvement in some areas, although the improvement is much less significant than the losses. The use of Inuktitut, the Inuit language, has increased 7.5 percent in 2001

TABLE 2.1 Aboriginal-Identity Population Using an Aboriginal Language at Home Compared with Their Knowledge of an Aboriginal Language, for Selected Languages with 2000 or More Speakers, Canada, 2001[a]

Aboriginal languages[b, c]	Know an aboriginal language	Use aboriginal languages regularly at home	Percentage of those who know an aboriginal language who use it regularly at home
Cree	92 630	69 210	74.7
Inuktitut	31 945	29 350	91.9
Ojibwe	27 955	17 140	61.3
Dene	10 500	9 275	88.3
Montagnais-Naskapi	10 285	9 765	94.9
Mi'kmaq	8 625	6 820	79.1
Oji-Cree	5 610	4 490	80.0
Attikamekw	4 935	4 620	93.6
Dakota/Sioux	4 875	3 535	72.5
Blackfoot	4 415	2 870	65.0
Salish languages not included elsewhere	2 675	1 125	42.1
Algonquin	2 340	1 490	63.7
Dogrib	2 265	1 895	83.7
Carrier	2 000	950	47.5

[a] Data adjusted for incompletely enumerated Indian reserves in 1996 and 2001.

[b] Four reserves in Manitoba had changes in reporting patterns for Cree, Ojibwe, and Oji-Cree between 1996 and 2001. Consequently, data for these reserves have been excluded.

[c] Due to changes in reporting patterns and coding between 1996 and 2001, North Slave (Hare) and South Slave are not shown.

Source: Adapted from Statistics Canada (2003, January 31).

over 1996, and Dene 6.8 percent. Both Inuktitut and Dene are languages of the North and may be less influenced due to isolation from English or French. Mi'kmaq is making a minor comeback with a 2.3 percent increase, and there is a 4.1 percent increase in the use of Oji-Cree.

In off-reserve situations, the lack of opportunity to practise an aboriginal mother tongue and the need to learn English or French to function within the larger society have caused a crisis in the use of aboriginal languages off-reserve:

> among those of all ages, the percentage of non-reserve North American Indian people with the ability to speak an Aboriginal language well enough to conduct a conversation fell from 20% in 1996 to 16% in 2001. At the same time, the use of an Aboriginal language at home declined from 8% to 6%. In addition, the proportion of North American Indian people with an Aboriginal mother tongue fell from 16% to 13%. (O'Donnell & Tait, 2003, p. 28)

These figures are startling. If one considers that only 16 percent of off-reserve North American Indians can converse well in a Native language, it also means that 84 percent can't converse in a Native language. The 4 percent gap between 1996 and 2001 will widen dramatically as those Native language speakers and their children

TABLE 2.2 Aboriginal-Identity Population with Knowledge of an Aboriginal Language and with an Aboriginal Language as Mother Tongue, for Selected Languages with 2000 or More Speakers, Canada, 1996 and 2001[a]

	Knowledge of an aboriginal language			Mother tongue		
Aboriginal languages[b, c]	1996	2001	Percentage change 1996–2001	1996	2001	Percentage change 1996–2001
Cree	95 555	92 630	−3.1	82 420	77 285	−6.2
Inuktitut	29 400	31 945	8.7	27 615	29 695	7.5
Ojibwe	29 735	27 955	−6.0	24 455	21 980	−10.1
Dene	9 525	10 500	10.2	8 955	9 565	6.8
Montagnais-Naskapi	9 335	10 285	10.2	9 065	9 790	8.0
Mi'kmaq	7 975	8 625	8.2	7 240	7 405	2.3
Oji-Cree	5 480	5 610	2.4	4 980	5 185	4.1
Attikamekw	4 075	4 935	21.1	3 970	4 710	18.6
Dakota/Sioux	4 710	4 875	3.5	4 270	4 280	0.2
Blackfoot	5 530	4 415	−20.2	4 140	3 020	−27.1
Salish languages not included elsewhere	2 285	2 675	17.1	1 825	1 730	−5.2
Algonquin	2 555	2 340	−8.4	2 105	1 840	−12.6
Dogrib	2 430	2 265	−6.8	2 080	1 920	−7.7
Carrier	2 830	2 000	−29.3	2 185	1 425	−34.8

[a] Data adjusted for incompletely enumerated Indian reserves in 1996 and 2001.

[b] Four reserves in Manitoba had changes in reporting patterns for Cree, Ojibwe, and Oji-Cree between 1996 and 2001. Consequently, data for these reserves have been excluded.

[c] Due to changes in reporting patterns and coding between 1996 and 2001, North Slave (Hare) and South Slave are not shown.

Source: Adapted from Statistics Canada (2003, January 31).

have fewer and fewer Native language speakers to converse with, and as the need to converse in French or English predominates.

When a Native language or any other language disappears, it is irretrievably gone, except for what is written down. The nuances, the intricate overlaying of meanings that are part of any language, can never truly be captured in print. Fear of losing European languages in Canada will not become a reality, as long as the countries from which those languages originated continue to exist. Without the means and support to sustain them, the loss of Native languages is real and potentially imminent.

GROUP DISCUSSION

It has been suggested in this chapter that the disappearance of a Native language could result in the loss of the culture associated with that language. Yet, Mohawk writer Brian Maracle believes that Mohawk identity exists even if people are speaking English. The culture is bound up with speaking Mohawk, yet transcends it. Which point of view would you accept? Can a culture survive the loss of its language? Give reasons.

Discussion Note

After this discussion, you should have made some observations about the difficulty — if not impossibility — of maintaining the distinctiveness of a culture without the existence of the language from which the culture grew and expressed itself. Although language is often discussed as a separate entity, it must be remembered that language is the primary means by which the members of a culture communicate and exchange information about their culture. Language, for all cultures, is important in maintaining the distinctiveness of a culture from others.

CONCLUSION

In this chapter, we have seen the characteristics of traditional Native cultures and their world views. Native cultures were similar and different in many ways but they undeniably had their own way of life, forms of leadership and rules, and languages. With European contact, however, many traditions and ways of being have become lost to many Natives. One key concern of Natives today is the rapid decline in the number and use of Native languages, which will continue without intervention. In future chapters, we will discuss the external influences that accelerated the loss of the languages — for example, assimilation policies and residential schools. As well, we will look at efforts undertaken to maintain the languages by various Native language groups across Canada.

WORKSHEET

1. Compare and contrast two different cultural groups that were discussed in the chapter. (4 marks)
2. Describe a situation today where the quality of interdependence exists within society. How does your answer compare with the interdependent relationship that existed within Native cultures before contact with Europeans? (4 marks)
3. Identify one characteristic from each of the Native cultural groups that sets that group apart from the other groups, and was a product of the environment from which the Natives came. (6 marks)
4. Identify three differences between the migratory and the agricultural Woodland groups. Explain your answers. (3 marks)
5. Why would alliances like the Three Fires Council and the Six Nations Confederacy be beneficial to the Native groups involved? List three benefits and explain your answers. (3 marks)

TOTAL — 20 MARKS

KEY TERMS

egalitarian society

holistic

language

linguistics

reserve

Seven Grandfathers

PART II

Effects of European Arrival on Native Peoples and Cultures

CHAPTER 3

Impact of Colonization on Natives

Chapter Objectives

After completing this chapter, you should be able to:

- Identify the general effects of colonization on Native peoples and their traditional ways of living.
- Identify the changes introduced by the settlers that affected the lives of the Native peoples in northern Ontario.
- Compare and contrast changes that occurred within specific Native groups of northern Canada as a result of the fur trade.
- Relate the effects of Native contact with religious groups — in particular, throughout the residential school system in Ontario.
- Describe other socioeconomic and spiritual issues that resulted from contact with Europeans before the 20th century.

INTRODUCTION

The arrival of Columbus to the New World in 1492 changed the lives of Native peoples irrevocably and permanently from that time on. Native peoples were profoundly affected by their contact with Europeans and the very basis of the cultures, which we looked at in chapter 2, was altered. Changes, new technologies, and new diseases, combined with the European nations' quest for new lands, put Native nations at a disadvantage from the start. As a result, cultural and traditional changes and the erosion of Native sovereignty were inevitable. This chapter focuses on the key European groups that contributed to the inevitable changes, and the beginnings of conflicts, especially with regard to land.

THE FIRST EUROPEANS

While the arrival of Columbus in 1492 is seen as a benchmark of sorts in terms of contact with the New World, there were doubtless previous contacts made between

North American Natives and Europeans. Written records are scarce; however, pre-1492 European records do exist that describe North American Natives; Native oral tradition also indicates contact before 1492.

Claims have been made for the sighting of Canada's Atlantic coastline by the Irish monk St. Brendan in the 6th century, and Norse settlements existed in Newfoundland as early as 1000 CE, according to archeological evidence. It's possible that sailors from Bristol, England may have reached Canada's east coast in the 1480s. The first reliably documented evidence of English contact with North America occurred in 1497, when John Cabot reached the shores of Maine and the maritime provinces.

Contact with North American Natives was documented after 1497 as fishers used Newfoundland as a supply base while fishing off the Grand Banks. Diamond Jenness (1932) describes the Beothuk Indians who were found in Newfoundland:

> The word "Beothuk" meant probably "man" or "human being," but early European visitors to Newfoundland considered it the tribal name of the aborigines who were inhabiting the island. They gave them also another name, "Red Indians," because they smeared their bodies and clothing with red ochre, partly for religious reasons, apparently, partly as a protection against insects. They may have been lighter in colour than the Indians of the Maritime Provinces, from whom they differed in several ways. Thus, they had no dogs, and did not make pottery, but cooked their food in vessels of birch bark. For sleeping places within their bark wigwams they dug trenches which they lined with branches of fir or pine. Their canoes, though made of birch bark like those of other eastern tribes, were very peculiar in shape, each gunwale presenting the outline of a pair of crescent moons; and they speared seals with harpoons modelled on an archaic Eskimo [Inuit] type. Many of their graves contain bone ornaments of curious shapes and etched with strange designs. We know nothing of their political organization except that they were divided into small bands of closely related families, each with its nominal leader. Some meagre vocabularies of their language suggest that they spoke two or three dialects of common tongue, although the entire tribe could hardly have numbered more than five hundred individuals ... in 1497.

Métis legend has it that the first Métis appeared on the east coast nine months after the first Portuguese fishers came ashore in the late 1480s.

The first true voyage of discovery into Canada occurred when Jacques Cartier explored the Gulf of St. Lawrence in 1534. Cartier's journals described a trading session in the Bay of Chaleur in that year:

> The next day part of the saide wilde men with nine of their boates came to the point and entrance to the Creeke, where we with our ships were at road. We being advertised of their comming, went to the point where they were with our boates: but so soone as they saw us, they began to flee, making signs that they came to trafique with us, shewing us such skinnes as they cloth themselves withall, which are of small value. We likewise made signes unto them, that we wished them no evill: and in signe thereof two of our men ventured to go on land to them, and carry them knives with other Iron wares, and a red hat to give unto their Captaine. Which when they saw, they also came on land, and brought some of their skinnes, and so began to deale with us, deeming to be very glad to have our iron ware and other things, stil dancing with many other ceremonies, as with their hands to cast Sea water on their heads. They gave us whatsoever they had, not keeping any thing,

> so that they were constrained to go back againe naked, and made signes that the next day they would come againe, and bring more skinnes with them.

On his second voyage during 1535–36, Cartier reached Stadacona (Quebec) and Hochelaga (Montreal). Cartier's journals record a close but uneasy relationship with the Natives there, particularly the Iroquois, who pointed out to Cartier that the St. Lawrence River provided a pathway to the interior of the continent, and also introduced Cartier to the idea that, in addition to the fisheries of the east, the furs of the interior offered unlimited opportunities for wealth.

Thus, the Europeans began to move toward North America, craving fish and furs, but still convinced that vast resources of gold lay somewhere in the unexplored interior. These explorers and opportunists cared not at all that they were invaders, that the land was occupied by the Natives, and that they were becoming nothing more than a foreign occupying power.

The first Europeans who came to the Americas saw potential and possibilities in the new land. As time passed, droves of Europeans, both governments and individuals, were drawn to the New World, the opportunities to become wealthy and/or to acquire land, or to experience freedom from social, religious, political, and/or economic plights and restrictions that plagued the different groups within their own countries. These reasons continue to be the primary impetus for immigrants to come to North America (see figure 3.1).

Initially, the Natives vastly outnumbered the first non-Natives they encountered and were considered either threats or saviours. The European governments – particularly those of Britain and France – thought the Natives were forces to be reckoned with. Diplomacy was used to develop and perpetuate their political ties with Native powers. As European immigrants began to arrive in increasing numbers, however, the manner in which the British and French dealt with the Natives also changed; they became more insistent in their claims to the land.

Over the course of the next few centuries, settlements and colonies of various European groups sprung up in North America, predominantly along the Atlantic east coast. Some of the earlier European communities disappeared. Because of their lack of knowledge and experience in an often hostile and alien environment, they were likely overcome by the elements or killed by the Natives upon whose territory they settled. One of the first New World colonies, La Navidad, was founded by Christopher Columbus. For political reasons a fort had been hastily erected during his first voyage to the New World – to reinforce the land claim for Spain. This first fort was burned to the ground and, when Columbus returned, all of the 39 men he had left to guard the fort had either disappeared or died at the hands of hostile Natives or from diseases.

Columbus initiated subsequent settlements, but they did not last because of disease epidemics, in-fighting among the colonialists, and the severity of the climate.

Thus, in some colonies, the newcomers and their settlements thrived in part because of their decision to adapt to the harsh new environment and by adopting some of the implements, tools, ways of hunting, and manner of dress that were used by the Native groups they befriended or with whom they came into contact. One of the earliest groups to become acculturated were men referred to as "coureurs de bois" (runners of the forest) or "voyageurs." They incorporated indigenous ways of dressing for the climate, their modes of transportation, and their languages, and even married or raised families with Native women. To survive, to develop commercial

FIGURE 3.1 European Penetration of North America

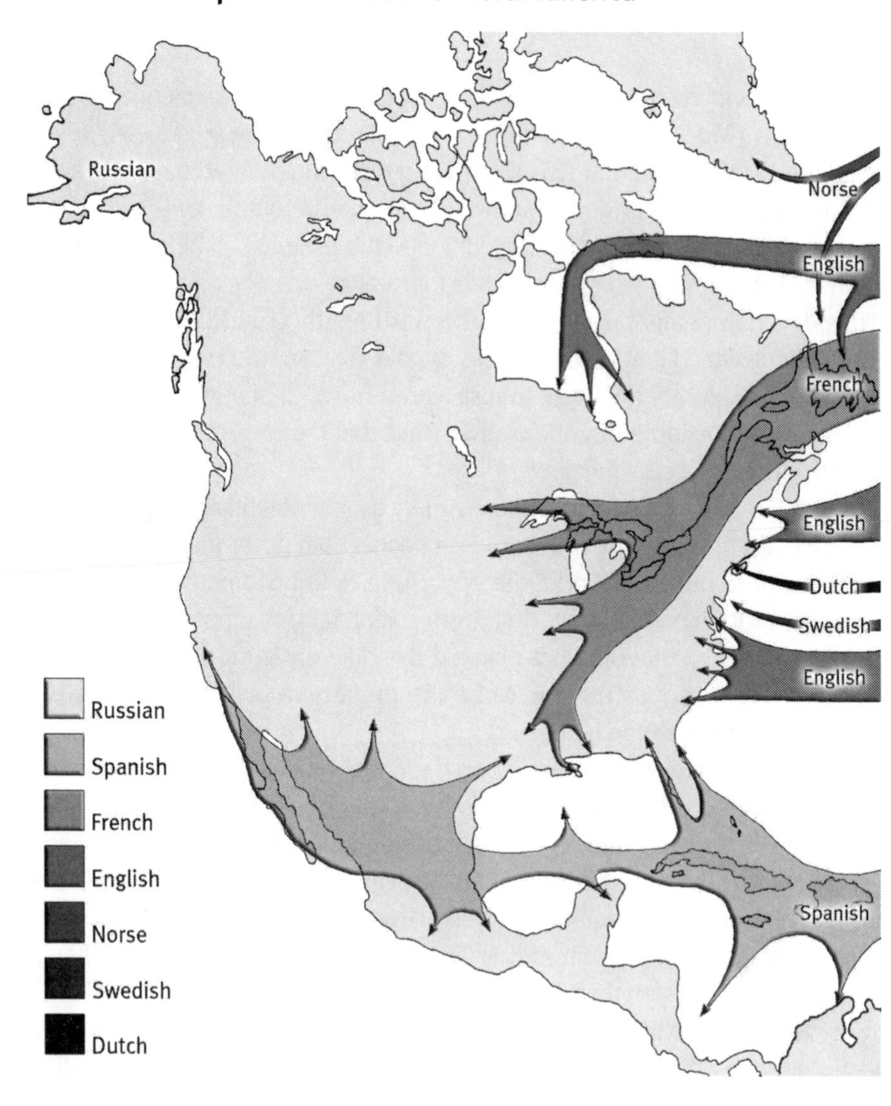

Sources: Waldman (n.d.); Barraclough (1978, p. 161).

contacts, and to be accepted by the Native groups, the coureurs de bois adjusted more successfully by imitating the people who had survived and thrived for countless centuries in the harsh and imposing land.

acculturation
the merging of cultures as a result of prolonged contact with each other; in essence, the cultures develop cultural modifications

indigenous
living or occurring naturally in a region; similar to aboriginal, but can be applied to non-native groups

To some extent, all of the European people who chose to settle in the Americas incorporated some of the foods and ways of living of their Native hosts. Conversely, Native peoples adapted some of the ways of the Europeans. This is referred to as **acculturation** – a natural process that occurs when individuals from different backgrounds are given the opportunity to get acquainted and to share their cultures. As a result, each side may choose to incorporate some parts of the other group into its own ways of being. This explains why cultures remain dynamic and ever changing.

Acculturation was not the only influence to bring changes to the Native ways of living and the direction of Native–European relations. The majority of the European groups that encountered Native people had their own world views, which were distinct from those of **indigenous** cultures. They came to acquire land or goods and, in the process, effected changes to the lives and cultures of Natives, imposing, often by force, European cultures, traditions, and ways of life onto the Natives. This process is referred to as **assimilation** – a concept discussed further in chapter 5. We will examine the key groups of Europeans who exerted the most influence on Native peoples – primarily the European governments and, later, the Canadian government, the settlers, the fur traders, and various religious groups.

assimilation
an act, process, or instance of absorbing a population or a cultural group into another's distinctive cultural traditions

IMPACT OF FRENCH AND BRITISH GOVERNMENTS ON NATIVES

The French and the British represented the predominant European influences in North America. They struggled for dominance by establishing settlements. The two powers also assisted in the formation of the French Compagnie du Nord (French) and the Hudson's Bay Company (British), each vying for the right to purchase furs from specific Native groups and for the right to claim specific territory for trade and hunting purposes. As a result, legal documents were created to reinforce these rights. The Hudson's Bay Charter is an example of a European government's claim to territories and the natural resources located within the territories. The two fur trading companies were in direct competition, each vying for control – first, of the Hudson Bay and surrounding area trade, and then the inland trade. They brought new tribes into their loose association of Native hunters and trappers from the various bands. Both fur companies built forts to establish their claim to specific fur trading routes and lands.

The two countries were fierce rivals, and conflict, now known as Queen Anne's War, broke out between them in 1702, and lasted until 1713. The battles they fought with each other occurred on both sides of the ocean. During the War of 1756 (referred to as the Seven Years' War), Native groups, based on their historical relationships, were enlisted as allies for both the French and the British. In 1763, the French were defeated on both continents and were required to relinquish their claims to North American lands, in addition to their right to officially trade within specific waterways. After 1763, when the British won the war against the French, a group of British and American free traders began to assume control over previously held French canoe routes. They competed with the Hudson's Bay Company by offering more goods to the Natives for the furs they brought. After a number of power struggles, the two groups joined to form the North West Company, which became a strong influence on the more northern Natives (Crowe, 1992).

In 1763, Britain drew up an important piece of legislation called the Royal Proclamation. One of the intentions of the proclamation was to reserve a large piece of land for Native occupation and use only.

IMPACT OF EUROPEAN SETTLERS IN NORTHERN ONTARIO

In northern Ontario, contact with Europeans increased in the 17th century. Before this, European influence focused mainly on the United States, along the coasts, and in the southern parts of what would become Upper and Lower Canada (Ontario and Quebec). Europeans began to edge farther north into the colder and harsher climate of Ontario to seek new lands and ore and mineral bodies. Some of these settlers were missionaries looking to convert the Natives, and fur traders seeking new sources of fur. We will look at these groups more closely to see their effect on the Native peoples with whom they came into contact.

Migration to North America began soon after its "discovery" by Columbus. Pockets of non-Native settlements could be found all over what is now Canada. However, the major influx of settlers and settlements within Canada did not occur until the 1700s and 1800s. This influx was in direct correlation to the British government's intention to validate its claim to the northern lands for the British empire. It was also a response to the British concern over what could happen to the rest of its land holdings in North America after its defeat in the 1776 American Revolution. In addition, colonists loyal to Britain who were living in American territory fled to Canada after their defeat in the revolution. The new settlers were referred to as Loyalists. They included the Scottish, Irish, German, English, Indian allies (the Iroquois, in particular), and African Americans. Most of the Loyalists settled in the areas known as Upper and Lower Canada. The lands that they settled on were along the north shore of the St. Lawrence River, near the Bay of Quinte, and the Niagara River (Ontario, 2001). Many blacks, recently freed from slavery, settled in New Brunswick and Nova Scotia.

The British concern over their New World lands was validated when the newly formed United States sought to claim ownership of all of North America. The War of 1812, fought in Upper and Lower Canada, resulted in the defeat of the Americans. From then on, the British began to aggressively campaign for people to settle in the New World. As we will later see, the British government then entered into treaties with Native nations to accommodate the large influx of new settlers. As more and more lands were removed from Native control, their sovereignty, which was based in part on the land, also diminished. By the late 1700s and early 1800s, settlers locating in northern Ontario had increased considerably.

FUR TRADE AND NORTHERN ONTARIO NATIVES

The fur trade was probably the most influential in the establishment of non-Native settlements across northern Canada. Wherever the North West Company and the Hudson's Bay Company erected a trading post, a small community was established to house their employees, as well as government officials. Why did the fur trade move north, despite being so strongly entrenched farther south? The first reason was the nation-building intentions of the British Crown. Another reason was the depletion of animal furs elsewhere. The increasing demand for furs compelled the fur companies to expand their activities farther north. In addition, and of more interest, the furs acquired north of the St. Lawrence were found to be superior. The cold climate provided these northern animals with thick and glossy pelts that were coveted by the European fashion market. The demands for these furs and the subsequent attraction of Native peoples in this area (Ojibwe, Cree, and other Woodland Native groups) for European goods provided the fur companies with a climate in which to set up shop.

Development of Permanent Dwellings

Although the trading posts were influential in creating non-Native communities across the north, they also had a tremendous effect on the Native peoples who came to them to barter. The fur trade brought many changes, among them the manner in which Native groups lived. Migratory Woodland Indians were traditionally nomads, seeking game for survival. As the trading posts became more fixed in their lives – a place where they would bring their furs in exchange for goods – more Natives began to develop permanent dwellings around the trading posts. These dwellings were often deliberately erected to coincide with places Natives frequented, such as their summer or winter campsites. For example, Sault Ste. Marie was populated with Native peoples because of its abundance of fish and access to water travel between Lake Huron and Lake Superior. The place became an early non-Native community for the same reasons.

The establishment of permanent Native dwellings started a chain reaction that led to many other significant changes.

HOMEWORK ACTIVITY

Use the Internet to research facts about a specific Hudson's Bay Company trading post. Give reasons for the location of this particular trading post, such as its proximity to well-used waterways, Native communities, and other trading posts. Present your findings to the class.

Changing the Barter System

The fur trade with non-Natives led to major changes in the traditional trading relations that the various Native groups had with each other. While the Native hunters and trappers continued to barter in their traditional manner, many of the types of goods for which they bartered changed. As a result, their immediate quality of life improved. The barter system did not, however, sustain long-term economic prosperity of their communities. The profits earned by the foreign traders were taken back to their home countries. From the Natives' viewpoint, trading posts received more benefits from their trading arrangements than Natives did, exemplifying the inequity of the trading system.

Development of the Notion of Wealth

Traditionally, northern Ontario Native groups did not consider furs to be a sign of wealth. The animals were killed for food, shelter, clothing, and tools. Anything that the family did not need was given to other community members. In fact, when a deer or moose was killed by a hunter, the whole community and/or the elders were given a share of the meat or other parts of the animal, as needed. Given their nomadic existence, collecting and storing the hides would have been impractical. The people travelled with what they could carry, so the concept of wealth – that one person could have more material goods than another – was inconsequential to their way of life.

Communal distribution of wealth is still a part of many Native cultural practices. Material goods are given to other community members in a number of ways. One of these practices is referred to as "giveaways." At a pow wow, a social event where people gather to share their songs and dance, giveaways are always held at the end of the celebration. At this time, all the elders, drummers, and dancers receive a gift, followed by other community members and guests who have attended the pow wow. Examples of giveaway items are crafts, tobacco, and linen.

Another instance of the Native custom of giving to other community members is in the distribution of wild meat. It is still not uncommon in northern communities for a hunter to give meat to other people in the community. In fact, some of the bands are attempting to reinstate this practice. In Wikwemikong, Manitoulin Island, the band encourages hunters and fishers to give meat and fish to the elders in the community. As a personal memory, co-author Pam Williamson remembers spending summers with her grandmother on the reserve. Whenever anyone visited, she would give items such as food, towels, and clothing to them when they left.

After the fur companies became established in northern Ontario, Native peoples began to change some of their practices. They began to see the accumulation of goods or wealth as a societal motivator. As some individuals in the community became wealthier than others, the community began to experience more disputes and violence over hunting and trapping territories and the encroachment of Native trappers onto other members' areas for hunting and trapping.

Selection of Leaders

The accumulation of wealth affected the manner in which leaders were selected. Traditionally, leaders were selected on the basis of their clan. For example, many leaders were selected from the Bear (Mu-kwa') clan or the Crane (Ah-ji-jawk') clan for their leadership qualities. Leaders were not selected for their admired qualities or for any social standing that they had attained; social classes almost did not exist in the traditional Ojibwe and Cree cultures. As wealth became a motivating factor within the communities, the selection of leaders became influenced by the material goods amassed by the individual.

Disappearance of the Clan System

clan
a group of people who share a common ancestor

Another change that occurred in Native cultures was the slow disappearance of the **clan** system. Before contact with Europeans, the system of clans maintained the tribes or communities as cohesive groups with clearly delineated roles and responsibilities. According to the teachings that author E. Benton-Benai (1998) received, the Creator gave the Earth's people the clan systems to form a framework for strength and order. The Ojibwe clan system comprised seven original clans: the Crane (Ah-ji-jawk'), known as chieftains or leaders; the Loon (Mahng), known as chieftains or leaders; the Fish (Gi-Goon'), known as the intellectuals or teachers; the Bear (Mu-kwa'), known as police, protectors, or herbal medicine people; the Martin (Wa-bi-zha-shi'), known as warriors; the Deer (We-we-shesh'-she), known as gentle people; and the Bird (Be-nays'), known as spiritual leaders. Each of these clan members was responsible for serving and acting as a clan representative.

The clans were guided by strict rules and social mores. For instance, clan lineage was passed down paternally (on the father's side of the family), which meant that each child assumed the clan of his or her father, while the mother maintained her own clan. Clan members did not necessarily know all the people to whom they were related because the lineage was too extensive and the members were spread out extensively. The only means of confirming their relationships was through the maintenance of the clan system, which included cousins, aunts, uncles, grandparents, and even distant relatives, following a lineage that had never been recorded on paper. As part of the introduction to a community, when a clan member visited another Native community, he or she would be asked to identify his or her clan. If the visitor identified himself or herself as belonging to a clan of the visited community, members of that clan were obliged to receive the person as a family member and invite him or her to eat and stay with them.

If a person fell in love with someone from the same clan, the couple would not be allowed to marry. This practice prevented intermarriage and potential problems caused by inbreeding.

The clan system also benefited from ceremonies and celebrations that brought together many Native groups at different times of the year. However, after Native hunters and their families settled in permanent dwellings, the various groups did not have as much contact. The ceremonies and celebrations among the various communities became less frequent. Stationary settlements also meant fewer opportunities to meet and marry people from other communities. Together with other factors, the clan system lost its influence and became ineffective. Today, although a number of Native people may know their clan identity, many do not.

Growing Dependence on Europeans

Another change that affected Natives was their growing dependence on European traders. Before the establishment of trading posts, Natives were proficient hunters who survived in a harsh land using traps, bows and arrows, spears, and other hunting tools to kill the animals that provided them with sustenance and shelter. If they required other goods, they bartered among themselves and with other Native nations. For example, tobacco was considered a sacred medicine and was used by the Ojibwe and the Cree. While few within these nations grew tobacco, they primarily bartered for it with the Iroquois who did. When the fur trading posts were established, their lure was undeniable to the Natives, who could then acquire things that they never had, which mostly enhanced the quality of their lives. Sewing needles, guns, shells, gunpowder, ceramic or glass beads (ornamentation for their clothing and moccasins), iron pots, axes, nails, tea, flour, sugar, alcohol, knives, kettles, blankets, and cloth were some of the goods they received from the European traders. These items made hunting, cooking, and making clothes easier for Natives. However, the introduction of alcohol created new societal problems and its impact continues to reverberate through Native communities today.

Thus, as Natives became less dependent on their environment for their survival, they became more dependent on the goods at the trading posts. For some years, this arrangement appeared to have been positive for both sides: the traders received the hides from which they made a profit in Europe, and the Native people acquired an improved standard of living. The shift from a reliance on the environment to a dependence on European goods, however, resulted in problems that would later plague Native communities and lead to the erosion in their ability to govern and make decisions about their ways of living.

To further elaborate on the extent of Native dependence on the trading posts, the actual goods they purchased were not things that they themselves could manufacture or replicate. To illustrate this point, we will examine the musket, and the pellets, flint, and gunpowder required to use it. In the 17th century, Native people did not have the skills or technology to melt ore, remove the impurities, and place the metal into moulds to create guns, nor could they make the pellets or gunpowder to discharge the guns. Isolated in North America, unlike the Europeans, Native peoples had not been exposed to other cultures and the developments that occurred within them. These technological advances were the result of the integration of inventions and concepts developed by people from a variety of nations. As a result of their relative isolation in the Americas, Natives came to rely totally on the trading posts for these purchases. From a business perspective, the suppliers or trading companies operated from a position of strength, with a monopoly on the prices and the quantities of the products. It is easy to see how the Native reliance on European products became so deeply entrenched.

Because the fur market was unstable, it eventually collapsed. Today, the market is a mere shell of its former existence. Discrepancies in fur prices were common and this resulted in unstable incomes for Natives. Fur price variations were merely the response of the fur companies to the changing demands and tastes of the fashion markets. For example, beaver pelts would be in fashion one season, and mink would replace it the next. Responding to these shifts in the market, fur companies would change the monetary value of the furs they purchased from the Natives. Consequently, Native trappers did not receive the same amount of goods or money for the furs each time they brought fur to the traders.

To add to the market's erratic nature, the trappers depended on the environment for the number of furs they could obtain. If animal populations were deficient due to overtrapping or natural causes — for example, disease, fire, and overpopulation of predators — hunters were unable to acquire furs with which to trade for the goods their families had become accustomed to and dependent on. In effect, the Natives were the ones caught in the middle — reliance on the whims of an ever-changing market, complicated by a dependence on a changing and unpredictable environment.

Growing Dependence on Government

Over time, Native trappers and hunters learned to use the gun almost exclusively, relying less and less on their traditional hunting skills. The demand for fur, overhunting, and the use of new weapons caused near extinction of some animals — for example, the beaver in the 1800s. Many trading posts closed. In 1870, the government of Canada assumed control of the Hudson's Bay Company, ending the influence of a private company (Frideres, 1993). Native peoples who had settled and developed ties with these posts began to experience hardships — some Natives died from starvation and related diseases. The government saw fit to intervene, providing food and other goods to the Natives.

paternalism
a system under which an authority undertakes to supply the needs and/or regulate the conduct of those under its control in matters affecting them as individuals, as well as in their relations to authority and to each other

Many Natives, though, considered this assistance as **paternalism**. Queen Victoria was referred to as "Your Queen Mother" in many treaties as well as in correspondence with many Native groups. Thus, in this fashion, Natives were maintained as dependants, leaving their guardian, the government, to control their destinies. Natives continue to resent this treatment because it implies that they cannot care for themselves and make their own decisions. Another complaint was that the government often provided help and intervention only because of political or public pressure, often without Native input or with minimal consideration of what the Native peoples wanted or needed. The help often came only when situations were at their most desperate or extreme.

As we study the relationship between Native peoples and the government further, we will note the recurring theme of ward and guardian as it occurs in various legislation and actions taken by the government with First Nations peoples.

IMPACT OF RELIGION

Religious orders came to the new lands to convert the indigenous peoples, whom they thought of as "pagans." Of the Christian religions that came across the sea to the northern regions of Ontario, the two most dominant groups were the English Protestants and the French Catholics. The Roman Catholic Church was linked to the government of New France, and its Jesuit and Récollet priests travelled and lived among the various Native groups seeking converts. Initially, the Native peoples did not welcome the missionaries as openly as they had the traders. The value of guns, iron pots, and other tools was obvious, whereas the value of new spiritual beliefs was not. However, northern tribes in general respected the spiritual beliefs of their European counterparts and began to accept the missionaries into their communities, adopting some or all aspects of the new religions.

Despite their good intentions, the missionaries restricted or forbade many Native cultural ceremonies, teachings, and practices, deeming them to be evil. For example, they discouraged any type of drumming; ceremonies — for example, Shaking Tent Ceremony, Full Moon Ceremony, and Healing Lodge Ceremony; smudging; and other Native practices. They also brought their cultural practices and tried to impose restrictions on the Natives' way of living, which had very little to do with biblical teachings — for example, ways of dressing.

The missionaries were, however, very influential and they were able to assist in positive changes within the communities. They helped reduce deaths by providing rudimentary health services and introducing health awareness. They also attempted to decrease alcohol-related problems. Unfortunately, the religious groups were also responsible for a number of rifts among the various community members and families. Sometimes, the various religious orders would become rivals for "Indian souls" and would compete with each other to see who could convert the most Natives. At times, they undermined each other's efforts. Evidence of the territorial or competitive nature of the religious orders still exists. In many reserves, particularly in the north, Native communities have one dominant church that forbids other religions or makes them unwelcome in the community. In the book *The History of the Original Peoples of Northern Canada*, K.J. Crowe (1992) noted, "Rival missionaries eager to convert the same cannibal are apt to behave like rival cannibals stalking the same missionary" (p. 149). An elderly non-Native woman from Manitowaning, on Manitoulin Island, recounted a time when the churches in the town would compete to see who could provide the most or best baking at Christmas so that Natives from the nearby reserve of Wikwemikong would attend their church festivities (and not their rivals').

Residential schools were one of the legacies of religious zeal and assimilation policies. These schools are discussed in chapter 5.

CONCLUSION

In this chapter, we saw the impact of European contact on First Nations peoples. We also examined the role of Euro-Canadian governments and the impact of their policies on Natives' lives. Missionaries had profound effects – both positive and negative – on the Native peoples they came to minister and convert. In most Native communities today, influences of the various churches can still be seen.

J.R. Miller (2002) summarizes the effects of contact between Europeans and Natives quite succinctly. Trade, he points out, brought Natives and Europeans together, as did the desire on both sides to establish a continuing relationship. This "continuing relationship," however, meant different things to each group. For the Europeans, the relationship meant Christian evangelization and military alliances, diseases that caused great loss of Native life, and resource exploitation that brought great loss of Native land and culture:

> The onset of settlement ... everywhere led to the dispossession, economic marginalization, and attempted assimilation of aboriginal peoples at the hands of the ... state and the Christian churches. (Miller, 2002, p. 80)

The Native population declined drastically, community cohesion withered, and individuality and culture suffered.

Europeans found other ways of subduing Natives, mainly by killing them off. The competition in the fur trade, as outlined in the following sections, led to violence, promoted by the Hudson's Bay Company and the North West Company, to gain an advantage in the fur trade. Alcohol was introduced, and inter-tribal violence became common. Britain and France sought Native allies in their wars with each other, causing many Native deaths. The contributions of the Natives in these wars, including the American Revolution and the War of 1812, the French and Indian Wars, and many others, were never acknowledged, and land grants that were offered to the Natives by the victors were rarely fulfilled.

In the next chapter, we will review the specific policies and legislation that were created by various governments to deal with Native peoples. We will also look at how the French and British governments and, later, North American governments treated Native populations and influenced the way in which their citizens responded to and interacted with indigenous populations. In part, the manner in which government officials, soldiers, fur traders, religious groups, and settlers treated Native people was based on their governments' actions, policies, and laws toward Natives.

WORKSHEET

1. Discuss the role that commerce played in Native–European government relations. Explain your answer fully and provide an example. (2 marks)
2. Identify two changes brought to the Native people by Europeans that were intentional and two changes that occurred unintentionally. Cite examples. (4 marks)
3. Describe fully the economic advantages for Europeans settling in northern Ontario. (4 marks)

4. List four items or goods that Natives did not have before contact with the fur traders. Consider the impact of these items individually and how they would have contributed to changes in Natives' ways of life. (4 marks)

5. Consider the effect that the following items or goods, which they had not used previously, had on Europeans following their contact with Native populations. Select three and describe the changes they made to the European way of life. (3 marks)

   potatoes

   unlimited access to land

   unlimited access to natural resources — for example, furs, timber, etc.

   tobacco

   canoes, snowshoes

6a. Assess the dangers of a partnership where one partner has the upper hand or most of the advantages. Use the Native–European relationship in trading as your example. (2 marks)

6b. Describe the outcome of this arrangement on the players. Support your answer. (1 mark)

TOTAL — 20 MARKS

KEY TERMS

acculturation

assimilation

clan

indigenous

paternalism

CHAPTER 4

Treaty Making: Loss of Native Lands and Autonomy

Chapter Objectives

After completing this chapter, you should be able to:

- Identify the significance of the land and land appropriation in Native and non-Native relationships.
- Explain the various types of treaties between the Natives and the government.
- Identify the specific treaties that the British and Canadian governments entered into with various Native groups for the area of Canada.
- Describe how the current process of land claims developed.

INTRODUCTION

Prior to European contact, Natives were sovereign, self-governing, and lived within their traditional territories. As discussed in previous chapters, the Native concept of the land differed from the Europeans'. This difference led to misunderstandings and contentions, the effects of which are still felt. Soon after contact, Europeans began to approach various Native groups to enter into nation-to-nation agreements to reconcile their different interests and aspirations. Changes to the Native way of living on the land began with these first **treaties**. Most important, the loss of Native sovereignty and right to self-government is strongly linked to the treaties. From the start, the Natives voiced concerns about disruptions to their traditional ways and cultures, and these concerns are reflected in the words of the treaties to which they became party.

Treaties and now land claims have dominated and flavoured the interaction and relationships between Native peoples and various non-Native governments from the beginning. Most treaties in Canada were signed between 1800 and the early 1900s. They are non-Native documents that have been approved of through

treaty
"an international agreement between States in written form and governed by the international law, whether embodied in a single instrument or in two or more related instruments and whatever its particular dimension" (Morse, 1985)

the Canadian legislative process as legally binding. Today, the treaties provide a legitimate claim for the Native peoples' fight for the injustice of, irregularity of, and the lack of treaty promises, and the failure to fulfill them. These circumstances have plagued the treaties from the beginning. We will examine the treaty process, its evolution, its format, and its existence in Native–Canadian relationships today.

BACKGROUND TO THE NEGOTIATION PROCESS

Treaties were not new to the First Nations peoples prior to the *Royal Proclamation of 1763*. Treaties had been made among tribes to settle wars and land disputes, to provide trading opportunities, and even to negotiate marriage arrangements.

One of the first recorded treaties, negotiated before 1450, involved the Seneca, Mohawk, Onondaga, Oneida, and Cayuga peoples. This treaty was called the Great Law of Peace of the People of the Longhouse, and it set down a code of law and form of government, along with other things, among the five nations. It was passed on orally and not recorded until 1880.

Before 1763, Natives had entered into negotiations with fur traders, with the Métis acting as intermediaries in many cases. The negotiations, which offered furs for trade goods, were characterized by mutual respect and equality between the parties. Native ceremonies were often part of the negotiations to establish a harmonious relationship. The Natives expected the principles that had been established long before negotiations over land began with the Europeans to carry over into these discussions. To them, mutual respect and understanding were essential components of any negotiations.

This was not the case with treaty negotiations. Europeans and the First Nations peoples had different cultural contexts for negotiations. In the first place, the Natives felt that no one could own the land; the land was a gift from the Creator, and they were its guardians, not owners. The land was their means of survival.

Second, language difficulties between Native people and Europeans meant that the Natives didn't fully understand the terms of any agreements that were negotiated. They weren't aware that they were selling the land, since it wasn't theirs to sell. They were unaware that they were giving up anything. To the Natives, treaties were intended to lay out the terms of a mutual sharing of resources and their compensation for sharing these resources. While both sides had translators present, it was impossible to translate decades of tradition. These and other factors in the negotiations put the Native people at a distinct disadvantage. In many cases, it wasn't until the Europeans began the process of removing them from their land that the Native people fully understood what they had signed. However, in the eyes of the government, a deal was a deal; treaties were a form of land surrender, the first step in the assimilation process.

ROYAL PROCLAMATION OF 1763 AND THE ENSUING TREATIES

> My heart is a stone. Heavy with sadness for my people; cold with the knowledge that no treaty will keep the whites out of our land; hard with determination to resist as long as I live and breathe. Now we are weak and many of our people are afraid. But hear me; a single twig breaks but the bundle of twigs is strong. Someday I will

embrace our brother tribes and draw them into a bundle and together we will win our country back from the whites. (Tecumseh, Shawnee Chief, circa 1795)

GROUP DISCUSSION

1. What is Tecumseh's general feeling about the treaties that were created between his people and the whites?
2. Does he hold any hope that the situation will improve? What is his final strategy to improve the situation?
3. What would be your strategy if you were in the same situation?

Since the *Royal Proclamation of 1763* formally established the treaty-making process in 1763, it is important to review what precepts were set down in this document that would affect the Natives throughout the treaty-making era up to present-day land claims. It is also important to examine what led up to the Royal Proclamation to understand the form and structure of the treaties that followed.

In 1763, the British government issued the Royal Proclamation to address a number of situations it faced. (For more information on the Royal Proclamation, refer to appendix 4.1.) First, with their recent victory in the Seven Years' War against the French (their main rivals for the New World), the British set out to organize the conquered French territories in North America and to set boundaries between the newly acquired province of Quebec and the American colonies. Second, the British were concerned about the potential eruption of a war between France's former Native allies and British Native allies. Finally, the British were concerned about the growing resentment of Natives toward the growing settlement of whites on Native lands. To address this last point, the British Crown developed a number of **policies** with regard to relationships with First Nations: no European, immigrant, or local government could purchase or settle land that was recognized as property of the Native peoples; a large tract of land was reserved for the exclusive use of Native peoples; any settlers on these designated or protected lands were to be removed; and the military was to "seize and apprehend all persons" in violation. The *Royal Proclamation of 1763* served to:

policy
a plan of action that has been chosen and that guides or influences future decisions

> Conciliate the Affection of the Indian Nations, by every Act of Strict Justice and by affording them His Royal Protection from any encroachment on the lands they have reserved to themselves, for their hunting Grounds and their own Support and Habitation.

In addition, the Crown clearly outlined a treaty-making process that was grounded in the principles set down in the Act. The law ensured that no one could approach Native peoples for land identified as Native-owned, with the exception of the Crown or representatives of the Crown. The land could then be sold or given by the Crown to settlers and other Europeans. The rationale given was that Native lands would be safe from unscrupulous individuals who might try to cheat Native peoples out of their lands. The Crown in effect assumed a paternal, authoritarian role in making decisions on the land transfer and how much Native peoples would be compensated for their lands.

The Crown not only initiated the treaty process but also declared itself to be the only one that could approach and purchase land that the Crown had decreed was "Indian land" from the various Native groups — in essence, a broker. Consequently, the government held a firm monopoly on any land transfers. Native people had to accept what the government offered. For example, many of the Numbered Treaties (discussed later in the chapter) that were signed after Confederation in 1867 included farming implements as part of what the Native groups received in return for their lands. The people in these areas were nomadic at this time and had no practical use for agricultural tools. However, the Canadian government concentrated on establishing permanent Native settlements and encouraged the people to become farmers — hence, the farming implements.

GROUP DISCUSSION

Weigh the benefits and drawbacks to the Crown's assuming the role as sole negotiator.

Did the *Royal Proclamation of 1763* recognize the sovereignty of Native peoples (that they were self-governing)? This question continues to be debated. Native peoples assert that their sovereignty as nations has never been **extinguished**. They argue that the Royal Proclamation, even though it placed boundaries on land reserved for Natives, continued to recognize Native sovereignty. Natives were not seen or referred to as Crown subjects in this document, nor in any later Crown documents. Native peoples were recognized as separate and distinct peoples and nations. They were promised in treaties by various European governments that their traditional ways, which included the right to their own laws, territories, and forms of government, would not be violated.

extinguish
to end something permanently by process or agreement

TREATIES AND TREATY NEGOTIATIONS

No other **legislation** or policies were created by the Crown between 1763 and 1830 that specifically addressed Native peoples. However, during this period, the British imperial government created and assumed responsibility for Natives through a department called Indian Affairs. The creation of this department reinforced the paternalistic attitude that the government had assumed in its dealings with Native peoples. Despite the influence of the government, however, Native peoples continued to be self-governing, looking after the needs of the people in their communities at a political, economic, social, and cultural level. The only legal documents created during this time between Natives and the British government were the treaties that amassed large tracts of land under British possession.

legislation
laws passed by the federal and provincial governments; a way of defining the powers of an institution

The European-Canadian–Native treaties are agreements between the Crown and Native groups across the country. There are three categories of treaties: Pre-Confederation Treaties, the Numbered Treaties, and the Modern Treaties. The Pre-Confederation Treaties were agreements made before Canada became a country. Many of these earlier treaties or copies of the actual surrender documents have never been found or were poorly documented. Examples of those that survived or were better documented are the Robinson–Huron, Robinson–Superior, and Williams treaties. A second group of treaties, the Numbered Treaties, which were signed between

1871 and 1921, were intended to provide cohesion to the vast interior of Canada and to formally recognize these territories as part of Canada. The third set of treaties is the Land Claim Agreements, which have been in existence only since the Land Claims Policy was established in 1973 (University of Alberta, n.d.).

Why Treaties Were Established

Initially, the first treaties were negotiated between the European military personnel and Native groups to establish peace and friendship. The Native nations themselves had traditionally participated in many peace and trading treaties with each other over the years so that when European governments first approached them with these offers of peace or friendship, the Natives were familiar with the premise. One of the first peace and friendship treaties to be struck was in 1725 between the British and the Mi'kmaq First Nations peoples of Nova Scotia. The British secured neutrality and assistance from the Mi'kmaq in their disputes, at that time, with the French. What was negotiated? In return for military assistance or neutrality, the British agreed to facilitate Native trade in this area and promised to prevent any European intrusion into traditional hunting, trapping, and fishing practices.

Another reason why the Europeans initiated treaty negotiations was to establish exclusive trading alliances with the Native nations. These contracts were developed as a response to the competition between the various governments and the European fur trading companies to corner the fur trade market. For example, the Hudson's Bay Company negotiated with northern Native groups so that the Natives would only sell furs to the Hudson's Bay Company. In return, the Hudson's Bay Company assured Natives that they would receive quality goods from their trading posts.

The final and primary reason why the Europeans entered into treaties with Native nations was to acquire lands and the natural resources from those lands. All treaties were initiated by the Europeans; at no time did the Natives commence the negotiations to sell their lands. Treaty negotiations increased as more and more colonies were established. The beginning of the land treaties in southern Ontario occurred after the American Revolution in 1776. As pointed out in chapter 3, following their defeat, the British required land for their displaced Loyalist colonists and their Native allies, all of whom had been in danger of losing their lives had they remained in the United States. The British also needed land to reward their military personnel who had fought in the revolution. The Native allies were primarily tribes of the Six Nations Confederacy (Mohawk, Onondaga, Cayuga, Seneca, Oneida, and Tuscarora) who performed considerable military services for the British. Many of these refugees were resettled in southern Ontario and parts of Quebec. The Native groups who were displaced in these early treaties to give way to these refugees were given lump sum payments of money and goods for the land.

Following the American defeat in the War of 1812, another wave of settlers arrived in Upper Canada or southern Ontario. According to E.S. Rogers and D.B. Smith (1994), non-Native population doubled between 1815 and 1824 from 75 000 to 150 000. During this time, the government completed six major treaty negotiations for nearly 3 million hectares of land. The treaty terms changed during this time. Native military clout and political influence were waning and the British no longer needed the Natives during times of relative peace. As a result, the government began to offer them small annual payments referred to as **annuities** rather than a considerably larger one-time payment. On the other hand, based on their previous experiences,

annuities
yearly amounts of goods or moneys received by the Natives based on specific treaty agreements

the Natives became more sophisticated and wary of the treaty process. They demanded better terms. For example, in many of the later treaties, Natives negotiated for land reserved for their use exclusively, with the right to hunt and fish and the ability to access Crown land to hunt and fish.

Process and Terms of Treaties

No uniform practices existed in treaty-making negotiations, with the exception that a Crown representative was to be involved in all negotiations. This representative, initially a military officer and later a civil or government representative of Indian Affairs, would assemble a number of chiefs who represented the tribes who inhabited the lands that the government desired. Depending on the tribe, the government officials would be accompanied by an interpreter to act as a third party in conveying the wishes of the Crown to the Natives. The signings of treaties were treated as solemn and formal events. The chiefs would dress in their finest regalia and the military negotiators would wear their uniforms. Many of the community members of the tribes involved would assemble for the signing of the treaties. Upon signing, the Natives would receive the goods, money, and so on that were agreed upon in the treaty. For the Natives, treaty signings were often seen as festive occasions.

In exchange for transferring the land over to governments, Native peoples were promised a number of things. In the early treaties for land, Native peoples were mainly given goods such as blankets and guns. For example, the British negotiated a treaty with the Mississauga Native people on May 9, 1781 to provide land for the Loyalists and Native allies who fled territories that fell under American power after the revolution in 1776. In return for selling the Crown a strip of land, six and one-half kilometres deep, along the full length of the west bank of the Niagara River from Lake Erie to Lake Ontario, the Mississauga received 300 suits of clothing (Rogers & Smith, 1994). At times, no payment was made to or requested by the Natives. For example, in 1785, a number of Upper Canada chiefs declared that their people were very poor and all they desired was clothing. They left it up to the "Good Father" (the King) to determine the amount to be paid. It was not until later treaties that financial remuneration was included.

Some treaties also promised that the Natives' spiritual practices would be respected. An early treaty between the British and Hurons promised "free exercise of their religion, customs and trade with the English." Some treaties in the west included a medicine chest. As a result, these Native groups successfully lobbied for and received funding to build medical facilities on reserves. Most treaties included clauses relating to education. Therefore, Status Natives (those whom the government formally recognized and who were eligible for any treaty compensation, such as an annuity) had the right to apply for and receive educational funding to attend school within their bands. In later treaties, the Native peoples also began to receive annuities. Each year, for example, each member of the Wikwemikong First Nation receives $4 from the federal government.

GROUP DISCUSSION

Read the Robinson–Huron Treaty in appendix 4.2. Analyze it and discuss what was negotiated and what the Natives received.

THE NUMBERED TREATIES

After Confederation, treaty negotiations with a large number of Native groups across the vast area of Canada were undertaken. Commonly referred to as the Numbered Treaties, these treaties were made in the interests of nation building for Canada by acquiring the land to build a national railway. Signing of these treaties began in 1871 and ended in 1921. Eleven Numbered Treaties were written after Confederation. The Natives had to agree to accept settlement on reserves as part of the treaty negotiations. Most of the agreements included reserve land based on the number of Native peoples in a settlement. In addition, most of the Numbered Treaties included agreements for schooling, agricultural equipment, gifts, and annuities.

The Numbered Treaties covered most of Canadian lands and regularized Canadian land title (see figure 4.1). The treaties delineated whom the government recognized as a "Treaty Indian" or later as a "Status Indian." The delineation often divided families and omitted Indians whom the government considered to be troublemakers or who had not accepted the Christian religions or ideals of becoming "civilized." As a note of interest, the government did not approach a significant number of aboriginal peoples for treaty negotiations. The Inuit people never entered into treaty talks, and the First Nations peoples in most of the northern expanse of James Bay and British Columbia were not approached for treaty negotiations or settlements. Other lands that the Canadian government claimed but not through the treaty process automatically became territory owned by Canada. Many of these lands are presently under comprehensive land claim agreements (discussed later in this chapter). This is the first time that the Native peoples in these areas have been compensated for the government acquisition and use of their traditional lands.

Treaties 1 and 2 (1871) covered most of the lands in southern Manitoba. These Native groups were expected to adopt farming practices and discontinue their traditional practices of hunting, trapping, and fishing. They were given farm tools and seeds, as well as annuities. Hunting and fishing rights were excluded from these treaties. Treaty 1 was negotiated between the Ojibwe and Swampy Cree Indians of Manitoba and Lieutenant Governor Archibald.

One section of Treaty 1 reads:

> Your Great Mother wishes the good of all races under her sway. She wishes her Red children to be happy and contented. She wishes them to live in comfort. She would like them to adopt the habits of the whites, to til land and raise food, and store it up against a time of want. ... Your Great Mother, therefore, will lay aside for you "lots" of land to be used by you and your children forever. She will not allow the white man to intrude upon these lots. She will make rules to keep them for you, so that as long as the sun shall shine, there shall be no Indian who has not a place that he can call his home, where he can go and pitch his camp or if he chooses, build his house and til his land.

GROUP DISCUSSION

1. What promises did the Great Mother (Queen Victoria) make to the Native people in Treaty 1?
2. Based on what was promised, discuss whether it is feasible that all the promises have been kept.

FIGURE 4.1 Indian Treaty Areas, 1850–1930

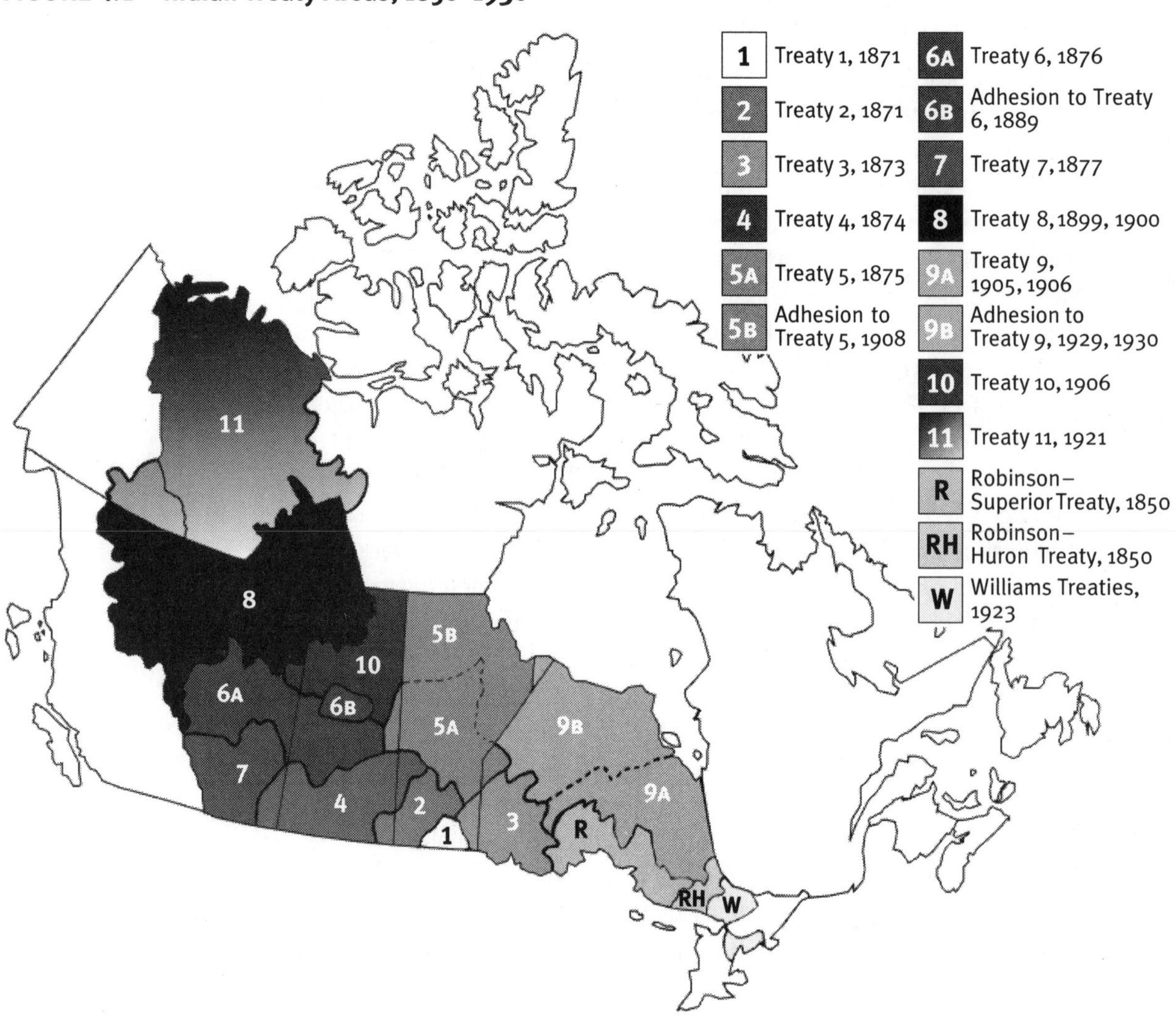

Source: Adapted from Energy, Mines and Resources Canada (1991).

Treaties 3 to 7 covered lands the government needed for the railway construction across the prairies. Treaty 3 (1873) was negotiated with the Ojibwe and included an area just north of Minnesota, also encompassing the Rainy Lake area.

Treaty 4 (1874) was negotiated primarily with the Cree, Ojibwe, and Saulteaux First Nations for the southern part of Saskatchewan. These treaties were intended to clear the way for the trans-Canada railway and to establish a clear Canadian presence in western Canada. At this time, the treaties encompassed areas that had been settled for many years by a strong Métis presence. The Métis were omitted from the treaties; their presence and their claims to the lands were largely ignored. Consequently, the treatment they received contributed to the uprisings, headed by Louis Riel, in the 1800s.

Treaty 5 (1875; Adhesions, 1908 and 1910) was signed by tribes of Ojibwe and Swampy Cree for lands that were approximately located from the middle of Lake Winnipeg and Lake Manitoba to just below the southwestern quadrant of James Bay. Two amendments were made in 1908 and 1910 to include bands within the treaty area that had been excluded in the original signing.

Treaty 6 (1876) was settled with the Plain and Wood Cree Natives and other tribes near Fort Carlton, Fort Pitt, and Battle River. This treaty contains the infamous "Medicine Chest" clause, which was intended to provide health care for the communities. Today, Native groups within this treaty have been fighting for greater on-reserve health care.

Treaty 7 (1877) was signed by the Blackfoot Confederacy (Blackfoot, Blood, Peigan, and Sarcee) and the Chipewyan and Assiniboine. The land given to the Canadian government included property located in the southern part of Alberta, near Bow River and west to the rise of the mountains, and all the way to Fort Macleod in the area of Saskatchewan.

In order to provide an overland route to the gold fields in the Yukon, Treaty 8 was negotiated and signed. The government acquired a vast territory called the Athabaska District, which encompasses most of the northern half of Alberta, the northwest corner of Saskatchewan, and a mountainous area north of British Columbia.

Treaty 9 (1905; amendments in 1929 and 1930) was signed by Natives in northern Ontario (Ojibwe and Cree), the former Hudson's Bay land grant, to open transportation routes and access to the natural resources such as timber in this area.

Treaty 10 transferred land title to the government of the two newly acquired provinces of Saskatchewan and Alberta from the Chipewyan and Cree in 1906.

Finally, Treaty 11 was signed in 1921 with the Slave, Dogrib, Loucheux, and Hare tribes for land in the Mackenzie District. This was the last of the Numbered Treaties to be signed and was initiated by the government to coincide with the discovery of oil at Fort William.

There were substantially more treaties, purchases, and Crown grants involving the First Nations than those listed as Numbered Treaties. Except for the Crown grants, most of them involved land surrender. In southern Ontario alone, there were 31 land surrender documents signed between 1781 and 1923 (Ontario, Archives of Ontario, n.d.):

1. Treaty No. 381, May 9, 1781 (Mississaugas and Chippewas);
2. Crawford's Purchase, October 9, 1783 (Algonquins and Iroquois);
3. Crawford's Purchase, October 9, 1783 (Mississaugas);
4. Crawford's Purchases, 1784, 1787, 1788 (Mississaugas);
5. John Collins' Purchase, 1785 (Chippewas);
6. Treaty No. 2, May 19, 1790 (Ottawas, Chippewas, Pottawatomys, Hurons);
7. Treaty No. 3, December 2, 1792 (Mississaugas);
8. Crown Grant to the Six Nations, 1793;
9. Crown Grant to Tyendinaga Mohawks, 1793;
10. Crown Grant No. 3 to Joseph Brant, October 24, 1795;
11. Treaty No. 5, 1795 (Chippewas);
12. Treaty No. 6, September 7, 1796 (Chippewas);
13. Treaty No. 7, September 7, 1796 (Chippewa Nation);
14. Treaty No. 13, August 1, 1805 (Mississaugas);

15. Treaty No. 13a, August 2, 1805 (Mississaugas);
16. Treaty No. 16, 1815 (Chippewas);
17. Treaty No. 18, October 17, 1818 (Chippewas);
18. Treaty No. 19, October 28, 1818 (Chippewas);
19. Treaty No. 20, November 5, 1818 (Chippewas);
20. Treaty No. 21, March 9, 1819 (Chippewa Nation);
21. Treaty No. 27, May 31, 1819 (Mississaugas);
22. Treaty No. 27, April 25, 1825 (Ojibways and Chippewas);
23. Treaty No. 35, August 13, 1833 (Wyandots or Hurons);
24. Treaty No. 45, August 9, 1836 (Chippewas and Ottawas);
25. Treaty No. 45, August 9, 1836 (Saugeens);
26. Treaty No. 57, June 1, 1847 (Iroquois of St. Regis [Akwesasne]);
27. Treaty No. 61, September 9, 1850 (Robinson–Huron Treaty: Ojibways);
28. Treaty No. 72, October 30, 1854 (Chippewas);
29. Treaty No. 82, February 9, 1857 (Sarawak Twp., Chippewas);
30. Williams Treaty, October 31, 1923 (Chippewas) and November 15, 1923 (Mississaugas); and
31. Williams Treaty, October 31, 1923 (Chippewas).

Varying Cultural Perspectives on Treaties

The aim of treaties differs, depending on whose perspective it is examined from — non-Natives' or Natives'. European–Canadian governments intended to secure clear title to the land for development and to guarantee that no future claim could be made by Native peoples to the land. It was likely that the Natives did not fully understand the implications of the land cessation agreements. As discussed in earlier chapters, the Natives' respect and communal approach to the land differed completely from the European perspective of land ownership. Second, each side drew on its world view in the treaty process, which resulted in deep and enduring misunderstandings about land tenure and political **autonomy**.

autonomy
self-government; independence

Did Native peoples fight over the land before contact with Europeans? The answer is "yes." However, we must examine the different rationales that existed between these two situations: Natives–government treaties and treaties between Native groups. Conflict between Native groups occurred especially when tribes claimed the right to certain territories. However, these conflicts were not over who had ownership of the land, but over who had the right to use the land for survival purposes. In comparison, the Crown, based on the world view of European culture, saw the land as transferable and subject to absolute ownership. According to M. Boldt (1993), the treaties were seen by Euro-Canadians as devices to acquire real estate.

As another interpretation of what a treaty is, treaties in the truest sense of the word are solemn agreements establishing the future basis of relationships between nations. For example, after the defeat of Germany in World War I, the allies met with Germany to sign the Treaty of Versailles, which required Germany to comply with a number of conditions. Though Germany lost the war, the nation continued to be recognized as a nation. Native peoples have fought to be recognized as independent nations that signed agreements or treaties, nation to nation. The ongoing debate is whether the treaties signed with Native peoples were based on this perspective. To date, the treaties do not easily fit into any category recognized by Canadian law. In recent years, the Supreme Court of Canada has ruled that the treaties are unique documents for which unique rules of interpretation and enforcement must be developed and implemented by the courts. The difficulty is in interpreting the treaties in contemporary terms, while giving full recognition to their original spirit and intent. At present, each reserve in Canada describes itself as a First Nations community.

Finally, the approach taken by Natives to the agreements and further articulated in today's land claims is from the position that they were the original inhabitants of Canada and that the treaties would guarantee their continued social and cultural distinctiveness. They truly expected that signing the treaties and giving access to the land to other people would ensure their continued ability to maintain a way of living, including the ability to hunt, fish, and essentially to live as they had for centuries.

Effects of Broken Treaty Promises

Many of the terms negotiated for lands, however, have never been completely fulfilled by the government. For a long time, Native peoples were legally unable to fight for their treaty rights because the federal government had made laws to prevent them from filing legal complaints. To date, a number of land claims have been settled, but many more are pending. Existing treaties, signed in those early years, are still upheld as sound and legal documents recognized in any court of law in Canada. Thus, many Natives are still fighting to reclaim their rights or to receive some form of compensation.

As another example of unfulfilled promises, most treaties that were negotiated before and after Confederation included a provision for hunting and fishing rights. However, a number of other treaties extinguished this right. In recent years, the courts have been reluctant to recognize aboriginal or treaty rights to fish or hunt for commercial purposes, even though some treaties specifically mention the Native right to trap or fish. For example, under Treaty 9, the courts have maintained that Natives cannot be regulated by provincial trapping legislation because the treaty protects their right to trap. This matter remains unsettled because federal government policies say that **aboriginal rights** only include the traditional methods of hunting and fishing that Native peoples used prior to European contact. This issue continues to be one of the more contentious problems voiced by Native peoples today.

aboriginal rights
special rights, such as the right to hunt and fish, held by aboriginal people

Consequently, broken treaty promises, both before and after Confederation, have led to a number of disputes that are still being fought. The battles and tensions consistently share a common theme — the land. Many of the disputes are currently in the courts where Natives are attempting to resolve them. Unfortunately, a number of land issues have erupted outside the courts, causing ethnic tensions within a number of communities across Canada.

In hindsight, Native peoples seemed to have little control or influence in the treaty-making process, from the land re-location, to the size of the land, to the type and amount of remuneration they received in return. The following excerpt, which clearly indicates the vulnerability of Native peoples, was written by Chief Buckquaquet of the Rice Lake Mississauga in a negotiation for the Kawartha Lakes region:

> Father: If I was to refuse what our Father has requested, our Women and Children would be more to be pitied. From our lands we receive scarcely anything and if your words are true we will get more by parting with them, than by keeping them — our hunting is destroyed and we must throw ourselves on the compassion of our Great Father the King.
>
> Father: Our youth People and Chief have always thought of not refusing our Father any request he makes to us, and therefore do what he wishes. (Rogers & Smith, 1994, p. 43)

GROUP DISCUSSION

1. Compare this speech with the speech given by Tecumseh earlier in the chapter. What differences do you see in the speeches? What similar themes do they have?
2. Examine the child–parent roles of the Natives and the Crown. How would this affect the relationship between the Native and British — and later, Canadian — governments?

PRESENT NATIVE LAND CLAIMS

usufructuary right the right to use and benefit from the land, based on its traditional use and occupancy

Since early European contact and early land disputes, various Native groups have attempted to regain some control of their traditional lands. Native land claims are based on the argument that the land belonged to the aboriginal peoples of Canada and that the title to the land has never been extinguished. This right is referred to as a **usufructuary right** ("a right based on traditional use and occupancy"), a term used by Native leaders and educators to describe the Native right to the land. Natives argue that they have a legal right to the land based on the fact that Euro-Canadian governments never enacted specific legislation to extinguish Indian title to the land.

Before 1969, land claims were dealt with individually by either the Department of Indian Affairs and Northern Development or by the Department of Justice. For the most part, the claims were held up or stymied because of the federal government's refusal to pass the necessary legislation to deal with Native claims to the land. As mentioned earlier, the Canadian government had not formally acknowledged aboriginal entitlement to the land or that Natives had a legal basis for making claims.

After 1969, a claim by the Nisga'a Indians became a precedent-setting case that initiated the beginning of recognition for the aboriginal claim to the land. The government, through the Supreme Court, formally recognized the fiduciary (guardian–child) relationship between the Crown and the Natives. The government also became obligated to guarantee the rights and freedoms of all of its citizens, which provided further support for land claims. In 1973, the Supreme Court of Canada finally recognized the Nisga'a Indians as the historical inhabitants of the land and that they had to be compensated for its loss.

Two separate agencies were formed to look after Native land claims: the Indian Claims Commissioner and the Office of Indian Claims. Recognition of Native land claims from the Canadian government became a formal process in the early 1970s soon after the Nisga'a case had been taken to the Supreme Court. The government agreed to negotiate settlements where aboriginal title was never extinguished by treaty. At this time, the Office of Indian Claims categorized the land claims under two specific categories: comprehensive and specific.

Comprehensive Land Claims

Comprehensive land claims refer to the Natives' right to their traditional land and resources. They formally recognize some form of aboriginal title to the lands covered by the treaty. However, land is a key issue to contemporary Native land claims. The claims are not based or backed by previous treaties, but these claims represent areas of Canada where treaties were never entered into with the Native groups who had lived there traditionally. (Note that over 50 percent of Canada was never included under any treaty.) Each claim is distinct with individual differences that reflect the needs and history of each area. Comprehensive land claims emphasize the cooperation between the Natives and the government for the purpose of ultimately extinguishing aboriginal title and providing the necessary restitution. There has, however, been much discussion about whether it is appropriate to require aboriginal parties to agree to extinguishment because this is an extremely controversial issue for First Nations peoples.

The first comprehensive land claim was the James Bay and Northern Quebec Agreement, signed in 1975. As of 2004, the federal government has settled 13 comprehensive land claims.

J.S. Frideres (1997) describes two further subcategories under comprehensive claims based on regions: northern and southern. Southern comprehensive claims exist in the more southerly regions of Canada and, as a result, are in the midst of heavily populated areas. These claims are difficult to settle because the land is already well used and "owned." Northern comprehensive claims are claims that originate primarily in the northern regions of the country where settlements are few. These claims are easier to process because the land involved is usually Crown land.

Another more current example of a comprehensive land claim is that of the Nisga'a First Nation in British Columbia in the summer of 1998. The Nisga'a treaty is the first of many land claims to be settled and it resolves one of a number of longstanding grievances of the aboriginal tribes in British Columbia. The treaty grants the Nisga'a $190 million in cash, 2000 square kilometres of land, and a share in the catch from the Nass River.

The treaty also provides for a system of self-government for the 5500 Nisga'a people. This system of self-government has not been seen before in Canada and differs from that found in Nunavut, the new Native territory. Self-government for the Nisga'a creates four village governments with one central Nisga'a government that will be responsible for the administration of services in the Nass Valley. To date, the majority of the people who live in the valley are Nisga'a. To describe it simply, the Nisga'a government will have many of the same powers as a municipality and will also have law-making authority in areas that normally fall under provincial or federal jurisdiction; however, it is not sanctioned to make any laws that supersede current federal legislation. Some non-Native groups oppose the treaty because the non-Native populations that are living in the Nass Valley will be directly affected by decisions of the Nisga'a government, yet will have no voting rights. Nisga'a leaders contend that the treaty does not allow them to tax non-Natives and that non-Natives will be "consulted" when making decisions that may affect them. Other non-Native residents do not perceive the treaty to be a threat and are pleased with the infusion of money and benefits into the area that will be enjoyed by all Nass Valley residents (Bell, 1998).

Specific Land Claims

Specific land claims are based on a lawful obligation and involve claims that relate to the management of Indian lands and assets. They deal with treaties, scrip (a certificate issued for compensation of land), and band claims. The main issues addressed in band claims are the loss of treaty lands and natural resources in established band lands and government stewardship over band assets. For instance, the government of Quebec did not enter into a treaty with the Natives indigenous to that area, and France did not have treaties with the Natives, so the issue is whether Native rights were extinguished. Some, including Natives, argue that the land in Quebec was given through imperial grace to all its people in its territories. But the French Crown handed the land to religious orders to be held in trust for Native peoples (and did not give them complete ownership). In both Quebec and the Maritimes, the lands given as reserves to the Natives could be reduced or sold with no agreement made or consent given by Native groups. Some Native groups claim that the treaty terms have not been fulfilled. For example, they argue that verbal promises were not kept. A number of reserve lands have been lost through resurveying, settling of non-Natives on Native lands, formal surrenders, and government expropriations (transferring of another's property to one's own possession). Native groups also claim that, based on unfairness in the way that the treaties were negotiated, treaty terms were inadequate.

Examples of specific land claims include the following situations. In 1901, the Assiniboine were forced off two different reserves and were settled in a Cree settlement. The government made a handsome profit on the real estate. Under a grievance by the Natives, settlement of $119 million was made. In another situation, the Ojibwe of Kettle Point near Sarnia, Ontario received $2.4 million in 1980 for land for a military camp surrendered at below-market prices. The status of specific land claims in Ontario as of 2004 can be seen at http://www.ainc-inac.gc.ca/ps/clm/onm_e.pdf.

RESOLVING LAND CLAIMS

The greatest difficulty encountered in resolving land claims is the number of parties involved in various aspects of any land claim. Negotiations for the resolution of land claims might involve the federal and provincial governments. Regional governments, municipal governments, private corporations, and individuals who have an interest, either political or economic, in the results of a specific land claim may also be involved.

For instance, in any area affected by a land claim, there may be a variety of federal and provincial services that would be involved: highways, pipelines, railways, policing services, power generation stations, educational facilities, provincial parks, and the like, that have to be negotiated. An entire city or town may be located within the boundaries of an area covered by the land claim. Private and individual businesses may also be located within that area. All of these stakeholders must be involved in negotiations, and it is certain that each of them will be affected in different ways.

Paul Baxter (2004) offers a comprehensive analysis of this division of powers and solutions to the land claims issue. As Baxter states, it is very difficult to achieve any kind of agreement over how to resolve a specific land claim, and it often takes decades to reach an agreement. Of all the stakeholders that may be involved, the greatest obstacle to the resolution of land claims often rests with the higher levels of government, both federal and provincial.

First Nations negotiators can't simply ignore the governments; under the *Constitution Act, 1982*, the federal government has exclusive jurisdiction over First Nations peoples who are registered and live on reserves. Therefore, in a land claim, the federal government must be involved. However, the constitution also states that the provinces have control over natural resources and Crown land, among other things, and responsibility for civil law, law enforcement, protection of property, and public works. Section 88 of the ***Indian Act*** (discussed in chapter 5) states that First Nations peoples are subject to all of the laws that fall under provincial jurisdiction, such as hunting and fishing laws, that may have been negotiated in earlier treaties. The federal government cannot deny provincial jurisdiction in the resolution of land claims.

Indian Act
the principal federal statute dealing with Indian status, local government, and the management of reserve lands and common moneys

Bill C-6

Bill C-6 introduced the *Specific Claims Resolution Act* in the House of Commons in October 2002. This bill was an attempt to overcome some of the difficulties encountered in settling land claims. By way of background to Bill C-6, between 1927 and 1951 it was illegal for aboriginal people to bring any claim against the government without the prior permission of the federal government. It was not until 1973 that the federal government began to consider specific land claims from various First Nations.

It would be difficult to characterize the process of considering land claims as objective, since the government accepted, validated, and negotiated land claims against itself. One result of the Oka situation in 1991, however, was the establishment of the Indian Claims Commission, which held public inquiries into specific land claims that had been rejected by the government. Since the commission held only advisory powers, and since it could be disbanded by the government at any time, the commission's powers were limited. This was not the answer to the specific land claims dilemma.

Bill C-6 was introduced as legislation to resolve the specific land claims process. The intention of the legislation is to create a Canadian Centre for the Independent Resolution of First Nations Specific Claims, providing a process through which specific claims can be settled without litigation. The centre will provide information and expertise on the land claims process and will act as a mediator for specific claims.

Bill C-6 establishes the criteria under which a First Nation can launch a specific claim:

1. A breach of the Crown's legal obligations, including
   a. fiduciary responsibilities to the First Nation,
   b. legislation affecting reserve lands,
   c. administration of reserve lands;
2. The illegal use or lease of Crown land;
3. The failure to provide adequate compensation for the use of reserve land;
4. Fraud or other white-collar crimes by employees of the government or its agents.

The exclusions under this legislation include:

1. No claim can be launched involving actions by the government after December 31, 1973.
2. No claim can be launched involving any government actions in the 15 years prior to the filing of a claim.
3. Acts of Parliament and previous agreements are exempted.
4. No claims can be launched relating to law enforcement or policing.
5. No claims can be launched concerning issues that are being adjudicated by other means.

Bill C-6, then, means that claims can be launched that extend back prior to 1850, the time of the Robinson–Huron Treaty, and indeed as far back as colonial times. However, most of the First Nations' opposition to Bill C-6 concerns the first exclusion, that no claim can be launched involving actions by the government after December 31, 1973. This means that no agreements made between the government and a First Nation after that date can be renegotiated, despite any irregularities or perceived unfairness of the result of the negotiation.

The Assembly of First Nations is only one First Nations group that opposes Bill C-6:

> The position of the Assembly of First Nations on the development of an independent claims body has been clear and consistent. The Assembly of First Nations wants to develop a truly fair, efficient, and effective independent claims body. The *Specific Claims Resolution Act* [Bill C-6] does not accomplish these objectives, and as a result the AFN is calling on the Government of Canada to withdraw the legislation and return to a joint table with First Nations. This cooperative approach produced a legislative framework for a truly independent Claims Body that was agreed to by all parties, and is described in the 1998 Joint Task Force Report on Claims.

The reasons for wanting Bill C-6 withdrawn are numerous, and include government control over appointments to the negotiating process, a lack of funding to address claims, and conflict of interest on the part of the government:

> The Assembly of First Nations has concluded that the *Specific Claims Resolution Act* is so seriously flawed that it cannot be fixed by amendments and must be withdrawn.

Despite these and other objections, Bill C-6 was passed by Parliament November 4, 2003.

PROFILE OF A LAND CLAIM

The following two articles illustrate the difficulties involved in resolving land claims. The Temagami claim began in 1877 and was not fully resolved until 2002.

Temagami First Nation and Teme-Augama Anishnabai Re-enter into Land Claim Negotiations with Ontario

By Abby Cote, *Anishnabek News* (July 2000)

In its 1991 decision on Bear Island, the Supreme Court ruling stated that, while the Temagami Aboriginal community did not have title to the land it claimed, the Crown had failed to comply with some of its obligations to the Indians. The obligations arose from arrangements the Crown made with the Temagami Indians by which the Indians adhered to the Robinson Huron treaty in exchange for treaty annuities and a reserve, states the Temagami Land Claim Report issued by the Ontario Native Affairs Secretariat, Spring 2000.

In 1877, the Chief of the Temagami people approached representatives of the Federal Government to ask for a reserve and Treaty. In 1883, the Federal Government recognized the omission of the Temagami Indians from the Robinson Huron Treaty of 1850 and commanded payment of annuities without paying any formal cession of rights to lands. A promise to survey a reserve was also made at that time.

In 1884 Canada petitioned Ontario to provide Crown land to create a reserve of approximately 100 square miles [260 square kilometres]. This did not happen. In 1971 a reserve of one square mile [2.5 square kilometres] was created on Bear Island. Current figures for combined Teme-Augama Anishnabai (TAA) and Temagami First Nation (TFN) membership stands at about 1200 people, about 192 of which reside on Bear Island.

The Supreme Court of Canada decision of 1991 stated that although the Temagami Indians did not have Aboriginal title to the land they claimed as "n'Daki Menan," their traditional lands, the Crown had outstanding obligations to the Temagami Aboriginal community. These obligations stemmed from the Crown's failure to provide an adequate reserve and a failure to make annuity payments.

By 1993 Ontario and the Temagami Aboriginal community had reached an Agreement-In-Principle to settle the claim. However, the Aboriginal community did not ratify the agreement, and the negotiation process collapsed.

The current negotiation process started in 1988 when the TFN and TAA asked Ontario to return to the negotiating table. On March 25, 2000, TFN and TAA members voted on a Framework Agreement. Ontario and representatives of TAA and TFN signed a Framework Agreement on June 21, 2000, to define issues and set out the negotiation process.

"We have entered into the beginning of formal land claim negotiations. This is set out as a 30-month process. The Framework Agreement sets out the process, general parameters and timeframe for negotiations to settle the claim. We are negotiating two different categories of land, 'Settlement Lands' and 'Traditional Family Lands.' The Settlement Lands will comprise not more than 112 square miles [290 square kilometres] and will be located from within the 149 square miles [386 square kilometres] of unpatented land set aside for this purpose by the Ministry of

Natural Resources in 1996," explains Chris Cameron, Daki Menan Negotiation Office communications officer.

Reprinted with permission.

Milestone Reached in Temagami Land Claim Settlement

Ontario Native Affairs Secretariat, December 18, 2002

TORONTO — Negotiators for the Ernie Eves government, the Temagami First Nation and the Tene-Augama Anishnabai have reached agreement on the elements to settle the Temagami land claim, David Young, Attorney General and Minister Responsible for Native Affairs, announced today.

The key elements include 127 square miles [329 square kilometres] of land for the creation of a reserve and an economic development package worth approximately $4 million, including a land component. Ontario will also pay $20 million in financial compensation ... .

Ontario and the Temagami Aboriginal community have agreed to ensure the protection of the Temagami shoreline by the creation of a waterway park, or by another appropriate legal designation. Shoreline areas designated as having high mineral potential will not be included in the park and will still be available for mineral exploration.

The proposed reserve will be located within 149 square miles [386 square kilometres] of land set aside for settlement purposes by the Ministry of Natural Resources in 1996.

As next steps in the process, the lawyers for the parties will draft a legally binding settlement agreement incorporating the elements of settlement that have now been agreed upon. Then negotiators for the parties will initial the proposed settlement agreement to indicate their approval of it. The parties [intend to] ratify the agreement [in] 2004.

CONCLUSION

Land claims share a number of general characteristics. A land claim is a formal process that is enacted into law by Parliament. Aboriginal title is exchanged for such things as monetary compensation, land ownership, hunting and trapping rights, control of social programs, economic participation, interim protection, and environmental protection. Native groups also seek a number of other terms and conditions in land claim settlements. These may include the ability to maintain as much as possible their traditional lifestyle and culture; to participate in the decision-making process with regard to land and resource management within their claim area; and to receive a fair share of the economic opportunities and benefits that may exist in the claim area. The Natives' basic concerns are the protection and enhancement of their social, cultural, and economic well-being.

In conclusion, due to different aims of the negotiators representing the government and the Native groups, the land claims process has been long and contentious. The government would like to extinguish aboriginal rights to the land and achieve a final settlement of historical claims. The aboriginal people would like to have aboriginal rights affirmed and be guaranteed a unique place in the country of Canada.

WORKSHEET

1. Discuss the benefits and drawbacks of the treaties for both sides: Native and British — and later, Canadian — governments, and the ability of each party to enforce the terms of the contract. Consider that the Canadian government would not legally allow Natives to take land issues to court in the first half of the 20th century. (5 marks)

2. Summarize the sections of the *Royal Proclamation of 1763* that pertain to Native peoples (see appendix 4.1). (2 marks)

3a. Briefly describe the purpose of each of the Numbered Treaties. (5.5 marks)

3b. Identify the benefits of the treaties to both sides (Canadian government and the Native groups) and, from your list, determine which party benefited the most. Support your answers. (3.5 marks)

4. Identify the implication of the precedent-setting 1969 Nisga'a Indian case on further land claim negotiations. (2 marks)

5. Describe the differences between a specific and a comprehensive land claim. (2 marks)

TOTAL — 20 MARKS

KEY TERMS

aboriginal rights

annuities

autonomy

extinguish

Indian Act

legislation

policy

treaty

usufructuary right

APPENDIX 4.1

The Royal Proclamation of October 7, 1763

Purpose

Whereas We have taken into Our Royal Consideration the extensive and valuable Acquisitions in America, secured to our Crown by the late Definitive Treaty of Peace, concluded at Paris the 10th Day of February last; and being desirous that all Our loving Subjects, as well of our Kingdom as of our Colonies in America, may avail themselves with all convenient Speed, of the great Benefits and Advantages which must accrue therefrom to their Commerce, Manufactures, and Navigation, We have thought fit, with the Advice of our Privy Council, to issue this our Royal Proclamation, hereby to publish and declare to all our loving Subjects, that we have, with the Advice of our Said Privy Council, granted our Letters Patent, under our Great Seal of Great Britain, to erect, within the Countries and Islands ceded and confirmed to Us by the said Treaty, Four distinct and separate Governments, styled and called by the names of Quebec, East Florida, West Florida and Grenada, and limited and bounded as follows, *viz.*

First – The Government of Quebec bounded on the Labrador Coast by the River St. John, and from thence by a Line drawn from the Head of that River through the Lake St. John, to the South end of the Lake Nipissing; from whence the said Line, crossing the River St. Lawrence, and the Lake Champlain, in 45 Degrees of North Latitude, passes along the High Lands which divide the Rivers that empty themselves into the said River St. Lawrence from those which fall into the Sea; and also along the North Coast of the Baye des Châleurs, and the Coast of the Gulph of St. Lawrence to Cape Rosières, and from thence crossing the Mouth of the River St. Lawrence by the West End of the Island of Anticosti, terminates at the aforesaid River of St. John.

Secondly – The Government of East Florida, bounded to the Westward by the Gulph of Mexico and the Apalachicola River; to the Northward by a Line drawn from that part of the said River where the Chatahouchee and Flint Rivers meet, to the source of St. Mary's River, and by the course of the said River to the Atlantic Ocean; and to the Eastward and Southward by the Atlantic Ocean and the Gulph of Florida, including all Islands within Six Leagues of the Sea Coast.

Thirdly – The Government of West Florida, bounded to the Southward by the Gulph of Mexico, including all Islands within Six Leagues of the Coast; from the River Apalachicola to Lake Pontchartrain; to the Westward by the said Lake, the Lake Maurepas, and the River Mississippi; to the Northward by a Line drawn due East from that part of the River Mississippi which lies in 31 Degrees North Latitude, to the River Apalachicola or Chatahouchee; and to the Eastward by the said River.

Fourthly – The Government of Grenada, comprehending the Island of that name, together with the Grenadines, and the Islands of Dominico, St. Vincent's and Tobago. And to the end that the open and free Fishery of our Subjects may be extended to and carried on upon the Coast of Labrador, and the adjacent Islands, We have thought fit, with the advice of our said Privy Council to put all that Coast, from the River St. John's to Hudson's Streights, together with the Islands of Anticosti and Madelaine, and all other smaller Islands lying upon the said Coast, under the care and Inspection of our Governor of Newfoundland.

We have also, with the advice of our Privy Council, thought fit to annex the Islands of St. John's [now Prince Edward Island] and Cape Breton, or Isle Royale, with the lesser Islands adjacent thereto, to our Government of Nova Scotia.

We have also, with the advice of our Privy Council aforesaid, annexed to our Province of Georgia all the Lands lying between the Rivers Alatamaha and St. Mary's.

New Governments To Have General Assemblies and Make Laws

And whereas it will greatly contribute to the speedy settling of our said new Governments, that our loving Subjects should be informed of our Paternal care, for the security of the Liberties and Properties of those who are and shall become Inhabitants thereof, We have thought fit to publish and declare, by this Our Proclamation, that We have, in the Letters Patent under our Great Seal of Great Britain, by which the said Governments are constituted, given express Power and Direction to our Governors of our Said Colonies respectively, that so soon as the state and circumstances of the said Colonies will admit thereof, they shall, with the Advice and Consent of the Members of our Council, summon and call General Assemblies within the said Governments respectively, in such Manner and Form as is used and directed in those Colonies and Provinces in America which are under our immediate Government: And We have also given Power to the said Governors, with the consent of our Said Councils, and the Representatives of the People so to be summoned as aforesaid, to make, constitute, and ordain Laws, Statutes, and Ordinances for the Public Peace, Welfare, and good Government of our said Colonies, and of the People and Inhabitants thereof, as near as may be agreeable to the Laws of England, and under such Regulations and Restrictions as are used in other Colonies; and in the mean Time, and until such Assemblies can be called as aforesaid [see *Campbell v. Hall* (1774), 1 Cowp. 204; 98 ER 1045], all Persons Inhabiting in or resorting to our Said Colonies may confide in our Royal Protection for the Enjoyment of the Benefit of the Laws of our Realm of England; for which Purpose We have given Power under our Great Seal to the Governors of our said Colonies respectively to erect and constitute, with the Advice of our said Councils respectively, Courts of Judicature and public Justice within our Said Colonies for hearing and determining all Causes, as well Criminal as Civil, according to Law and Equity, and as near as may be agreeable to the Laws of England, with Liberty to all Persons who may think themselves aggrieved by the Sentences of such Courts, in all Civil Cases, to appeal, under the usual Limitations and Restrictions, to Us in our Privy Council.

Grants for Settlement

We have also thought fit, with the advice of our Privy Council as aforesaid, to give unto the Governors and Councils of our said Three new Colonies upon the Continent, full Power and Authority to settle and agree with the Inhabitants of our said new Colonies or with any other Persons who shall resort thereto, for such Lands, Tenements and Hereditaments, as are now or hereafter shall be in our Power to dispose of; and them to grant to any such Person or Persons upon such Terms, and under such moderate Quit-Rents, Services and Acknowledgments, as have been appointed and settled in our other Colonies, and under such other Conditions as shall appear to us to be necessary and expedient for the Advantage of the Grantees, and the Improvement and settlement of our said Colonies.

Soldier Settlement

And Whereas, We are desirous, upon all occasions, to testify our Royal Sense and Approbation of the Conduct and bravery of the Officers and Soldiers of our Armies, and to reward the same, We do hereby command and impower our Governors of our said Three new Colonies, and all other our Governors of our several Provinces on the Continent of North America, to grant without Fee or Reward, to such reduced Officers as have served in North America during the late War, and to such Private Soldiers as have been or shall be disbanded in America, and are actually residing there, and shall personally apply for the same, the following Quantities of Lands, subject, at the Expiration of Ten Years, to the same Quit-Rents as other Lands are subject to in the Province within which they are granted, as also subject to the same Conditions of Cultivation and Improvement; *viz.*

To every Person having the Rank of a Field Officer — 5,000 Acres.

To every Captain — 3,000 Acres.

To every Subaltern or Staff Officer — 2,000 Acres.

To every Non-Commission Officer — 200 Acres.

To every Private Man — 50 Acres.

We do likewise authorize and require the Governors and Commanders in Chief of all our said Colonies upon the Continent of North America to grant the like Quantities of Land, and upon the same conditions, to such reduced Officers of our Navy of like Rank as served on board our Ships of War in North America at the times of the Reduction of Louisbourg and Quebec in the late War, and who shall personally apply to our respective Governors for such Grants.

The Indian Provisions

And whereas it is just and reasonable, and essential to our Interest, and the Security of our Colonies, that the several Nations or Tribes of Indians with whom We are connected, and who live under our Protection, should not be molested or disturbed in the Possession of such Parts of Our Dominions and Territories as, not having been ceded to or purchased by Us, are reserved to them, or any of them, as their Hunting Grounds — We do therefore, with the Advice of our Privy Council, declare it to be our Royal Will and Pleasure, that no Governor or Commander in Chief in any of our Colonies of Quebec, East Florida, or West Florida, do presume, upon any Pretence whatever, to grant Warrants of Survey, or pass any Patents for Lands beyond the Bounds of their respective Governments, as described in their Commissions: as also that no Governor or Commander in Chief in any of our other Colonies or Plantations in America do presume for the present, and until our further Pleasure be known, to grant Warrants of Survey, or pass Patents for any Lands beyond the Heads or Sources of any of the Rivers which fall into the Atlantic Ocean from the West and North West, or upon any Lands whatever, which, not having been ceded to or purchased by Us as aforesaid, are reserved to the said Indians, or any of them.

And We do further declare it to be Our Royal Will and Pleasure, for the present as aforesaid, to reserve under our Sovereignty, Protection, and Dominion, for the use of the said Indians, all the Lands and Territories not included within the Limits of Our said Three new Governments, or within the Limits of the Territory granted to the Hudson's Bay Company, as also all the Lands and Territories lying to the Westward of the Sources of the Rivers which fall into the Sea from the West and North West as aforesaid.

And We do hereby strictly forbid, on Pain of our Displeasure, all our loving Subjects from making any Purchases or Settlements whatever, or taking Possession of any of the Lands above reserved, without our especial leave and Licence for that Purpose first obtained.

And We do further strictly enjoin and require all Persons whatever who have either wilfully or inadvertently seated themselves upon any Lands within the Countries above described, or upon any other Lands which, not having been ceded to or purchased by Us, are still reserved to the said Indians as aforesaid, forthwith to remove themselves from such Settlements.

And whereas great Frauds and Abuses have been committed in purchasing Lands of the Indians, to the great Prejudice of our Interests, and to the great Dissatisfaction of the said Indians: In order, therefore, to prevent such Irregularities for the future, and to the end that the Indians may be convinced of our Justice and determined Resolution to remove all reasonable Cause of Discontent, We do, with the Advice of our Privy Council strictly enjoin and require, that no private Person do presume to make any purchase from the said Indians of any Lands reserved to the said Indians, within those parts of our Colonies where We have thought proper to allow Settlement: but that, if at any Time any of the Said Indians should be inclined to dispose of the said Lands, the same shall be Purchased only for Us, in our Name, at some public Meeting or Assembly of the said Indians, to be held for that Purpose by the Governor or Commander in Chief of our Colony respectively within which they shall lie: and in case they shall lie within the limits of any Proprietary Government, they shall be purchased only for the Use and in the name of such Proprietaries, conformable to such Directions and Instructions as We or they shall think proper to give for that Purpose: And we do, by the Advice of our Privy Council, declare and enjoin, that the Trade with the said Indians shall be free and open to all our Subjects whatever, provided that every Person who may incline to Trade with the said Indians do take out a Licence for carrying on such Trade from the Governor or Commander in Chief of any of our Colonies respectively where such Person shall reside, and also give Security to observe such Regulations as We shall at any Time think fit, by ourselves or by our Commissaries to be appointed for this Purpose, to direct and appoint for the Benefit of the said Trade:

And we do hereby authorize, enjoin, and require the Governors and Commanders in Chief of all our Colonies respectively, as well those under Our immediate Government as those under the Government and Direction of Proprietaries, to grant such Licences without Fee or Reward, taking especial Care to insert therein a Condition, that such Licence shall be void, and the Security forfeited in case the Person to whom the same is granted shall refuse or neglect to observe such Regulations as We shall think proper to prescribe as aforesaid.

And we do further expressly conjoin and require all Officers whatever, as well Military as those Employed in the Management and Direction of Indian Affairs, within the Territories reserved as aforesaid for the use of the said Indians, to seize and apprehend all Persons whatever, who standing charged with Treason, Misprisions of Treason, Murders, or other Felonies or Misdemeanors, shall fly from Justice and take Refuge in the said Territory, and to send them under a proper guard to the Colony where the Crime was committed, of which they stand accused, in order to take their Trial for the same.

Given at our Court at St. James's the 7th Day of October 1763, in the Third Year of our Reign.

GOD SAVE THE KING

APPENDIX 4.2

The Robinson–Superior Treaty

THIS AGREEMENT, made and entered into on the seventh day of September, in the year of Our Lord one thousand eight hundred and fifty, at Sault Ste Marie, in the Province of Canada, between the Honorable William Benjamin Robinson, of the one part, on behalf of Her Majesty the Queen, and Joseph Peandechat, John Iuinway, Mishe-Muckqua, Totomencie, Chiefs, and Jacob Warpela, Ahmutchiwagabou, Michel Shelageshick, Manitoshainse, and Chiginans, principal men of the Ojibewa Indians inhabiting the northern Shore of Lake Superior, in the said Province of Canada, from Batchewanaung Bay to Pigeon River, at the western extremity of said Lake, and inland throughout that extent to the height of land which separates the territory covered by the charter of the Honorable Hudson's Bay Company from the said tract, and also the Islands in the said Lake within the boundaries of the British possessions therein, of the other part, witnesseth:

That for and in consideration of the sum of two thousand pounds of good and lawful money of Upper Canada, to them in hand paid, and for the further perpetual annuity of five hundred pounds, the same to be paid and delivered to the said Chiefs and their tribes at a convenient season of each summer, not later than the first day of August at the Honorable Hudson's Bay Company's Posts of Michipicoton and Fort William, they the said chiefs and principal men do freely, fully and voluntarily surrender, cede, grant and convey unto Her Majesty, Her heirs and successors forever, all their right, title and interest in the whole of the territory above described, save and except the reservations set forth in the schedule hereunto annexed, which reservations shall be held and occupied by the said Chiefs and their tribes in common, for the purposes of residence and cultivation, — and should the said Chiefs and their respective tribes at any time desire to dispose of any mineral or other valuable productions upon the said reservations, the same will be at their request sold by order of the Superintendent-General of the Indian Department for the time being, for their sole use and benefit, and to the best advantage.

And the said William Benjamin Robinson of the first part, on behalf of Her Majesty and the Government of this Province, hereby promises and agrees to make the payments as before mentioned; and further to allow the said Chiefs and their tribes the full and free privilege to hunt over the territory now ceded by them, and to fish in the waters thereof as they have heretofore been in the habit of doing, saving and excepting only such portions of the said territory as may from time to time be sold or leased to individuals, or companies of individuals, and occupied by them with the consent of the Provincial Government. The parties of the second part further promise and agree that they will not sell, lease, or otherwise dispose of any portion of their reservations without the consent of the Superintendent-General of Indian Affairs being first had and obtained; nor will they at any time hinder or prevent persons from exploring or searching for mineral or other valuable productions in any part of the territory hereby ceded to Her Majesty as before mentioned. The parties of the second part also agree that in case the Government of this Province should before the date of this agreement have sold, or bargained to sell, any mining locations or other property on the portions of the territory hereby reserved for their use and benefit, then and in that case such sale, or promise of sale, shall be perfected, if the parties interested desire it, by the Government, and the amount accruing therefrom shall be paid to the tribe to whom the reservation belongs. The said William Benjamin Robinson on behalf of Her Majesty, who desires to deal liberally and justly with all Her subjects, further promises and agrees that in case the territory hereby ceded by the parties of the second part shall at any future period produce an amount which will enable the Government of this Province without incurring loss to increase the annuity hereby secured to them, then, and in that case, the same shall be augmented from time to time, provided that the amount paid to each individual shall not exceed the sum of one pound Provincial currency in any one year, or such further sum as Her Majesty may be graciously pleased to order; and provided further that the number of Indians entitled to the benefit of this treaty shall amount to two-thirds of their present numbers (which is twelve hundred and forty) to entitle them to claim the full benefit thereof, and should their numbers at any future period not amount to two-thirds of twelve hundred and forty, the annuity shall be diminished in proportion to their actual numbers.

Schedule of Reservations made by the above-named subscribing Chiefs and principal men

First — Joseph Pean-de-chat and his tribe, the reserve to commence about two miles from Fort William (inland), on the right bank of the River Kiministiquia; thence westerly six miles, parallel to the shores of the lake; thence northerly five miles; thence easterly to the right bank of the said river, so as not to interfere with any acquired rights of the Honorable Hudson's Bay Company.

Second — Four miles square at Gros Cap, being a valley near the Honorable Hudson's Bay Company's post of Michipicoton, for Totominai and tribe.

Third — Four miles square on Gull River, near Lake Nipigon, on both sides of said river, for the Chief Michimuckqua and tribe.

[*Signatures deleted*]

The Robinson–Huron Treaty

THIS AGREEMENT, made and entered into this ninth day of September, in the year of Our Lord one thousand eight hundred and fifty, at Sault Ste Marie, in the Province of Canada, between the Honorable William Benjamin Robinson, of the one part, on behalf of Her Majesty the Queen, and Shinguacouse Nebenaigoching, Keokouse, Mishequonga, Tagawinini, Shabokishick, Dokis, Ponekeosh, Windawtegowinini, Shawenakeshick, Namassin, Naoquagabo, Wabakekik, Kitchepossigun, by Papasainse, Wagemaki, Pamequonaisheung, Chiefs; and John Bell, Paqwatchinini, Mashekyash, Idowekesis, Waquacomick, Ocheek, Metigomin, Watachewana, Minwawapenasse, Shenaoquom, Oningegun, Panaissy, Papasainse, Ashewasega, Kageshewawetung, Shawonebin; and also Chief Maisquaso (also Chiefs Muckata, Mishoquet, and Mekis), and Mishoquetto and Asa Waswanay and Pawiss, principal men of the Ojibewa Indians, inhabiting and claiming the eastern and northern shores of Lake Huron, from Penetanguishene to Sault Ste Marie, and thence to Batchewanaung Bay, on the northern shore of Lake Superior, together with the Islands in the said Lakes, opposite to the shores thereof, and inland to the height of land which separates the territory covered by the charter of the Honorable Hudson's Bay Company from Canada; as well as all unconceded lands within the limits of Canada West to which they have any just claim of the other, witnesseth:

That for and in consideration of the sum of two thousand pounds of good and lawful money of Upper Canada, to them in hand paid, and for the further perpetual annuity of six hundred pounds of like money, the same to be paid and delivered to the said Chiefs and their tribes at a convenient season of each year, of which due notice will be given, at such places as may be appointed for that purpose, they the said Chiefs and principal men, on behalf of their respective tribes or bands, do hereby fully, freely and voluntarily surrender, cede, grant, and convey unto Her Majesty, Her heirs and successors forever, all their right, title, and interest to, and in the whole of, the territory above described, save and except the reservations set forth in the schedule hereunto annexed; which reservations shall be held and occupied by the said Chiefs and their tribes in common, for their own use and benefit.

And should the said Chiefs and their respective tribes at any time desire to dispose of any such reservations, or of any mineral or other valuable productions thereon, the same will be sold or leased at their request by the Superintendent-General of Indian Affairs for the time being, or other officer having authority so to do, for their sole benefit, and to the best advantage.

And the said William Benjamin Robinson of the first part, on behalf of Her Majesty and the Government of this Province, hereby promises and agrees to make, or cause to be made, the payments as before mentioned; and further to allow the said Chiefs and their tribes the full and free privilege to hunt over the territory now ceded by them, and to fish in the waters thereof, as they have heretofore been in the habit of doing; saving and excepting such portions of the said territory as may from time to time be sold or leased to individuals or companies of individuals, and occupied by them with the consent of the Provincial Government.

The parties of the second part further promise and agree that they will not sell, lease, or otherwise dispose of any portion of their Reservations without the consent of the Superintendent-General of Indian Affairs, or other officer of like authority, being first had and obtained. Nor will they at any time hinder or prevent persons from exploring or searching for minerals, or other valuable productions, in any part of the territory hereby ceded to Her Majesty, as before mentioned. The parties of the second part also agree, that in case the Government of this Province should before the date of this agreement have sold, or bargained to sell, any mining locations or other property, on the portions of the territory hereby reserved for their use; then and in that case such sale, or promise of sale, shall be perfected by the Government, if the parties claiming it shall have fulfilled all the conditions upon which such locations were made, and the amount accruing therefrom shall be paid to the tribe to whom the Reservation belongs.

The said William Benjamin Robinson, on behalf of Her Majesty, who desires to deal liberally and justly with all Her subjects, further promises and agrees, that should the territory hereby ceded by the parties of the second part shall at any future period produce an amount as will enable the Government of this Province, without incurring loss, to increase the annuity hereby secured to them, then and in that case the same shall be augmented from time to time, provided that the amount paid to each individual shall not exceed the sum of one pound Provincial currency in any one year, or such further sum as Her Majesty may be graciously pleased to order, and provided further that the number of Indians entitled to the benefit of this treaty shall amount to two-thirds of their present number, which is fourteen [hundred and twenty-two]. And should they not at any future period not amount to two-thirds of fourteen hundred and twenty-two, then the said annuity shall be diminished in proportion to their actual numbers.

The said William Benjamin Robinson of the first part further agrees, on the part of Her Majesty and the Government of this Province, that in consequence of the Indians inhabiting French River and Lake Nipissing having become parties to this treaty, the further sum of one hundred and sixty pounds Provincial currency shall be paid in addition to the two thousand pounds above mentioned.

Schedule of Reservations made by the above-named subscribing Chiefs and principal men

First — Pamequonaishcung and his band, a tract of land to commence seven miles, from the mouth of the River Maganetawang, and extending six miles east and west by three miles north.

Second — Wagemake and his band, a tract of land to commence at a place called Nekickshegeshing, six miles from east to west, by three miles in depth.

Third — Kitchiposkissegan (by Papasainse) from Point Grondine westward, six miles inland, by two miles in front, so as to include the small Lake Nessinassung — a tract for themselves and their bands.

Fourth — Wabakekik, three miles front, near Shebawenaning, by five miles inland, for himself and band.

Fifth — Namassin and Naoquagabo and their bands, a tract of land commencing near Quacloche, at the Hudson Bay Company's boundary; thence westerly to the mouth of the Spanish River; then four miles up the south bank of said river, and across to the place of beginning.

Sixth — Shawenakishick and his band, a tract of land now occupied by them, and contained between two rivers, called Whitefish River, and Wanabitaseke, seven miles inland.

Seventh — Windawtegawinini and his band, the Peninsula east of Serpent River, and formed by it, now occupied by them.

Eighth — Ponekeosh and his band, the land contained between the River Mississaga and the River Penebewabecong, up to the first rapids.

Ninth — Dokis and his band, three miles at Wanabeyakokaun, near Lake Nipissing and the Island near the Fall of Okickandawt.

Tenth — Shabokishick and his band, from their present planting grounds on Lake Nipissing on the Hudson Bay Company's post, six miles in depth.

Eleventh — Tagawinini and his band, two miles square at Wanabitibing, a place about four miles inland, near Lake Nipissing.

Twelfth — Keokouse and his band, four miles front from Thessalon River eastward, by four miles inland.

Thirteenth — Mishequanga and his band, two miles on the lake shore east and west of Ogawaminang, by one mile inland.

Fourteenth — For Shinguacouse and his band, a tract of land extending from Maskinonge Bay, inclusive, to Partridge Point, above Garden River on the front, and inland ten miles, throughout the whole distance; and also Squirrel Island.

Fifteenth — For Nebenaigoching and his band, a tract of land extending from Wanabekineyunnung west of Gros Cap to the boundary of the lands ceded by the Chiefs of Lake Superior, and inland ten miles throughout the whole distance, including

Batchewanaung Bay; and also the small island at Sault Ste Marie used by them as a fishing station.

Sixteenth – For Chief Mekis and his band, residing at Wasaquesing (Sandy Island), a tract of land at a place on the main shore opposite the Island; being the place now occupied by them for residence and cultivation, four miles square.

Seventeenth – For Chief Muckatamishaquet and his band, a tract of land on the east side of the River Naishconteong, near Pointe aux Barils, three miles square; and also a small tract in Washauwenega Bay – now occupied by a part of the band – three miles square.

APPENDIX 4.3

Vote on Indian Treaties Sparks Anger in Canada

By Allan Dowd, Reuters

VANCOUVER – Residents on Canada's Pacific Coast will be asked this week [April 3, 2002] to endorse a tougher provincial government line in a century-old battle over Native land rights, but the referendum may prove as much of a quagmire as treaty talks have been.

The British Columbia government wants voters to endorse eight principles, including opposition to the expropriation of private land claimed by Indians for treaty settlements and limiting Native self governments to the same powers the province grants to local non-Native communities.

Supporters of the mail-in referendum say it will engage citizens directly in the treaty process. Critics call the vote an attack on minority rights and warn it will lead to civil disobedience and economic uncertainty .... [Voters] will be asked to vote yes or no on eight questions the government says will guide its negotiating position if approved.

According to the government, there are 197 native bands and tribal nations in British Columbia, ... but the aboriginal population comprises only about 3 per cent of the province's 4.09 million people .... Indians are among the province's poorest residents. Unemployment is high on reserves, and many Natives have ended up destitute in urban neighbourhoods such as Vancouver's drug-infested Downtown Eastside. Native leaders often blame the situation on the loss of territory and traditional culture as European settlers began spreading across Western Canada in the mid-1800s.

British Columbia was the only Canadian province to officially ignore a 1763 directive from the British Crown that required land treaties to be signed with native Indians. In 1973, the Supreme Court of Canada ruled Indians ... had aboriginal title to their traditional lands, and in 1990 British Columbia agreed to enter three-way negotiations with the tribes and with the federal government in Ottawa.

Treaty talks, however, have stalled on issues such as the legal structure of native self-government, how much land Indian nations should receive, compensation resources, and whether natives should be allowed to retain their current tax free status.

[British Columbia signed a treaty with the Nisga'a in 1999, giving them self-government rights over 1930 square kilometres and $490 million in compensation. Many non-Natives thought this was too much. The Liberal Party in British Columbia in 2001 promised to hold a referendum on future negotiations. There have been no further negotiations with Indian bands as yet.]

CHAPTER 5

Native Assimilation Laws and Practices — Prior to and Within the Indian Act

Chapter Objectives

After completing this chapter, you should be able to:

- Describe existing traditional Native government and political structures.
- Outline significant historical events that led to the erosion of Native sovereignty and political systems before the Confederation of Canada.
- Identify specific, historical assimilation policies and legislation of the British and the Canadian governments regarding Native peoples before the Confederation of Canada.
- Describe the original *Indian Act* and subsequent amendments that contributed to the loss of sovereignty of Natives.
- Describe specific incidents and events that negatively affected Native sovereignty and quality of life as a result of the *Indian Act*.
- Identify significant events that resulted in the awakening of a collective Native voice and vision toward self-determination.
- Cite key Native organizations and their mandates at the national, provincial, regional, and band levels.

INTRODUCTION

The imperial civil administration for British North America was dominated by two ideas concerning Natives in 1830: that as a people, they were disappearing, and that those who remained should either be removed to communities isolated from Euro-Canadians, or else be assimilated (Dickason, 2002).

The treaty era passed when the Canadian government was satisfied that all the lands within its jurisdiction could be claimed for itself and its non-Native populations. Natives argue that the reason why the Canadian government had worked so diligently to assimilate Natives and their lands into the framework of Canada was to remove the uniqueness and differences that set apart the Natives and their lands. After all, they contend, these differences support the Natives' claim to **sovereignty** (the right of Native peoples to govern themselves). We will look at specific strategies used by the British and Canadian governments to assimilate Natives and their lands to become part of Canada.

sovereignty
self-government

In this chapter we will also look at the connection between the slow erosion of Native sovereignty in Canada and the government acquisition of aboriginal lands. We will study the loss of Native sovereignty through the process of assimilation and through the introduction of Acts, such as the *Enfranchisement Act* of 1869 and the *Indian Act* of 1876. To understand what sovereignty or self-government means to the Natives, we will examine their traditional political structure and their struggles today, through the creation of various organizations, to reclaim their right for self-government. In this chapter, our focus will remain on the indigenous populations in Ontario.

LOSS OF NATIVE SOVEREIGNTY

Viable aboriginal governments existed long before contact and were in place when Europeans arrived. Initially, the European effects on the lives of Native peoples were minimal. Had the first Europeans arbitrarily imposed changes to the Native's way of living at any level, they would have been met openly with hostility and rejection. As it was, for a long while after contact, the Native peoples were valued as allies and as resource people in the Northern Hemisphere of the New World. For instance, in many of the early skirmishes among European nations for the procurement and protection of land, resources, and settlements, the outcome of these conflicts was often decided by the number of Native allies a European group had. As well, aboriginal peoples were highly skilled in surviving in their homelands and were intimately familiar with the land and its resources. It was because of their proficiency in hunting and trapping that the fur trade enterprises flourished. As a result of their value in these capacities, Native autonomy and political structures remained fairly intact, uninterrupted by European influence for a long time.

This did not mean, however, that Native sovereignty was respected. The French, for instance, while not raising issues of sovereignty, considered that France had sovereign rights in Acadia and New France, even though the Native people did not consider themselves subject people. Europeans were seen as partners in some cases and allies in other cases. At no time did the Natives feel that the French had claim to Native land, or that they owed any allegiance to the French king.

Even from the beginning of European contact, forces seemed to undermine Native nations' autonomy in the Northern Hemisphere. European attitudes toward Natives were, from the start, a result of differing and often opposing values and beliefs. The Europeans had distinctive lifestyles and traditions not shared by their Native neighbours. As a result, ethnocentrism played a significant role in the manner in which they approached and dealt with Native peoples. From their earliest contacts,

Europeans generally viewed the aboriginal cultures as inferior and primitive and expected the Native tribes to adopt their ways. Resentment of non-Native attitudes contributed to the Native distrust for non-Native authority, which lingers today.

Despite their differences, Native peoples traded their furs for things such as European tools, metal pots, weapons, and clothing, that made their lives easier. In most circumstances, the Native peoples in the northern part of North America shared their territories and resources with the Europeans. However, Native tribes varied in their acceptance of the religions and social customs that the Europeans tried to impose. As we will see in this chapter, European and North American governments consistently and aggressively imposed assimilation practices on Native peoples through policies and legislation.

Change was inevitable as the newly introduced cultural groups began to interact. The sharing of specific and tangible things, as well as the exchange of more intrinsic aspects such as values, beliefs, and ways of behaving, gradually transformed the participants in some manner. The European and, later, the Canadian governments and the industries and companies that came to claim the land and/or natural resources had an agenda to replace traditional Native political and social cohesion and substitute them with European-based models. The expansion of Canada shortly after Confederation is an example. Canada, as a newly formed country, forged a number of treaties with the Native groups to extend and establish its territorial borders across the continent. As the Canadian government began an aggressive campaign for immigrants to settle in these new lands, it began to seek a resolution with its Native populations — for example, where to put disgruntled and displaced Natives and how to address Natives who were experiencing hardship due to reductions in the buffalo and beaver populations. The government's response to these problems was to accelerate the assimilation practices started by the British government in an attempt to absorb the Native peoples into the cultural mainstream. As a result, the government created specific policies within the *Indian Act* intended to remove Indian status from Natives — without the Natives, the reserves and lands protected for Native peoples under the treaties would also disappear.

There were a number of early campaigns for Native sovereignty. For instance, at the close of World War I the Six Nations began to campaign for sovereignty. The federal government responded by amending the *Indian Act* in 1920 to abolish tribal governments. In 1924, an elected council was imposed upon the Six Nations of the Grand River near Brantford, Ontario as a result of the 1920 amendment. In 2004, there is still a division among the people of Six Nations over this policy; some still adhere to the hereditary council, and some follow the elected council at Six Nations. The government deals only with the elected council.

GROUP DISCUSSION

1. Consider the rationale behind the assimilation policies. Why did the government choose assimilation as a means of dealing with Native peoples?
2. What other options other than assimilation might have been available to the Canadian government?

TRADITIONAL NATIVE GOVERNMENTS AND POLITICAL STRUCTURES

As discussed in chapters 1 and 2, before contact with Europeans, there were many different self-governing groups of Native people, speaking many different languages and having different cultures, economies, and forms of governments. Let's look at two of the governments of the eastern Woodlands Native groups — the Ojibwe and the Iroquois.

Ojibwe Traditional Form of Government

The Ojibwe possessed a loosely based political structure that conformed to their nomadic lives. Each band had its own leader who generally acquired his rank (all chiefs were male) from his father, but leaders could also be selected by the council of elders on merit alone. In most cases, the chief of the band was also the war chief. If a raid or battle was planned against another nation, the chief would consult his followers. Decisions were made by consensus, within a highly formalized system of protocol and debate. The chief would send an envoy or personal lieutenant with a pipe and tobacco to invite participation from allied tribes. Those who did not want to join in the war party would pass the pipe on without smoking it and those who smoked the pipe indicated their involvement and commitment (Jenness, 1932). No chieftain controlled or governed the entire Ojibwe nation. Each tribe was an independent, self-sustaining community.

Prior to European contact, the political organization of the Ojibwe people was closely integrated with their spiritual practices. The Midewiwin Society of the Ojibwe people, for example, was a secret religious organization that maintained and performed elaborate healing ceremonies for maladies. As a unique part of the culture, the Midewiwin kept records — for example, prophecies and medicines — on birchbark scrolls. Beyond their function as healers, the Midewiwin also provided political leadership by binding the Ojibwe groups together ("Ojibwe History").

The clans, as discussed in chapter 2, bound all of the groups together. Group unity was important, considering the nomadic lifestyle. Since members of each clan were distributed among all of the bands, it provided the Ojibwe nation with a certain unity. Warring with neighbouring bands may have meant fighting against one's own clan members.

In addition, the Ojibwe shared a history with the Ottawa (with whom history has caused confusion by erroneously labelling the two as one tribe) and the Potowatomi. According to traditional stories, these nations migrated together from the St. Lawrence Valley. They split up when they came to the Great Lakes, the Ojibwe settling around Bawating or Lake Superior, the Ottawa living on Manitoulin Island and in the Georgian Bay region, the Mississauga (an Ojibwe group) remaining in the Mississauga River area (along the North Shore of Lake Huron), and the Potowatomi relocating on the west side of Lake Huron or the Lower Peninsula of Michigan. The three nations, the Superior Ojibwe, the Ottawa, and the Potowatomi, maintained a tribal alliance, which is referred to as the Three Fires Confederacy or the Council of the Three Fires (Jenness, 1932). In times of conflict, each tribe would assist and defend the others.

GROUP DISCUSSION

Describe the benefits each tribe derived from the Three Fires Confederacy.

Iroquois Traditional System of Government

To discuss the Iroquois political system, it is important to outline how its system of government evolved. According to Iroquois oral tradition, the Haudenosaunee (the Iroquois) became established as a confederacy as a result of the work of a man called the Peacemaker. Born on the northwest shores of Lake Ontario, he journeyed among the Iroquois when they were caught in horrific civil wars and feuds. While among the Mohawk, he met an exile named Hiawatha (an Iroquois name that was used erroneously by the poet Henry Wadsworth Longfellow as an Ojibwe hero in his "Song of Hiawatha"). The two men mediated among five of the warring tribes and were able to persuade them to join together in a "Great Peace." As the story goes, they had to conquer a wizard who had snakes in his hair and who stood in the way of a peaceful outcome. With 50 chiefs of the first Grand Council assembled on the shore of Lake Onondaga, the Peacemaker planted The Tree of Peace, a white pine, under which all of the warriors of the Five Nations buried their weapons.

From this beginning of Great Peace, the original Five Nations Confederacy was born. Each of the Five Nations formed a government whose principles are still adhered to today. The League of Five Nations operated successfully for a number of centuries as a confederation. The Five Nations, and later the Six Nations when the Tuscarora joined, had a central government authority that provided general laws and structure for the confederacy as a whole but allowed each nation to pursue its own interests. Each nation had an obligation to maintain and uphold the confederacy but were responsible for the daily care and operations of their own communities. For example, when any separate nation faced danger from other tribes, all of the warriors from the other nations of the confederacy were obligated to fight together. The Iroquois were well known for their military prowess.

As pointed out in chapter 2, the leadership of the Iroquois was chosen by their women. Nominated by the clan mothers who had complete power over their selection, the Iroquois leadership fell into two categories: sachems or war chiefs. Sachems held office in times of peace, and war chiefs obviously were chosen during times of war. Once the war ceased, the position was dissolved. All leadership roles were assumed by the men and were generally lifetime positions. However, if the chief proved to be incompetent or inappropriate, the clan mother could remove the leader from office and select another leader.

GROUP DISCUSSION

The concept of women choosing the leaders is unique for most cultures. Describe the pros and cons of this system if it were incorporated into our society today.

The League would come together a number of times during the year to discuss issues and make decisions affecting the entire confederacy. All decisions of the council had to be unanimous. In essence, the Iroquois system of government was based on the strength of its union and incorporated such themes as free expression and order through free speech and compromise. Benjamin Franklin cited the Iroquois confederacy as an example of a successful union of sovereign states. According to many sources, it was no coincidence that the American constitution bears similar features to the philosophical principles and laws set down by the Six Nations Confederacy. Franklin was quoted as saying (Hall & Madison, 1987, p. 342):

> It would be a very strange Thing if six Nations of ignorant Savages should be capable of forming a Scheme for such a Union and be able to execute it in such a Manner, as that it has subsisted Ages, and appears indissoluble: and yet that a like Union should be impracticable for ten or a Dozen English Colonies.

ASSIMILATION POLICIES AND LAWS

After the *Royal Proclamation of 1763*, the Native peoples continued to live autonomous lives, with little or no interference from the British government. Slowly, however, with every treaty and the subsequent loss of traditional lands, with the decimation of Native populations due to European-introduced diseases, and with conflicts and wars, the traditional ways and authority of Native peoples began to diminish. Exclusion of Native peoples from the decisions that affected them and the land issues also contributed to further erosion of Native sovereignty. Assimilation policies and intentions began to dominate British–Native relations, becoming more pronounced in the 1800s.

The British and then Canadian governments created policies and legislation that attempted to integrate Natives into non-Native society. The logic of such endeavours seemed rational at the time: to provide the Natives with Euro-Canadian cultural ways so that the Natives could more successfully adapt to the changing times. The following quotation articulates a commonly held thought of the day:

> In order to strengthen the Colony in the manner you propose, by bringing the isolated settlements into parishes, it appears to me, without waiting to depend on the new colonist who may be sent from France, nothing would contribute more to it then to endeavour to civilize the Algonkians, the Hurons, and other Indians who have embraced Christianity, and to induce them to come and settle in common with the French, to live with them and raise their children according to our manners and customs. (O'Callaghan, Commissioner, 1856–57, p. 35)

GROUP DISCUSSION

1. On the basis of the above quotation, what qualities did O'Callaghan identify for a "civilized" person? Conversely (and by inference), what qualities did he deem to be uncivilized?
2. Does this type of categorization still continue today? Give an example to support your answer.

Sir John A. Macdonald wrote that the aim of the government was to "wean [the Natives] by slow degree, from their nomadic habits, which have become almost an instinct, and by slow degrees absorb them on the land." The latter part of the phrase meant that Canada intended to resolve its Native problem by turning them into farmers. As part of what they received in the treaty negotiations, they were given farming implements, cows, etc. But the farming scheme was not as successful as the government had hoped it would be. While many Native peoples began to grow crops and raise animals, other Natives were reluctant or determined not to leave their traditional way of life and settle on specific plots of land assigned to them. Many government officials concluded that the Natives were lazy in nature, intellectually backward, and resistant to change. Clifford Sifton, minister of the interior in 1902, referred to Natives as a "horde of savages" (Francis & Morantz, 1983). To combat this kind of resistance to the changes imposed by the Canadian government, the government began to more aggressively enforce assimilation practices.

A number of laws were enacted by the British to facilitate the assimilation process. In 1830, the Indian civilization policy was developed to train Native peoples to use European skills. For example, children in residential schools were taught such skills as sewing, farming, and blacksmithing. During this time, Native governments continued to make decisions on whether schools were to be allowed on reserves, on agriculture and resource development, and on control over populations and land. Another Act, the *Gradual Civilization Act*, was passed in 1857 and was designed to "christianize and civilize" Native peoples in Ontario.

The *Enfranchisement Act* of 1869 was a policy intended to remove special status from the Natives. The premise behind **enfranchisement** was that if Native peoples gave up their legal status as "Indians," then they would be more readily absorbed into the rest of the Canadian population. On giving up their status, the government would pay the Natives money and land. Any Native who became enfranchised would gain 20 hectares (approximately 100 acres) of land, which was removed from their band's reserve base. The enfranchised Indian would then be entitled to all the rights accorded to other Canadians, such as voting in provincial and federal elections. In effect, the government was taking Native reserve lands to further its assimilation plans. The outcome was erosion of Native sovereignty.

enfranchisement
loss of Native status through the *Indian Act* of 1876

Native leaders were against this legislation and few Native peoples signed up to be enfranchised. Essentially, the Act was deemed unsuccessful and subsequent enfranchisement policies became more aggressive.

The ***British North America Act*** was introduced in 1867. It was drawn up during the Confederation of Canada and during a time of extensive nation building. The British imperial government transferred responsibility for Indian affairs to the government of the United Canadas during this time. Native peoples were not included in the drawing up of this Act, a statute that did not recognize Native self-government. Section 91(24) of the *British North America Act* enabled the Canadian government to arbitrarily assume extensive control of reserves and tribal nations for the first time in Native and non-Native relations. As a result, traditional Native governments were dismissed and replaced with Indian agent–controlled governments.

British North America Act
a statute enacted on March 29, 1867 by the British Parliament providing for the confederation of Canada

What did this mean for Native peoples? With Confederation, the power of Native governments was reduced to less authority than municipalities and the diversity of Native peoples and cultures were treated as one homogeneous group.

GROUP DISCUSSION

Summarize the relationship Britain maintained with the Indian nations and compare it with the relationship between Native peoples and the Canadian government after 1867. Keep in mind that the Native nations were not party to the Confederation talks.

THE INDIAN ACT OF 1876

Slowly, as the influence of the fur trade began to wane and the treaty era ended, the new Canadian government was firmly established as the decision maker over the destinies of Native groups within Canada. In 1876, the Canadian government created and passed the *Indian Act*. Native peoples were not consulted in the development of this Act, which had specific legislation that gave the Canadian government the right to dictate every aspect of Native life. The legislation was contrary in many ways to any legislation written for the general Canadian populations. Many Natives felt that the most degrading aspect of this Act was that the Canadian government assumed **fiduciary responsibility** over Native peoples and Native lands, making them and their lands wards of the government.

fiduciary responsibility
legal duty to act in the best interest of another person; usually seen in the relationship between guardian and ward

GROUP DISCUSSION

1. What current terms are used to describe a government that arbitrarily dictates the actions of and places restrictions on the people within its borders? Cite examples where these conditions exist today.
2. Could the Canadian government have imposed similar conditions on the rest of Canadians?

Dictates of the Indian Act of 1876 on Natives

Until this point, the bands had still practised their own forms of government and had made decisions for their people. With the *Indian Act*, however, the Canadian government imposed changes on the way Native chiefs and councils could operate. The Canadian government dictated specific duties for which each chief and council were responsible and the decisions they could make. The government made decisions on such things as road maintenance, construction and repairs to band schools, and "suppression of intemperance and immorality."

The government developed legal parameters on how Native peoples could select their leaders. This law was in direct conflict with the manner in which a chief was traditionally selected, which was often through direct, hereditary lineage. Additionally, the Act clearly delineated the time, the place, and the manner in which Native chief and council elections could occur. In addition, the chief and/or council could be removed by the superintendent general of Native affairs, for dishonesty, intemperance (selling, purchasing, making, or drinking alcohol), immorality (living common law, having a child out of wedlock, having an extramarital affair, etc.), or incompetence. The government refused to recognize customary practices for selecting chiefs and councils and would not honour the treaty annuities and other services to bands that did not follow the dictates of the *Indian Act*.

Purposes of the Indian Act of 1876

First, the *Indian Act* defined who was an Indian. Only people who were listed in a registry or roll that was maintained by Ottawa were legally recognized as Indians. Who could legally call themselves Indians in 1876?

- All persons of Indian blood belonging to a tribe, band, or body of Indians and their descendants;
- all persons residing among such Indians whose parents were or are descended from either side from Indians and the descendants of such a person; and
- all women lawfully married to an Indian and their children. Native women who married non-Native men lost their status rights but could receive band annuities (because of the treaties).

Second, the 1876 *Indian Act* "protected" Native lands. The manner in which the government did this was to introduce Indian agents who were responsible for carrying out terms of the Act. These agents were non-Natives who generally lived within the Native communities as an enforcer, authority, financial manager, and money leader (jahoonyaa gemah). Reserve land was held in trust by the Crown and could not be mortgaged or seized in lieu of a debt. Surrender of land could only be done if all male band members over the age of 21 agreed to this at a meeting. At this time, the government needed band consent to issue licences for removal of timber or stone. These moneys were held in trust for the band and up to 10 percent of them could be paid directly to band members.

GROUP DISCUSSION

Read "What Did the Indian Agent Think of Native People in 1921?" in appendix 5.1 and answer the following questions:

1. Why did the deputy superintendent general want Native peoples to stop recreational activities?
2. What indications are there that the Indian agent thought Native peoples had poor hygiene?
3. What kind of control does this indicate that the Indian agents had over Native populations at this time?

Third, the *Indian Act* gave the government concentrated authority over Native peoples. Examples of their power over Native populations included enforcing children to attend school until the age of 16, policies of enfranchisement, maintenance of laws, and presiding over chief and council meetings. In addition, the Indian agents, on behalf of the government, made final decisions with regard to education, health care, and social services that were to be provided by the federal government. Other Canadian citizens were provided these services by the provincial government.

The *Indian Act* also introduced laws with regard to Indian tax exemption that only applied to Natives living on reserves. Natives had the right to be exempted from any federal tax if they purchased items while living on the reserve. This was in recognition of the special status accorded to the reserves. While this law is often maligned by non-Natives as an unfair privilege given to Native peoples, most Native peoples who are aware of the history behind this law are proud of this treaty right because it recognizes their status as aboriginal peoples. This law exists today.

Another statute included in the *Indian Act* dictated that Native peoples were forbidden to sell, manufacture, or possess liquor. A Native could be arrested if he or she was caught in an intoxicated state. It was illegal for Natives to drink alcohol in any quantity. The sellers of alcohol to Natives also faced legal consequences and, if caught selling alcohol to a Native, they could receive up to six months in jail. With the exception of Prohibition (in the 1920s and 1930s), other Canadians have experienced no such ban.

Finally, the enfranchisement laws created prior to Confederation were reintroduced into the *Indian Act* with a few modifications. A number of procedures were included in the Act to speed up the assimilation of Native peoples into Canadian society. For one thing, a Status Native had to receive permission from his or her band before he or she could begin enfranchisement. An application also had to be made to the superintendent general and, if the application was approved, the individual and his or her family would be granted a location ticket and placed on probation for three years. The rationale for the probation was to determine whether the Native lived in a manner that was worthy of enfranchisement. What type of behaviour was considered acceptable? The Native person had to show that he or she received a steady income through employment, such as farming. As an incentive, each enfranchised Indian received an individual allotment of land, which was subdivided from reserve or treaty land. The land would then cease to be reserve land. (As a note of interest, western Natives were not eligible to apply for enfranchisement at this time, because the government deemed them unready to become enfranchised.) By inference, then, if enfranchisement was seen as a promotion in status, then Natives unwilling to give up their status might be considered inferior to the rest of Canadians.

The government passed amendments to the *Indian Act* in an effort to accelerate assimilation. Regulations became increasingly coercive. For example, officials were given the authority to spend money belonging to the reserves without the members' permission. The Indian agent could impose an elected system of government on bands, and depose leaders of whom he did not approve. In the early part of the 20th century, it became law that an Indian agent of the office could be elected as chief and become a non-Native chief. To this day, this law remains on the books. The minister of Indian affairs (all have been non-Native to date) can legally become chief of a Native community if he or she is voted in. Until 1954, Natives were not allowed to leave the reserve without approval from the Indian agent. As pointed out earlier, in many ways Natives living on reserves experienced restrictions that have never been imposed on any other group within Canada.

Because the government was unsatisfied by the lack of success of their existing assimilation policies, it developed further amendments to their enfranchisement policies. As recently as 1985, enfranchisement could have potentially happened to any Status Native, which meant that the Native could lose his or her Indian status forever. As an example, in 1920, the government had legal authority to enfranchise Natives against their will and take away their rights as a Status Native. What this meant was that if the Indian agent felt that a Native person was successfully integrating into mainstream society, then the Indian agent had the right to remove the Native's name from the Indian registry that recognized who was an Indian and who was not. This law was repealed two years later but later re-enacted in the 1930s.

GROUP DISCUSSION

What potential for abuse existed in the role of the Indian agent?

Residential Schools

For many years after Britain assumed control of Canada, Native education was controlled by the military, acting on behalf of the Crown. Legislation was passed in 1830 that transferred the responsibility for education to the provincial or local governments. However, because Natives were seen as wards of the Crown, the British government and later the Canadian federal government was responsible for financing Native education (this is a part of Native treaty rights, which will be discussed later). The federal government was unwilling to supervise the daily operation of the schools for Natives and passed this responsibility primarily onto religious agencies. It became mandatory for Native children to attend schools (*Indian Act* of 1876, ss. 113–122). Four churches, the Roman Catholic, the Anglican, the United, and the Presbyterian, were selected to educate Natives in **denominational** schools. A few bands established schools for their children on the reserve. However, most Native communities had neither the financial means nor the knowledge of such things as curriculums and federal and provincial laws to develop their own schools. Moose Deer Point, an isolated Native community near Mactier, was one Native community in Ontario that took on this task. It built its own school, provided lodgings for the teacher, and maintained its school for years during the early part of the 20th century.

denomination
a religious organization

PURPOSE OF RESIDENTIAL SCHOOLS

The residential and industrial school system (industrial schools were later phased out) was advocated for and financed by the British and later the Canadian governments to "educate" Native children, away from the influence of their parents, communities, languages, and customs. The creation of residential schools was one of the actions that the government implemented toward their goal of Native assimilation. We will discuss a number of other actions they took in the next chapter.

At the time when treaty signings were the most prolific, a number of prairie Natives requested the inclusion of educational rights. They foresaw the need to provide an education for their children in order for their peoples and cultures to survive in a changing world. The manner in which the residential schools were developed, however, was not based on any input from Natives themselves. The government did not consult with Natives about their assimilation policies and their intention to use the schools to carry out assimilation. As a result, Natives contend that the children became pawns in the government's plan to "fix" their Native problems and to "mainstream" the Native peoples within their territories.

The residential schools were built to house and educate Native children and provide them with basic skills and religious teaching. According to the *Indian Act*, Native children were legally obligated to attend these schools. From 1867 to 1945, inclusively, Native children were not allowed to attend any other educational institution except one that was legally recognized as a Native school. Native students were not allowed to attend a public, separate, or private school, unless their parents wished to become enfranchised — that is, to give up their Native status. The schools in effect maintained Native children in isolation and in limited contact with their families and communities, as well as other Canadians. In hindsight, the potential for abuses can clearly be seen, given the power and control of the schools' administrators. Only in recent years have the experiences of what some term as "residential school survivors" come to light.

STRUCTURE OF RESIDENTIAL SCHOOLS

All of the residential schools had a number of things in common. Children were forbidden to speak their Native language as soon as they began attending the schools. They were punished if they spoke their Native language. Boys were segregated from girls, and siblings were intentionally separated from each other. Students were required to wear a European style of clothing. In addition, they received food and meals that were primarily Euro-Canadian. The traditional foods to which they had been accustomed, such as wild meats and wild rice, were sometimes available when food donations were made to the school. From the time they awoke until the time they went to sleep, the school life of the children was highly regimented. Academically, the religious groups supervising the schools were far more concerned with teaching useful and practical skills — such as blacksmithing, sewing, woodworking, reading, writing, and so on — and made few attempts to prepare Native students for professional careers such as judges, administrators, lawyers, doctors, and other leadership roles.

Until 1945, Native schooling was referred to as "education in isolation." Before this period, schools and hostels for Native children were established with scant attention paid to developing a curriculum geared to either their language difficulties or their sociological needs (Frideres, 1997). One school, Brandon Industrial School, expressed the state's education purpose as "preparation of Indian youth for the duties, privileges and responsibilities of citizenship ... [through] the industrial arts, the development of the moral and intellectual faculties, the formation of good habits, the formation of character ... learning is a secondary consideration; but what we give him should be adapted to his immediate practical needs" (Wotherspoon & Satzewich, 1993, p. 118). In certain instances and in individual schools, some commitment was made to enhancing Native educational levels. However, for the most part, the schools served to provide Native youth with the basic elements of reading, writing, and arithmetic, and an industrial education, supplemented with religious training.

THE TOTAL INSTITUTION

Paul Baxter of Georgian College applies Rick Ponting's definition of the total institution to residential schools. Ponting (1997) describes a total institution as "a confining formal organization usually intended to forcibly change people's behaviour and self-conduct by means of the rigid structuring of daily routines and assault upon their personal dignity and autonomy." Ponting relates the residential schools to the seven elements of the total institution:

1. **Mortification of self:** the invocation of horror or disgust (children at residential schools were forced to eat their own vomit), humiliation, beatings for minor offences such as bed wetting or using Native languages, losing face, uniforms, and censorship of personal mail.
2. **Anxiety over physical safety:** bullying, sadistic corporal punishment, and rape, at the hands of older children, faculty, and staff of the residential schools.

3. **Manipulation by a system of punishments and rewards:** punishments and rewards were meted out arbitrarily at residential schools; it is a hallmark of the ways in which rules are changed arbitrarily to lower self-esteem.
4. **Participation in activities which are incompatible with the students' self-conception:** even though they weren't Christian, and did not have the concept of "sin" in the Christian sense, children were forced to go to confession, to deny their own spiritual beliefs, and to denounce their parents and grandparents as "pagans."
5. **Loss of privacy:** mail was censored, visits were monitored, students were regularly inspected along with their underwear and beds for personal hygiene, and students were forced to take communal showers, often under the supervision of someone of the opposite sex.
6. **Regimentation:** there were standard times for waking and sleeping, forced silences, forced attendance at religious services, mandatory prayers, mandatory chores, fixed meal times, and the like.
7. **The asymmetry of the power relation:** there was a clear distinction between those with power and those without power at the residential schools, resulting in resistance from Native students, often in the form of escape attempts.

EFFECTS OF RESIDENTIAL SCHOOLS

The children of the residential schools have related many of their experiences. For a number of these children, the missionary school, as some referred to it, was seen as an opportunity to be in an exciting and entirely different world from the one they experienced in their tribal villages. Despite memories of homesickness and loneliness, some students have retained positive memories of the years spent in the residential school. Other students experienced traumas that continue to affect them today. Some received physical beatings, others were raped, while others suffered from food deprivation, long hours of isolation as a means of punishment, and bouts of back-breaking labour.

Physically, most of the schools were located far from any settlement. The distance from which the children were required to come left them isolated, vulnerable, and far removed from their communities and home camps. Children came from as far away as Walpole Island, Ontario (the most southern area of Canada) to attend the Shingwauk Residential School, in Sault Ste. Marie, Ontario. This was roughly 1200 kilometres away from their homes. To put this into perspective, a journey of this magnitude at that time (late 1800s to mid-1900s) made maintaining family contact virtually impossible. Earlier modes of transportation were by water or by rough roads in horse and buggies. Later, given the poverty in which most of the Native people lived, the costs of travelling to see their children were exorbitant. As a result, some children did not see their families for years. They felt abandoned, lonely, and powerless. Many who ran away were merely found and returned to the place from which they were fleeing.

GROUP DISCUSSION 1

Consider the impact that enforced separation from your family for an extended period of time would have on you as a child. What effects might it have on you later as an adult?

Children often boarded with non-Native families during vacations. They often lost contact with their parents, families, and communities, and, in many situations, these relationships became distant. Many children returned home, only to find that their parents could not speak English. Many described their communities as backward, with squalid living conditions. The children and their families found that they had nothing in common after such a long separation. These youths were caught in the middle of two cultures, feeling as if they did not "fit" into either one.

Issues and discord within Native families and communities continue today as a result of the residential school experience. It is generally accepted that the family plays a significant role in the development of an individual into a productive and happy member of society. The children, however, were not raised with their parents, siblings, and other families to learn how to raise children. Removal from such supports often leads to personal and interpersonal dysfunctions. Today, many Native communities cite this deprivation as the cause of community problems such as spousal abuse, child abuse (physical, sexual, mental, and neglect), elder abuse, violence, and suicide.

In the late 1990s, a number of churches involved in residential schools attempted to make amends. The United Church was quoted in the *National Post* (Bell, 1998) as calling the Indian residential school system "cruel" and "ill-conceived." The church's national council stated that it needed to continue mending the ties that it has with First Nations peoples. It also felt that the apology was "not an end in itself" but was a step toward a long healing process. The church established a $1 million healing fund, among a number of initiatives aimed at healing residential school survivors.

royal commission
an official inquiry appointed by Parliament to investigate matters of public concern

The federal government responded to the 1997 **Royal Commission** *Report on Aboriginal People* by acknowledging the mistreatment and abuse that occurred in the residential schools. In January 1998, the Government of Canada announced that it was committing $350 million to support community healing initiatives of physical and sexual abuses suffered by Native children attending residential schools (Indian and Northern Affairs Canada & Health Canada's Medical Services Branch, 1998). This was the first time that the government had assumed responsibility for the ill effects of the residential school system. The funding will assist in developing healing and wellness programs that are culturally specific and community based for survivors of residential schools. The concern of Natives with regard to this initiative is the failure to recognize the cultural and socialization losses created by the residential schools that have contributed to the loss of languages, culture, parenting skills, and other related issues. These issues, the communities contend, are equally critical and need to be addressed as well.

The residential school system has become a major embarrassment for the Canadian government. Despite assuming responsibility for some of the wrongs and initiating funding designed to help in the healing process, in the early 2000s, there were about 12 000 lawsuits in the courts seeking compensation for injustices dealt out at the residential schools. Many more lawsuits are likely to follow.

In June 2001, the government created a new federal department to deal exclusively with residential school issues, and in December of that year created an alternative dispute resolution process intended to allow lawsuits and claims to be handled with speed and efficiency. Yet, many difficulties remain. Even though the Anglican Church in Canada signed an agreement with Ottawa in March 2003 to cooperate with compensating claimants, the Anglican Council of Indigenous People renounced the agreement the same day because it required former students to waive any claims for loss of language and culture. This is not the only roadblock to a settlement of claims, but it is typical of the complexity of the issues. Finger-pointing, blame, shame, and guilt characterize the long and winding path to a resolution of residential schools issues.

GROUP DISCUSSION 2

Read the following poem written by Rita Joe (1998), a student of the Shubenacadie Residential School in Nova Scotia. Then discuss in groups the question: What did Ms Joe dislike about the residential school?

Based on what you know about residential schools from the reading, compare your formal education in elementary and secondary school with her experience. What differences do you see?

Hated Structure: The Indian Residential School

If you are on Highway 104
In a Shubenacadie town
There is a hill
Where a structure stands
A reminder to many senses
To respond like demented ones.

I for one looked into the window
And there on the floor
Was a deluge of a misery
Of a building I held in awe
Since the day
I walked into the ornamented door.

There was grime everywhere
As in buildings left alone or unused.
Maybe to the related tales of long ago
Where the children lived in laughter, or abused.

I had no wish to enter
Nor to walk the halls
I had no wish to feel the floors
Where I felt fear
A beating heart of episodes
I care not to recall.
The structure stands as if to say:
I was just a base for theory
To bend the will of children
I remind
Until I fall.

Residential schools became the primary tool that the government devised to accomplish assimilation of Native peoples. The term **cultural genocide** is often used by Natives to describe the life experienced by Native children within these institutions and the lingering effect that the residential schools have had on the lives of Natives and their communities.

cultural genocide
deliberate and systematic destruction of the culture, traditions, language, and ways of being of a specific cultural group

Outcome of the Indian Act of 1876

The *Indian Act* of 1876 had a number of outcomes. First, the unique relationship that Native peoples had historically maintained with the British Crown was not severed but transferred to the new Canadian government, which assumed responsibility for commitments and treaties with Native peoples. As a result, a large part of the *Indian Act* merely consolidated previous legislation and policies that had been developed by the British. As one new development, Native peoples became subject to the legislation of the province in which they were living.

Second, the unspoken agreement between the Natives and the British that had respected the Natives' right to govern themselves was abolished. Natives did not become citizens of the new country but became "minors." In retrospect, it was undoubtedly difficult for Native peoples who had never been consulted or responsible for contributing to the development of this Act to suddenly be faced with even greater restrictions in their lives by a newly formed non-Native governmental body.

Third, Native peoples lost their autonomy and were not allowed or provided with the means to maintain their unique cultures. As a result, a number of Native cultures and languages have become or are becoming extinct. The irony for Natives today is that, while the French-Canadian culture has been able to maintain its distinct forms of law, language, etc., in part because of their history in Canada, this same privilege has not been accorded to the indigenous nations. The French language, judicial system, and other French influences continue to exist and are protected under Canadian law. Many contend that the **Meech Lake accord** of 1987 ignored the reality of Native peoples as having distinct cultures with collective rights and a legacy of being the original inhabitants of North America. The readiness of the first ministers to concede to Quebec's demands to be recognized as a distinct society, and their readiness to ignore similar Native claims, resulted in strong opposition of Native peoples to the accord. Fortunately, for Natives, they were given the opportunity to influence the final decision on the Meech Lake accord, at a Canadian governmental level. One lone Native representative from the Manitoba legislature, Elijah Harper, refused to give his agreement for unanimous consent, thereby defeating the accord (Boldt, 1993).

Meech Lake accord
the 1987 agreement between the provinces and the federal government regarding amendments to the Canadian Constitution

Amendments to the Indian Act

An overview of changes to the *Indian Act* from its inception until recent times is given in the box on the following pages.

The definition of Indian changed over the years from before Confederation until the most recent revision. The evolution of the term is shown in appendix 5.2.

The most recent attempt to change the terms of the *Indian Act* is Bill C-7, *An Act Respecting Leadership, Administration and Accountability of Indian Bands, and To Make Related Amendments to Other Acts*. It was introduced into the House of Commons

HISTORICAL TIMELINE OF CHANGES TO THE INDIAN ACT AFTER 1876

1879 and 1880

First amendments were passed — half-breeds were withdrawn from the treaty agreements.

1879

- Curtailed prostitution of Indian women — women were not to be penalized but the men who solicited were.
- Native officials were debating over the type of schooling that they wanted offered to Native peoples.

1880

Indian Branch became own department with own "inside" and "outside" staff:

- Inside staff — worked at staff headquarters in Ottawa and included superintendent general, chief clerk, accountant, clerical staff, messengers, packer, etc. (amounted to less than 40 staff).
- Outside staff — 460 staff — worked in the field and were responsible for policy implementation — were called Indian agents.

Indian agents were responsible for directing farming operations, administering relief, inspecting residential schools and health conditions, presiding over band council meetings, etc.

Amendments made to Act required Native people to enfranchise if the Native:

- Held a university degree.
- Joined the clergy.
- Joined the armed forces.
- Voted in a federal election.
- If a Native woman married a non-Native man.

Further amendments made to the Act:

- Excluded Indians of British Columbia and the Northwest Territories from enfranchisement provisions.
- Would not recognize hereditary chiefs — only elected chiefs according to laws set down in the *Indian Act*.
- If a Native woman married a non-treaty Native or a university degree-holding Native, she was not able to keep her status.
- Native peoples of the west could not sell their products — wheat crops and vegetables.

Why not?

- The government did not want them to buy "liquor or other worthless items."
- According to Prime Minister Macdonald, "the wild nomad of the North West" could not be judged on the same basis as "the Indian from Ontario."

1881

Indian agents became justices of the peace and could prosecute and hand down sentences for Act violations.

1883

Sir Hector Langevin argued that the best way to increase Natives' knowledge of agriculture, mechanical skills, and general education was to remove them from the traditions and influence from their band.

Simon J. Dawson (MP for Algoma District) argued that the tribal system protected Natives from the "encroachment of the white man."

1884

- The Native peoples contended that they signed treaties for the government to borrow not to buy the land — the government was not fulfilling treaty obligations.
- Government conceded that not all the treaty promises had been lived up to but felt that bands were not sufficiently advanced to benefit from promised tools, livestock, and schools.
- Banned potlatch — could receive 2 to 6 months for contravening this law — not enforced until the 1920s — was not changed until 1951. (Note: This was the first law created by the Canadian government to protect the Natives from themselves.)
- Native peoples were given the right to create a will for property and personal effects. Bands had partial authority to consent to transfer of property. Second or third cousins were excluded from the estate. The superintendent general of Indian affairs could decide to exclude a Native woman/wife from a will if she was deemed to be "not a woman of good moral character." If there was no will, then ⅓ went to the wife and the remainder was evenly distributed among the children. Property of enfranchised Natives did not have to be taxed on the property left in the will.
- Introduction of the *Advancement Act* — transferred tribal powers into municipal laws.

1885

Issued scrip to half-breeds who were then discharged from treaty rights.

1889

Indian Act amended to allow the federal government to override a band who did not wish to lease land.

1894

Any land of Indians that was not worked due to illness or disability could be leased to non-Natives by the authority of the superintendent general — land seen as "idle" or "surplus" was viewed as fair game.

1905

Up to 50% of band land sold could be distributed to land members and the rest was placed in trust for the band. The rationale of this was to get Natives to sell more and more of their land.

1911

- Section 46 allowed portions of land to be taken by municipalities of companies for roads, railways without surrender — only needed consent of the superintendent general.
- Section 46(a) permitted removal of Indians from any reserve next to or partly within a town of 8000 inhabitants — referred to as the *Oliver Act*.

What impact did all of these laws have on the land negotiated in the treaties for Native peoples?

From July 1, 1896 to March 31, 1909, of identified Native lands in the west, $74 353 was given to Natives for surrendered lands — $2 156 020 was obtained by the Department of Indian Affairs for surrendered lands.

1918

- Natives could not be conscripted into army because not recognized as full citizens (*Military Act*) — but if Natives volunteered they would not lose status.
- Enfranchisement was made easier to encourage more Natives to apply. How? Natives who wished to enfranchise had to:
  a. Apply to superintendent general.
  b. Be self-supporting.
  c. Receive a share of band funds.
  d. Relinquish further claims to band property.

1921

Enfranchisement could happen against will of Native person by the department — if he or she was considered a "suitable" candidate.

1927

No person could raise money to fund land claims without the consent of the superintendent general of Indian affairs.

1933

Government could enfranchise a person without his or her consent.

1951

Indian Act was completely overhauled and changes included:

- Lifted ban on potlatches.
- Allowed Native peoples right to purchase and drink alcoholic beverages and the right to access public bars, pending provincial approval.
- The establishment of the Indian Register or Roll as a centralized record of all persons entitled to registration and was composed of band lists (Native people that lived on the reserves) and the general list (included any persons registered in the Indian Register who were not band members).

The registrar was a departmental official whose duties were to determine who was entitled to registration as Indians and band members — had the authority to add or delete names from the general or band lists.

- Band lists were to be posted.
- Band members and band councils had the right to protest additions or deletions or omission from the Indian Registry — within 6 months — after this time, the decision of the registrar was final.

Who was eligible to have their name in the registry?

a. When name of a Native was added or deleted from the band or general list, the names of his wife and minor children were also added or deleted.
b. Illegitimate male children of Indian males could be registered as well as legitimate children of Indian males.
c. The wife or widow of an eligible Indian was also eligible.
d. Persons who had lost their band membership prior to 1951 could regain it given the consent of the band council.

Who was not eligible to have their name in the registry?

a. Natives were not eligible if they were already enfranchised, owners or descendants of an owner of half-breed lands or money scrip.
b. Persons who lived in a "foreign residence" for a period over five years.
c. Any children born to a Native woman prior to her marriage to a non-Native male could also become enfranchised with a recommendation from the minister.

These changes did not include:

a. Changing enfranchisement policies.
b. Setting up a land claims commission requested by Native peoples.

Mid-1950s

Indian agents still controlled aspects of community life even to the point of issuing temporary passes from the reserves.

Early 1960s

Natives given the right to vote in federal elections.

1969

- White paper proposed to:
  - a. Repeal the *Indian Act*, ending federal responsibilities to First Nations.
  - b. Indian status and treaties would also end.
  - c. Eliminate reserve land.
  - d. Transfer all responsibilities for Native people over to the provinces.
  - e. Promised to look into land claims more closely.

The white paper was dropped due to consciousness raising and banding together of First Nation peoples in protest over this paper and, in turn, they produced extensive statements of their own positions. Native political organizations became stronger and more unified at this point.

- Indian agents were removed from the reserves.
- First Nation political groups were funded by the federal government (e.g., Assembly of First Nations, Union of Ontario Indians).

1970

The federal government began to fund First Nation groups and associations for research into treaty and Native rights.

1982

- The *Constitution Act, 1982* recognized "existing aboriginal and treaty rights" – guaranteed equally to aboriginal men and women.
- Section 25 of this act – the *Canadian Charter of Rights and Freedoms* – attempts to ensure that the protection of individual rights does not take away from the protection of "aboriginal, treaty or other rights or freedoms that pertain to the aboriginal peoples."

1985

Bill C-31 [see appendix 5.3] was introduced. It recognized the right of Native people to never lose their status – enfranchisement became obsolete. Many Native people, in particular the women who had married non-Native men, and their children, were returned their status.

Source: Adapted from Leslie & Maguire (1978).

Bill C-31
1985 amendment to the *Indian Act* that allowed for reinstatement of status to Natives who had lost it for a variety of reasons

on October 9, 2002. The *First Nations Governance Act* (Bill C-7) was referred to the House of Commons Standing Committee on Aboriginal Affairs after first reading.

First Nations representatives were almost unanimously opposed to the act. On November 19, 2003, First Nations representatives met in Ottawa to discuss the legislation, after the government, represented by Indian and Northern Affairs Minister Robert Nault, had recommended more than 50 changes to the proposed legislation.

Nault commented that "only 81 chiefs voted against this legislation," while failing to mention that only 10 chiefs voted for the legislation.

Presentations were made to the government before the 2003 Ottawa meeting by many Native groups, including the Northwest Tribal Treaty Nations, the Assembly of First Nations of Quebec and Labrador, the Six Nations of the Grand River, and the Dene Nation. The government recorded that there were more than 80 separate discussions being carried out over the legislation.

Opposition such as the following was typical of the responses from the majority of Native groups:

> The position of the Assembly of First Nations has been consistent in rejecting Bill C-7 and calling for the legislation to be withdrawn. Bill C-7 does not replace the *Indian Act* but instead entrenches the *Indian Act*. The *First Nations Governance Act* represents more tinkering with the *Indian Act*, an approach that has been condemned by such studies as the Royal Commission on Aboriginal Peoples and the Penner Report.
>
> The past failure of the one size fits all approach of the *Indian Act* is set to be repeated with the development of codes that have strict prescriptive measures ignoring the diversity of the First Nations across Canada. First Nations that do not or cannot develop codes based on the restrictive and prescriptive criteria will have codes developed by federal bureaucrats imposed on them. This is a direct infringement on Aboriginal and Treaty rights as recognized in Canada's *Constitution Act* of 1982. First Nations are also concerned with the capacity requirements that will be imposed and other subsequent requirements under this legislation. (Assembly of First Nations)

Other concerns of the Assembly of First Nations include the low threshold of 25 percent that is identified in the act for the ratification of codes, that the traditional positions of chief and councillor will be removed, that a First Nation will have the legal capacity of a natural person affecting treaty negotiations, and the fact that Bill C-7 does not include a non-derogation clause.

In the end, the government dropped Bill C-7. The process, however, serves to show the difficulties inherent in changing the *Indian Act*.

GROUP DISCUSSION 1

Read appendix 5.3 regarding Bill C-31 at the end of this chapter and answer the following questions:

1. Upon whom did Bill C-31 have the greatest impact?
2. What is the difference between band membership and Indian status?
3. What are the long-term effects of Bill C-31 on Native peoples?

GROUP DISCUSSION 2

1. Taking into account all of the changes to the *Indian Act* over the years, describe the revisions that enabled the Natives to experience freedom similar to that enjoyed by other Canadians.
2. After reading through the amendments to the *Indian Act*, which laws that affected or still affect Natives were you unaware of?

FIRST NATIONS CHIEFS AND COUNCILS TODAY

Earlier, we examined two traditional Native governments. As discussed, the Natives slowly lost their sovereignty and ability for self-determination. The Canadian government recognized only the powers granted to the bands under the *Indian Act* and other relevant Native legislation. The only Native government legally recognized by the Canadian government is at the band level, which we will look at in more detail in the following section. All other Native organizations, including ones at the federal level, Assembly of First Nations (AFN), which comprises chiefs across Canada, have no law-making powers. This does not mean that they are without power, but they must work as a unified front to influence and lobby for changes. Native self-government remains a key issue of the AFN today.

Legal Definition of "Band"

According to the *Indian Act*, a "band" is a body of First Nations for whom the government has set aside lands for their common use and benefit; for whom the government is holding moneys for their common use and benefit; and who have been declared a band by the governor in council for the purposes of the Act. A member of a band is a person whose name appears on a band list or who is entitled to have his or her name appear on such a list. A reserve, within the meaning of the Act, is a tract of land, the legal title to which is vested in the Crown, that has been set aside for the use and benefit of the band.

In total, Canada has 633 First Nation communities within its borders (Assembly of First Nations Brotherhood, 1999). The history of how each community came into existence has been unique to each community. Some communities show evidence of a settlement pattern that pre-dates European contact, while the majority of the First Nations communities were created as a result of the treaties or through federal or provincial government actions. This majority has been relocated by the government to places that were deemed appropriate. As of 1995, there were 116 government recognized reserves in Ontario. (Note: The federal government does not recognize the term "First Nations" but identifies Native communities as "Bands." In reference to their aboriginal rights that were never extinguished by the British or Canadian governments, Native people have come to refer to their communities as First Nations.)

Bands by their very nature are unique forms of government that exist nowhere else in the world. Imai, Logan, and Stein, authors of *Aboriginal Law Handbook* (1993, p. 103), describe why a band differs from any other municipality, province, or country:

> The band, as an enduring entity with its own government, is a unique type of legal entity under Canadian law. The rights and obligations of the band are quite distinct from the accumulated rights and obligations of the members of the band. What distinguishes a band from a club is that a band exists apart from any voluntary act of its members. In this respect a band is more like a nation state than a club. But no comparison is totally apt. In law a band is in a class by itself.

New bands can be and have been created since Confederation. The creation of a new band generally occurs when a larger community divides into smaller groups because of the distance between the reserve's lands. It is important to remember that not all reserves are based on a single land base but may comprise two or more areas. For example, Batchewana First Nation near Sault Ste. Marie, Ontario is composed of three different land bases roughly 80 kilometres apart. Another example is the Sachigo Lake Indian Reserves Nos. 1 and 2, which are located approximately 425 kilometres north of Sioux Lookout and are accessible only by air. Sachigo received separate band status in 1976 from the Big Trout Lake Band.

Decision-Making Power of Band Councils

Most decisions for the First Nations communities are made by the band councils. The chief and council formally pass bylaws called Band Council Resolutions (BCRs). In order to pass a BCR, a quorum of chief and council members must be present at a meeting. Band Council Resolutions can be declared to bind the band members to legally abide by what was passed and can affect the rights of the band members. The band council may not pass some decisions without community approval. These decisions include land surrender or designation, membership codes, and alcohol bylaws. To obtain community majority approval, the band council is obligated to hold a community meeting. After being told about the proposed changes, the community must then vote. A majority vote decides the outcome. As an example, Wikwemikong First Nation on Manitoulin Island, Ontario historically occupied a large territory of the lands on the north shore of Lake Huron. In 1836, the government moved a number of Native peoples to what is now Manitoulin Island and to 23 000 islands in the Georgian Bay area of Lake Huron to make these areas into reserves and fishing routes. The British government gave up claim on those islands. In 1850, after examining the extent of the lands on Manitoulin Island and to "avoid encroachment of the whites," the government signed another treaty with the Manitoulin Island Natives. The people of Wikwemikong did not take part in the treaties of 1862 and remain an "unceded" Native community. In 1968, the Point Grondine Band members joined the Wikwemikong Band, making Wikwemikong the legal representative in any issues of the Point Grondine Band. The Point Grondine Band had originally settled on the north shore of Lake Huron near Killarney, Ontario. The surveyors made a mistake in the measurement of the lands to be given to the Point Grondine Band in 1850. In the original agreement, the reserve was intended to be three times longer. From this perspective, the Wikwemikong First Nation took this land claim to court in 1994 and won. However, once the land claim negotiations were completed, the band members had the right to vote on accepting or rejecting the offer. In this situation, the band received a settlement for the land but not the amount of land they were entitled to or had initially negotiated for (Wikwemikong First Nation Land Claims Office, 1994).

Native peoples chafe under the restrictions and problems that arise from the band council resolution system. For one thing, 50 percent of the BCRs submitted to the federal minister are disallowed. Native peoples also contend that the resolutions are formalistic and government enforced. First Nations often find the federal law-making process to be in direct conflict with their traditional methods of decision making. Until recent years, the bands have felt they have not had the means by which to enforce these bylaws (lack of Native-based policing, etc.). In addition, any band council resolution may be superseded by other provincial legislation.

Elections of Chiefs and Band Councils

Under the *Indian Act*, bands must hold elections every two years to elect a chief and council by secret ballot unless they select their leaders by band custom elections. If the bands follow band custom, the bands can decide who will vote and when terms of office end. However, whenever a Native community faces conflicts within their boundaries, these traditional councils are easily dismissed by the Canadian courts. In fact, any election held under the *Indian Act* can be overturned by the federal Cabinet. In both types of band election process (*Indian Act* legislated or band custom), only reserve residents have the right to vote.

The *Indian Act* enforces specific guidelines for the elections of chief and council. Anyone who is 18 years of age or older and is a resident of the Native community may vote. An election can be called by an electoral officer, a neutral party, who must post a notice for a nomination meeting, prepare the voters' list, and post it at least 6 days before a nomination meeting or 12 days before an election. The elections are conducted from 9 a.m. to 6 or 8 p.m. The ballots are secret and, if there is a tie, the electoral officer may cast the deciding vote but does not have to vote. The election may be contested within 30 days in an appeal to the Department of Indian Affairs if the parties supply reasonable grounds for the appeal.

The minister of Indian affairs may deem that an election should take place to elect chief and council if he or she considers that an election is for the band's benefit. Each band can have only one chief and one band councillor for every 100 band members and they cannot have fewer than 2 band councillors or more than 12 band councillors.

Powers of the Band Council

According to s. 81 of the *Indian Act*, among other things, the band councils are responsible for the following:

- health of residents on reserve
- regulation of traffic
- observance of law and order
- prevention of disorderly conduct
- the control of trespass by cattle and other domestic animals
- construction of roads and other local works
- zoning for land use
- regulation of construction and repair of buildings
- surveying and the allotment of reserve lands to individuals
- control of "noxious" weeds
- regulation of bee-keeping and poultry raising
- control of public games and other amusements
- regulation of salespeople on the reserve
- management of game and fish on the reserve (Note: Courts are increasingly recognizing the mandate of First Nations to create BCRs to regulate fishing done by reserve members. Assuming control of hunting and fishing laws can be seen as a step toward self-government.)
- removal and punishment of trespassers on the reserve
- residence of band members (Note: It is important to remember that there are two provisions to this law: first, if a member of a First Nation has the right

to reside on the reserve, that right must also extend to the dependent children of that member, whether or not the children have status; second, no Natives have lawful possession of the land unless the chief and council have allotted the land and the minister has given approval.)

- application of bylaws to spouses and children of band members who reside on the reserve
- allowing all members of the band to vote on citizenship or membership codes (In 1985, the *Indian Act* was amended to provide bands with greater control over their citizenship; bands may now pass their own codes to determine who are their citizens. As of 1993, over 50 First Nations in Ontario had passed membership codes for their communities.)

GROUP DISCUSSION

After reviewing the powers given to the band council, identify any areas in which the bands have powers that are different from those of a municipality.

In summary, Native criticism of the system of band council government has been extremely vocal over the years. Bands feel that they function as agents of the federal government and must administer programs and follow policies set down by the federal government that are not culturally appropriate. In addition, they believe that band governments exercise limited and delegated power permitted by the *Indian Act*. The councils were created in part to promote the federal government's policy of assimilation by creating communities that were more like the dominant culture's concept of a community and its functions. For example, in the 1930s, the Canadian government abolished the hereditary council of the Iroquois and replaced it with an elected council. Finally, many Natives feel that the federal government has attempted to make bands work primarily as municipal governments with the limited powers that they possess. In fact, Native bands have authority and jurisdiction over areas that are unique to them.

DEVELOPMENT OF NATIVE PEOPLES' POLITICAL ACTIVISM

Most Canadians are not aware of the roadblocks and difficulties that Native peoples face in their striving for political recognition in Canada. Since the inception of Canada until now, Native peoples have struggled for the right to take part in Canadian constitutional developments or at least for the right to provide input in a law, the *Indian Act*, that controls so much of their lives. The long years of exclusion from the formal political process have meant that First Nations peoples must work quickly to overcome this gap to achieve the same level of political and legal knowledge that other ethnic and political groups in Canada appear to have. For example, the 1927 *Indian Act* prohibited Natives from forming any political organizations. Unawareness of facts like these might have contributed to the possible resentment and misunderstanding felt by some Canadians when First Nations peoples try to assert what they see as their rightful position in Canadian society.

Development of Native Organizations

The political response of aboriginal people to the *Indian Act* and its consequences resulted in the formation of various Native organizations. Before World War I, Native groups in British Columbia organized over land issues. Nationally, the League of Indians of Canada was organized after the war, but it failed due to lack of support. Native groups in the West took the lead in organizing on a political level between the wars; the League of Western Indians was formed in the 1920s, and in 1939 the Indian Association of Alberta was organized. Despite the limited success of these organizations, they did offer some form of organized resistance to government policies regarding First Nations peoples, and led to the success of the major post–World War II associations, the National Indian Brotherhood and the Assembly of First Nations.

The North American Indian Brotherhood (NAIB) was organized shortly after World War II but again lacked national support. In addition, the federal government provided no funding support for the organization and also seemed to work against any Native initiatives. Moreover, the NAIB suffered from internal administrative problems caused by regional factions. As a result, the NAIB disbanded in the early 1950s.

Native groups and communities continued to work toward the development of a new national lobby group and, in 1961, the National Indian Council (NIC) was formed. The NIC represented three of the four major aboriginal groups in Canada: treaty and Status Natives, non-Status Natives, and the Métis (the Inuit were excluded). The stated purpose of the NIC was to "promote unity among all Indian people." Carrying out this purpose was a challenge, especially because of the diversity of Native cultures, their issues, and their priorities. This recurring theme challenges any national Native organization today. As a result of disunity, the NIC split up. The treaty and Status aboriginal peoples formed the National Indian Brotherhood, and the non-Status and Métis groups formed the Native Council of Canada.

NATIONAL INDIAN BROTHERHOOD (NIB)

Soon after its inception, the National Indian Brotherhood (NIB) experienced "trial by fire" as a test of its mettle. The federal government introduced plans to pass the white paper of 1969. The paper had been developed by the recently elected prime minister of Canada, Pierre Elliott Trudeau, and his Liberal party. Under the terms of the paper, Native peoples were to be assimilated into mainstream Canadian society by removing the reserves, removing First Nations from the Canadian constitution, and revoking the *Indian Act*. Natives felt that this policy in effect removed all traces of laws or lands that recognize the presence of Natives as indigenous peoples of Canada. The resulting outcry from Native peoples, headed by the NIB, saw the development of the red paper. Although this paper proposed recommendations from the Natives' perspective, these recommendations received no response by the federal government. The National Indian Brotherhood came out of this crisis knowing how to better deal with the government and with the support of many Native communities across Canada.

From 1969 to the present (the NIB changed its name to the Assembly of First Nations [AFN] in 1982), this national organization has retained its role as a watchdog agency for Native interests. It has remained a voice to press for changes to federal and provincial aboriginal policies. Its greatest difficulty is in organizing and working for First Nations communities across Canada as one united body. For this reason, the essential structure of the organization will continue to mould and change as it strives to meet a myriad of needs; hence, the AFN will remain an organization in flux.

ASSEMBLY OF FIRST NATIONS (AFN)

One of the original goals of the Assembly of First Nations was to rewrite the *Indian Act*. The Department of Indian Affairs, the federal trustee over First Nations affairs, treated the First Nations people as children who needed care. Two tendencies developed. First, the AFN worked to gain control over Native education, which was achieved in 1973. Second, the AFN took a leading role in the land claims question and was instrumental in creating the two-tier land claims resolution dealing with comprehensive claims and specific claims in 1974. The land claims question was dealt with in chapter 4.

The Assembly of First Nations has been involved in other matters, including the 1969 federal white paper that called for the elimination of Indians as a separate legal category; constitutional renewal, which defined aboriginal rights; and self-government issues, which unfortunately detracted from the need to focus on Native housing, poverty, and health issues at the time.

The Assembly of First Nations (AFN) gives First Nations across Canada a collective voice to channel their concerns and desires for positive changes in the lives of Native peoples. The AFN enables the 633 First Nations across Canada to restore the nation-to-nation relationships among them. Any First Nations community that wishes to be represented in the assembly can be represented through its elected chief or council representative. The structure of the AFN is such that the various First Nations communities across Canada may present their views and issues in such areas as aboriginal and treaty rights, land claims, economic development, education, housing, health, social services, environment, and other commonly held concerns.

The AFN has been involved in the residential school situation, assisting the federal government in dealing with the problems created and compensation expected as a result of these schools. The government, through the minister of Indian affairs rather than the Prime Minister's Office, has apologized for the residential schools abuses. The national chief of the AFN did not accept the apology, requesting instead an order in council to act as a national forum for problems resulting from residential schools.

The chiefs of First Nations meet in the assembly at least once a year to set national policy and direction through the passing of resolutions (similar to a motion passed by any board). In this section, we will examine the organization to better understand its functions. The position of national chief is held for three years through an election held by the chiefs in the assembly. Each chief has the right to vote once when a decision is required. Their voting rights are not based on the size of their communities or the population of their reserves. The AFN executive committee is composed of the national chief and regional vice-chiefs and the chair of the elders council. The regional vice-chiefs are elected periodically by their chiefs, who reside in First Nations communities within specific regions. The elders council is composed of elders who counsel the AFN. The mere existence of the elders council indicates the organization's uniqueness. The AFN has incorporated the traditional value that elders be sought and be given respect for their input, knowledge, and experience before making any decision.

The AFN also has a nationally elected representative body of First Nations chiefs called the Confederacy of Nations, which meets every three to four months and provides direction for the AFN. This arm of the AFN is an integral part of its political structure. In turn, the AFN has become more directly responsible for carrying out the wishes of the communities via the First Nations Chiefs-in-Assembly.

Here are some examples of the positive influence that the NIB–AFN has had in decisions, policies, and laws affecting Native peoples and Native communities:

- First Nations presence at constitutional meetings between the prime minister and federal ministers, as well as at other meetings that relate to or affect Native peoples.
- Progress in self-government talks and related changes (despite consensus between First Nations groups with regard to the definition of self-government).
- Heightened awareness of the Canadian public about Native issues.

GROUP DISCUSSION

Based on the positive influences that we just examined about the AFN, discuss the potential benefits that the AFN can bring to the various First Nations they represent.

ISSUE OF SELF-GOVERNMENT

In s. 35 of the *Constitution Act, 1982*, it is stated that "the existing aboriginal and treaty rights of the aboriginal peoples of Canada are hereby recognized and affirmed" and that "[for the purpose of] this act, 'aboriginal peoples of Canada' includes the Indian, Inuit and Métis people of Canada." In 1985, the Supreme Court of Canada recognized that Native sovereignty and Indian rights were independent and separate from the Crown because of Indian title and occupation of the land from time immemorial. How have these precepts been received by the provincial governments of Canada? The federal government and some provincial governments (such as Alberta) have become more accepting of the issue of Native sovereignty and self-government than some other provinces (such as Quebec). Each provincial government has been dealing with Native claims of self-government in its own way, often based on the historical relationship maintained with the Native groups inside each province's borders.

The first attempt at what might be seen as self-government occurred in 1836 when, by treaty, Ojibwe living in the southern part of Canada were expected to move to Manitoulin Island after ceding their lands. While the Natives on Manitoulin Island were granted some rights that could be considered as part of self-government, the project was a failure. Over a century later, Native participation in World War II would, it was hoped, lead to more self-government. Natives' hopes were dashed, however, when the Canadian government looked at Native participation in the armed forces as a form of assimilation rather than proof of competence for self-government. In 1983, the Penner report urged the establishment of First Nations self-government, a report that the First Ministers Conference on Aboriginal Affairs reinforced. However, these efforts died with the Meech Lake accord.

Defining Self-Government

The issue of self-government itself is contentious. In fact, the very definition of self-government has never been agreed upon by either the government or the individual First Nations. Therein lies the problem. For many Native leaders, self-government as a national concept is impossible. Perhaps tired of waiting, a number of communities have contracted agreements with the federal government for their own forms of self-government.

The issue of Native self-government began in the early 1970s after the federal government's attempt to pass legislation based on the 1969 white paper. As a response to the white paper and as a direct result of the development of a stronger and more unified national Native political organization, the recurring theme in the early 1970s and 1980s was the call for Native self-government. As a concept, self-determination through self-government was seen by many Natives as a new order in the Canadian–aboriginal relationship, a means of resolving Native community issues and addressing human rights inequities. Many Natives argued that they never gave up their right to be independently governed and proposed that self-government become the means by which to sever the relationship between the government and themselves. Native peoples think they have received unfair and unethical treatment. Self-government, Natives argue, would provide them with greater autonomy, which would end their dependency and erase the debilitating experiences that many Native communities faced and are still experiencing.

Natives believe that self-government is feasible, despite their opposition to new government initiatives such as Bill C-7 (see discussion earlier in this chapter). The Assembly of First Nations has been leading the struggle for self-government, advancing the ideals that First Nations have an inherent right to self-government, that the right to self-government was not extinguished by treaty, and that the treaties and federal law contain provisions for self-government. These ideals are contained in the four pillars of the claim to self-government, according to Baxter (2004):

1. **The right to self-determination:** Aboriginal peoples have the right to self-determination. This basic human right was denied to Natives by the Crown for over 200 years.
2. **The dispute over extinguishment clauses:** A substantial number of First Nations have never signed any treaties with the Crown, and they demand self-government as one of the conditions of signing treaties today. First Nations further argue that the Crown was fraudulent, or at least dishonest, in both the negotiation and the implementation of treaties, both of which are sufficient conditions to nullify the treaties.
3. **Legislative record:** First Nations argue that various colonial legislation such as the *Royal Proclamation of 1763* and Treaty 4 contain an implicit recognition of Native self-government.
4. **Equality rights:** First Nations organizations point out the differences in the way Natives were treated by the Crown when compared with other

"national" minority groups, such as the Quebecois, who have received differential treatment since the *Quebec Act of 1774*. The AFN has pointed out the implicit cultural bias that this differential treatment demonstrates on the part of the Crown. To many Natives, it seems ironic that a European culture is allowed to keep its traditional laws and institutions while people indigenous to this country have not been granted the same rights.

GROUP DISCUSSION

1. Based on the information covered in this chapter, describe the similarities between Natives and French Quebeckers, to which the label of distinct society would apply.
2. Describe the qualities, if any, that the Native and French communities possess that would give them greater claim to the distinct society title. Any conclusions?

Common Grounds Among First Nations for Self-Government

Now that we have stated a number of reasons why Native peoples have the right to be self-governing, we will examine why many Native groups have stopped advocating for national self-government. The very definition of self-government and what it means to Natives collectively has never been established because Native tribal governments have not reached a consensus on this matter. Self-government means different things to the many Native cultures in Canada. As mentioned before, each First Nation has a different history and distinct cultural background; hence, they have diverse needs and concepts about what they require to be self-governing.

Despite the diversity in Native perceptions of what self-government is, Canadian First Nations also have similar visions with regard to self-government. Most important, all bands have expressed the desire to maintain their unique ways of being and living. From the early treaties to the present, Native peoples have spoken of their need to retain their culture. As well, the bands have demanded greater local control and decision making over services and programs that affect the communities. In response to pressure on the federal government over the past 20 years, Native communities are now assuming more control over the **administration** of services to their band members in areas such as education, medical care, social services, and community and economic development.

administration
the execution of public affairs as distinguished from policy making

In another shared vision of Native First Nations, many chiefs and councils want to be more accountable to local electors (community members) rather than the federal government. Bands must now seek the final approval of the federal government in all ventures and in all laws that they create. Many Natives would also like to have the right to govern their own people and regulate their affairs, including the land and its use, without interference. In recent years, bands have assumed control over what occurs within the parameters of the reserves. However, Native peoples are also concerned about decisions being made over Crown land, such as the Ontario **Lands for Life** initiatives, and the impact that these decisions will have on Natives and the treaty promises of hunting and fishing rights.

Lands for Life
land-use planning undertaken by the Ontario government for Crown lands; Crown lands are currently used by Natives as part of their treaty rights relating to hunting and fishing

Another concept on which most Native groups agree that relates to self-government is that Native self-governance exists within the territorial jurisdiction of the federal or provincial governments. Canadian Native peoples want to remain part of Canada. However, as distinct peoples who have experienced lives that are distinct from the rest of the Canadian population, many Native leaders want the opportunity to govern all aspects of Native life – political, economic, social, and cultural – with the hope that a better way of life may be provided for their citizens. At present, Native communities across Canada are seeking more control within these areas to improve the life of Native communities and people (both on-reserve and off-reserve). These actions are often identified as a path toward greater self-determination.

There are indicators that First Nations people continue to move toward self-government and self-determination. In the first place, a significant number of Native people have been elected to important posts in federal and provincial governments, giving the Native cause visibility and a voice in the affairs of the country. A partial list includes:

- Huron chief Ludger Bastien elected to the Quebec legislature, 1924;
- Nisga'a chief Frank Calder elected to the British Columbia legislature, 1949;
- Len Marchand appointed minister of state for small business, 1976; minister of state for the environment, 1977; Senate, 1984;
- Wilton Littlechild elected as the first treaty Indian member of Parliament, 1988; and
- Ethel Blondin Andrew elected member of Parliament, 1988; secretary of state, training, and youth, 1993; secretary of state, children, and youth, 1997.

Not to be overlooked is the number of aboriginal organizations that are contributing to Native self-determination, including

- Aboriginal Financial Officers Association of Canada,
- Aboriginal Healing Foundation,
- Aboriginal Human Resource Development Council of Canada,
- Aboriginal Nurses Association of Canada,
- Aboriginal Tourism Team Canada,
- Canadian Aboriginal Science and Engineering Association,
- Canadian Aboriginal Science and Technology Society,
- Canadian Council for Aboriginal Business,
- Canadian Indigenous and Native Studies Association,
- Centre for Aboriginal Policy Change,
- Centre for Indigenous Environmental Resources,
- Centre for Indigenous Sovereignty,
- First Nations Chiefs of Police Association,
- First Nations Child and Family Caring Society of Canada,

- First Nations Environmental Network,
- Indigenous Bar Association,
- Indigenous Women's Coalition of Canada,
- National Aboriginal Achievement Foundation,
- National Aboriginal Business Association,
- National Aboriginal Diabetes Association,
- National Aboriginal Health Organization,
- National Aboriginal Women's Association,
- National Association of Friendship Centres,
- National Association of Indigenous Institutes of Higher Learning,
- Native Psychologists of Canada, and
- Native Women's Association of Canada.

The Complexity of Self-Government

A common self-government scenario maintains each First Nations group under the jurisdiction of the federal and provincial governments. Hence, the principles of democracy, justice, freedom of speech, equal access to all services, equality of the people, etc., under the present governmental structure would be maintained. Under each Native government's jurisdiction would be the power to create laws in those areas that directly affect Native peoples, such as education, citizenship, land, water, forestry, minerals, conservation, economic development, health, and law enforcement. In their paper "Reluctant Citizens? First Nations in the Canadian Federal State" (1997), J. Cockerill and R. Gibbins describe the process of self-government as being one where First Nations peoples would speak and deal with the Canadian government through their own governments. The Assembly of First Nations envisions Native self-government to have a province-like government status within the current Canadian federation. This is referred to as a third order of government (Boldt, 1993).

Comparatively, any changes sought by Natives within the existing system can only be accomplished through a federal or provincial ballot. Native people would have to be a provincial legislative member or a federal Cabinet member in order to directly make changes. The reality of changing any law in this manner is almost impossible for Natives. Why? Representing less than 5 percent of the entire Canadian population, a Native running for government office on a Native platform has occurred only rarely. Elijah Harper is one of the few Native provincial MPPs and he sits in the Manitoba Legislative Assembly. Therefore, without authority to vote in changes, lobbying and protests become the only avenues left to Natives to make changes. Unfortunately, the process often gets bogged down or overturned by the whims and wills of changing Canadian or provincial governments.

The Royal Commission on Aboriginal Peoples (RCAP), formed in 1991, made a number of recommendations concerning Native self-government, including

- restructure the *Indian Act* (which is in the process of taking place),
- promote Native self-determination through self-government,

- create an aboriginal parliament,
- vest the right to self-determination through aboriginal nations rather than through smaller communities,
- develop an aboriginal system of taxation,
- foster aboriginal economic initiatives by providing First Nations with more land, and
- establish a national aboriginal bank (which has been done).

To date, Native peoples, in negotiation with the federal government, have failed to reach any agreement about collective Native self-government. Currently, the federal government recognizes the Native right to administer the needs of the individual communities — education, health, social services, and community and economic development — but that does not recognize the collective rights of Native peoples to be fully self-governing. Self-government has become obtainable by a few bands who have taken the initiative to seek self-government for themselves.

Since July 1994, self-government legislation has been enacted on behalf of a few First Nations, including the Sechelt Band of British Columbia, the Cree Naskapi of Quebec, the Nunavut territory, the Teslin Tlingit from British Columbia, and most recently the Nisga'a. Each First Nation has negotiated with the federal government to reach an arrangement that is most appropriate to their needs. As discussed in chapter 4, the Nisga'a Indians, for example, negotiated a treaty that provides them with ownership of land, self-governing powers similar to those of a municipality, and greater control over health care, education, and justice. The band will also receive $500 million in cash grants and program funds. In return, the band will give up its tax-exempt status (Meissner, 1998).

CONCLUSION

At present, Native peoples are subject to the laws of Canada as is every Canadian. Because Native organizations have no direct authority to change legislation, unlike the federal or provincial level of government, changes to legislation must be done through political pressure by lobbying, protesting, influencing bureaucrats, proposing legislation changes, etc.

In the past 20 years, the bands have enjoyed greater autonomy and control over the services and programs by being able to administer them within the communities. However, concerns such as the following remain: the government still controls the money that is provided to each band; because they are federally funded, band schools often lack the services that provincially funded public and private schools have; education dollars have remained at a constant rate while the number of Natives applying to attend postsecondary institutions has risen dramatically; and the government still controls who can be legally recognized as an Indian (a system that continues to be discriminatory to Native women and their offspring).

The life Native peoples experienced before contact with Europeans no longer exists in its truest form. The political dominance of European powers gradually eroded Native sovereignty. What exists today of Native power and statehood is a mere shell of its former self. However, the lives of Native peoples and the directions taken by the communities today, while still controlled by the government, are slowly becoming more directed by the wills of First Nations governments and Native organizations. Many Natives hope that as long as these political bodies band together as a unified force, Native nations and peoples will continue to develop into a self-determining presence in Canada and be strong, viable members of Canadian society.

WORKSHEET

1a. Describe the policy of assimilation in your own words and explain why this policy was selected by the British–Canadian governments to deal with the Native populations. (2 marks)

1b. Provide examples to prove that the British and the Canadian governments intended to assimilate Native populations into their culture. (2 marks)

2a. Contrast the two traditional Native political structures that are discussed in this chapter as they existed prior to European contact or influence. (2 marks)

2b. Research another Native cultural group and briefly describe its political structure and how it is similar to or different from the two discussed in this chapter. Information can be obtained in a library or on the Internet. (2 marks)

3. Draw a parallel between the governing structure of the Six Nations Confederacy and the federal government and the provinces today. (2 marks)

4. Describe the key changes to the situation in which Native peoples found themselves after Confederation. Explain how this would adversely affect their futures. (2 marks)

5. Describe briefly four of the reasons why the *Indian Act* was created by the Canadian government. Explain the rationale for this law as part of your answer. (2 marks)

6. Describe what aspects of self-government Native peoples agree upon collectively. (2 marks)

7. After reading "Reluctant Citizens? First Nations in the Canadian Federal State," compare the current relationship that Native peoples have with the federal and provincial governments with the relationship that would exist under Native self-government. (4 marks)

TOTAL — 20 MARKS

KEY TERMS

administration

Bill C-31

British North America Act

cultural genocide

enfranchisement

fiduciary responsibility

Lands for Life

Meech Lake accord

royal commission

sovereignty

APPENDIX 5.1

What Did the Indian Agent Think of Native People in 1921?

OTTAWA – (December 15, 1921) It is observed with alarm that the holding of dances by the Indians on their reserves is on the increase, and that these practices tend to disorganize the efforts which the Department is putting forth to make them self-supporting.

I have, therefore, to direct you to use your utmost endeavours to dissuade the Indians from excessive indulgence in the practice of dancing. You should suppress any dances which cause waste of time, interfere with the occupations of the Indians, unsettle them from serious work, injure their health or encourage them in sloth and idleness.

You should also dissuade, and if possible, prevent them from leaving their reserves for the purpose of attending fairs, exhibitions, etc., when their absence would result in their own farming and other interests being neglected. It is realized that reasonable amusement and recreation should be enjoyed by Indians, but they should not be allowed to dissipate their energies and abandon themselves to demoralizing amusements. By the use of tact and firmness you can obtain control and keep it, and this obstacle to continued progress will then disappear.

The rooms, halls or other places in which Indians congregate should be under constant inspection. They should be scrubbed, fumigated, cleansed or disinfected to prevent the dissemination of disease. The Indians should be instructed in regard to the matter of proper ventilation, and the avoidance of over-crowding rooms where public assemblies are being held, and proper arrangement should be made for the shelter of their horses and ponies. The Agent will avail himself of the services of the medical attendant of his agency in this connection.

Except where further information is desired, there will be no necessity to acknowledge the receipt of this circular.

Yours very truly,

Duncan Elliott
Deputy Superintendent General
Indian Affairs

Source: Council Fires (1994).

APPENDIX 5.2

Changes to the Definition of an Indian

(Definition changed with revisions made to the *Indian Act*)

1. 1850 – "any person deemed to be aboriginal by birth or blood, any person reputed to belong to a particular band or body of Indians and any person who married an Indian or was adopted by Indians."
   - A broad definition with no emphasis on male lineage.
   - Linked Indian status to band membership.
2. 1876 – "any male person of Indian blood, reputed to belong to a particular band, or child of such a person; any woman who is or was lawfully married to such a person."
   - Emphasized male lineage.
   - Woman who married non-Status or non-Indian would lose her status.
3. 1951 – "a person who is registered or entitled to be registered in an Indian registry."
   - Establishment of an Indian registry meant that if someone was to be identified as a Status Indian, he or she needed to fulfill a complex set of eligibility rules.
   - Indians who were members of a band were entitled to registration.
   - Emphasis on male lineage – illegitimate children and women were discriminated against.
4. 1985 – "person who is registered or entitled to be registered."
   - Rules for eligibility changed so those who lost status due to discrimination can get their rights back.

Source: Supply and Services Canada (1991, p. 22).

APPENDIX 5.3

Ramifications of Bill C-31, 1985 Amendment to the Indian Act

Indian status is one of the most important issues that First Nations need to address. The government, since the introduction of the *Indian Act*, has carefully laid out whom they will legally recognize as being an "Indian." For the most part, the Native peoples most affected by discrimination in the *Indian Act* have been Native women and their children.

Prior to 1985

The *Indian Act* of 1951 did not grant Native women the same rights as men. They

- lost their rights when they married non-Native males,
- lost their rights in their own band when they married a Native male from another band, and
- may not be entitled to their rights if they or their parents became enfranchised. If a man gave up his Native status voluntarily, his wife and children would automatically lose theirs.

Reasons for the Introduction of Bill C-31

Bill C-31 was introduced in Parliament after a reprimand was given to the Canadian government by the United Nations that Native women's rights were being violated. Jeanette Lavell, an Ojibwe woman, first took a discrimination case to the Supreme Court of Canada citing contraventions of the *Canadian Bill of Rights*. She lost her case in 1974 because the Supreme Court found that the *Indian Act* took precedence over the *Bill of Rights*. In 1977, Sandra Lovelace, from the Maliseit First Nations, took her case to the United Nations Human Rights Committee, which determined that Canada had violated the International Covenant on Civil and Political Rights. This proved an embarrassment to Canada. In 1985, the amendments contained in Bill C-31 were legislated into the *Indian Act* to become aligned with the *Canadian Charter of Rights and Freedoms*, which guaranteed equal rights for women.

Despite the changes, the federal government has retained control of who is registered as an Indian and the rights that flow from registration.

Implications of Bill C-31

1. Bill C-31 allows Natives, who had formerly lost their status, as well as their children, to be reinstated.
2. Bill C-31 separates Indian status from band membership. How? A Native may be eligible for
   - status but not band membership,
   - band membership but not status, or
   - both.
3. Not all Status Indians are eligible to transmit status onto their children.

4. The majority of Métis and non-Status Indians are not eligible for registration.
5. Bands now have the right to control their own membership.

Terms of the Indian Act

I Indian Register (Definition)

The Indian register has the name of every Native person recognized by the government as being entitled to be registered and the date in which he or she became registered or deleted from the list (s. 5(4)). This information is maintained by the Indian Affairs Department and by most band offices.

II Indian Status

If a Native has status, he or she can never lose it (s. 6):

- if he or she was registered or entitled to be registered before 1985,
- if he or she is registered as a member of a band,
- if he or she is not entitled to be on a band list but the band consents to it,
- by marrying a non-Native (a non-Native woman can no longer gain status through marriage to a Native man),
- by being born out of wedlock or his or her father has not been identified, or
- through enfranchisement.

III Eligibility for Status

Eligibility is granted to

- children whose parents are both Status Natives and are registered as s. 6(1) will receive a s. 6(1) classification, which means that they are entitled to band status and band membership; and
- children who have only one parent who is eligible for s. 6(1) classification will be registered under a s. 6(2) classification. What does this mean? These children have fewer rights and the parents cannot pass their status onto their children unless they marry someone with a s. 6(1) classification.

Who does not qualify?

- Descendants of people who accepted half-breed land or money from the government.
- Descendants of families or entire bands who were left off band lists (never registered).
- Women who gained status but lost it in re-marriage (children of these women also lost their status).
- Grandchildren of people who lost their status (referred to as the second generation cutoff).

IV Benefits of Status

A Status Native

- is recognized legally as a Native (has a status card);
- has the right to some health, dental, optical, educational, and economic development services;
- may enjoy treaty rights; and
- is entitled to a partial tax exemption, but not to provincial sales tax.

V Band Lists (Section 8)

- A band has the right to enter every person on a band list who is a member of the band.
- The government has the right to add names to or delete names from the band lists (s. 9).
- Protests from band members can be made with regard to the contents of band lists (s. 14.2(2)).

VI Band Membership

Band membership is controlled by each band (s. 10). Bands can pass bylaws to control residency rights of band members if they applied to the federal government to pass membership codes (as of 1993, over half of the bands in Ontario still did not have the right to their own membership codes).

To pass a membership code, the band

1. must draft a citizenship code with a membership committee,
2. give appropriate notice to band electors to vote on the code, and
3. must agree to take over the membership code from Indian Affairs and consent to the proposed membership code. Although the band lists will include members that are on the general or Indian Affairs lists, the bands can decide about the admission of new members.

Automatic eligibility of band membership is granted to

- women and their children who lost status due to marriage to a non-Native,
- children born outside of a marriage and who have a non-Native father,
- children born after the passage of Bill C-31, and
- persons with status before 1985.

Membership of Natives belonging to an amalgamated band is covered in s. 11(4).

An individual can only be on the band list of one band in one's life. Women who marry men from other bands can either keep their memberships with their bands or transfer their memberships to the husbands' bands (s. 13).

Conditional membership is decided by each chief and council for

- enfranchised Indians,
- children whose parents belong to different bands, and
- children with only one parent eligible to belong to the band.

VII Benefits of Band Membership

A band member

- can vote in band elections and/or run for office;
- enjoys treaty rights;
- is entitled to tax exemptions;
- is eligible to receive health, education, and economic development services provided by the Indian Affairs Department;
- has the right to be buried in the community;
- has the right to own property or live in the community; and
- has the right to moneys obtained by the band through logging, mining, land claims, etc.

Natives who live on a reserve but do not have band membership

- may enjoy partial rights;
- may have some tax exemptions;
- may have some privileges of membership if granted by the band – for example, the right to live in the community and to be buried there; and
- may be eligible for some health, educational, or economic development services by various provincial or federal agencies.

(Note: These Natives cannot participate in political affairs.)

VIII Problems with Band Membership

Some bands will not provide services to newly reinstated members (mostly women):

- These members are denied fishing rights.
- Their children are refused admittance to reserve schools.
- They are denied medical services.
- They are refused housing construction permits.
- They are not sold lands.

Reinstated Natives are less able to transmit their status and membership onto their children compared with those who never lost their status.

Because of these problems,

- fewer single Indian women give the name of their child's father, especially if the father is non-Native or a non-band member;
- greater advantages are given to males and their offspring, resulting in a real bias against women; and
- the resulting trend of men and women to marry outside the culture means that the number of Natives who will be eligible for status and band membership will continue to decrease with every generation.

APPENDIX 5.4

The Principles of Self-Government

Under the federal approach for self-government negotiations, all self-government arrangements will be based on the following key principles:

- The inherent right is an existing Aboriginal right recognized and affirmed under the Canadian Constitution.
- Self-government will be exercised within the existing Canadian Constitution. Canada's recognition of self-government does not mean sovereignty in the international sense. Aboriginal peoples will continue to be citizens of Canada and the province or territory where they live. However, they may exercise varying degrees of jurisdiction and/or authority.
- The *Canadian Charter of Rights and Freedoms* will apply fully to Aboriginal governments as it does all governments in Canada. The current provisions of the Charter that respect the unique Aboriginal and treaty rights of Aboriginal peoples will continue to apply.
- All federal funding for self-government will come from the reallocation of existing resources.
- Where all parties agree, rights in self-government agreements may be protected in new treaties under Section 35 of the *Constitution Act, 1982*. They may also be protected through additions to existing treaties, or as part of comprehensive land claims agreements.
- Federal, provincial, territorial and Aboriginal laws must work in harmony. Certain laws of overriding federal and provincial importance, such as the *Criminal Code*, will prevail.
- The interests of all Canadians will be taken into account as agreements are negotiated.

Source: Indian and Northern Affairs Canada (1997).

APPENDIX 5.5

Out of the Past: First Nations Need To Rebuild Both Their Economies and Their Identities

By Bernd Christmas, *Time* (July 28, 2003, p. 39)

Much has been said and written about the story of the victims of residential schools. Almost all of us of aboriginal descent have in some way been affected by Canada's assimilation policies, epitomized by a residential-school system that I believe can be described as emotional genocide. My father had his own experiences, in a past for him that is not spoken of, and a childhood about which he does not talk, other than to acknowledge that he was there. I think he must have decided to leave behind whatever it was that he suffered. I am proud of him for that, but I am also sad that a part of him that I could have known is lost, buried because of the hardship he endured. I wish I could give him his childhood back and that he could have had the joys he gave me when I was growing up.

I know that my father's experiences, however bitter their memory, gave him a stronger sense of who he is and the understanding that if you show determination, you will grow. My father's determination is embedded in me, and I carry it forward to this generation. There is a lesson there for all of us in the First Nation communities.

I do not mean to imply that the residential-school issue can be brushed under the rug. It has consumed the attention of churches and the government for decades, and court decisions have recognized that both institutions share the blame for what happened to thousands of children. The government, however, still appears to be concerned about the huge financial compensation that will eventually need to be paid to those whose lives were damaged. The Aboriginal Healing Foundation has been formed to assist aboriginal people in addressing the legacy of physical and sexual abuse in the schools and has got off to a good start. But the government nevertheless needs to recognize its fiduciary duty to our people. At the same time, we need to move on. We have the ability to empower our communities and, in so doing, honor those who suffered abuses in the residential schools. For their sake, we need to take back control of our destinies.

In today's world a strong economic base is essential. Our indigenous economies are based on the pillars of conservation, sustainability and innovation, and they can all be deployed to bring our people prosperity. ...

Our success [in the Membertou First Nation in Sydney, Nova Scotia] is the result of saying no. No to poverty, no to red tape, no to enforced government dependency, no to unemployment, no to poor health and no to the loss of our language, our culture and our heritage. We reclaimed our Mi'kmaw identity, one that goes back thousands of years. Our nation has never signed treaties that ceded our land away, and our past is a history of peace and friendship. We have not been afraid to assert our rights in court, using the legal system to claim access to the fishery in Atlantic Canada and to prevent the construction of a pipeline across our land. The cases won us a new respect from the government and the private sector. And we achieved all this in a region that had been known as one of the most economically depressed in all of Canada.

If we can do all that, so can other aboriginal peoples. We owe it to ourselves to call on our leaders to unite. Our communities must work together to become truly self-governing nations. In choosing to take a proactive stance, rather than dwell forever on the past, we can move beyond the memories of some of the bitter incidents of Canadian history.

There still needs to be a thorough accounting for the atrocities of the residential-school system, compensation for those who suffered and a recognition by the federal government that our culture was damaged by a policy that was cruel and destructive. But we must look to the future and build on our innate strengths and unique cultural heritage. That way, we will develop our indigenous economies. It is by our success in the coming years that we can best honor those who had their innocence stolen from them.

Bernd Christmas is CEO of the Membertou Band and manages the business interests of Membertou First Nation in Sydney, Nova Scotia.

PART III

Contemporary Native Issues

CHAPTER 6

Natives and Socioeconomic Issues

Chapter Objectives

After completing this chapter, you should be able to:

- Contrast the current health status of aboriginal peoples to other social demographics in Canada.
- Contrast economic realities of Native peoples both on-reserve and off-reserve to the general Canadian population.
- Describe the present system of administration for Native peoples under the devolution process.
- Identify strategies and programs currently developed or initiated by Native peoples intended to minimize and reduce social and economic issues facing Native populations.

INTRODUCTION

In the last chapter, we saw how Native struggles have created a number of national and provincial Native organizations, such as the Assembly of First Nations, to represent all indigenous peoples and to give them a collective voice. While the focus in chapter 5 was on sovereignty and politics, the attention will now move to the socioeconomic realities that face Natives today. Many of the realities that we will be studying in this chapter are direct results of the trials of the Native past. Exploring these topics will help us better understand aboriginal issues today.

NATIVE DEMOGRAPHICS

Before discussing the socioeconomic issues relating to Canada's Native people, it is important to look at the context for the figures that will be discussed.

According to Statistics Canada, the 2001 census shows that aboriginal people's share of the total Canadian population is on the rise, with 1.3 million people reporting some aboriginal ancestry in 2001, comprising 4.4 percent of the total Canadian population, compared with 3.8 percent in the 1996 census.

Of the 1 319 890 persons who claimed some aboriginal ancestry in 2001, a total of 976 305 of them claimed aboriginal identity (343 585 persons had some aboriginal ancestry but did not identify as aboriginal), up from 799 010 in 1996. North American Indians accounted for 608 850 (529 040 in 1996) persons, Métis were at 292 310 (204 115), and Inuit at 45 070 (40 220).

Aboriginal Growth Rates

The population of those reporting an aboriginal identity (North American Indian, Métis, Inuit) grew 22.2 percent since 1996, with a 15.1 percent growth rate among North American Indians, according to Statistics Canada (see table 6.1). This figure marks a tenfold increase since 1901 in the number of people who claimed aboriginal ancestry, while the total population rose by only a factor of six.

One of the main reasons for this increased growth rate among aboriginal peoples was an improved level of health care, which considerably reduced the infant mortality rate after 1960. During the first 50 years of the 20th century, the aboriginal population grew only 29 percent, while the population of Canada increased by 161 percent. However, after 1960, the aboriginal population increased sevenfold, while the Canadian population only doubled.

Another important reason for the dramatic increase in those persons who claimed aboriginal ancestry was a decrease in racism after 1960 and an awareness of aboriginal issues in this country. Before the 1960s, it was not "popular" to be aboriginal, and therefore many people who could have claimed aboriginal ancestry did not do so. After the 1982 **constitution** enshrined Métis as aboriginal people, the number of people claiming Métis ancestry grew dramatically, and continues to do so. For example, the number of persons claiming to be Métis in the Hamilton, Ontario census area grew by 87 percent between 1996 and 2001.

constitution
the core system of rules and principles by which a nation or group is governed

Statistics Canada also reports that an increased reporting of aboriginal issues since 1986, such as the Oka crisis, the Royal Commission on Aboriginal Peoples, the creation of Nunavut, and reporting on aboriginal land claims, human rights issues, and residential schools has increased an awareness and pride among Canadians in their aboriginal roots and has encouraged them to acknowledge their aboriginal ancestry.

Decrease in Birth Rate

The birth rate for Native peoples has been declining over the past 30 years. Native women, on average, tended to have 6.2 children 30 years ago. In 1986, the average Native woman had 3.2 children, while the average non-Native Canadian woman had 1.67 children. In 1999, the First Nations birth rate was 23.0 births per 1000 population, two times the comparable rate for Canada, according to Health Canada. Over one-half (58 percent) of First Nations women who gave birth in 1999 were under 25 years of age. Native peoples consistently have more children than the average Canadian and the trend continues today. Overall, the size of Native families contributes to a steadily increasing Native population, both on-reserve and off-reserve.

Increase in Life Expectancy

From 1956 to 1986, Native life expectancy increased by 10 years. For an aboriginal male, life expectancy increased from an average of 53.8 years to 63.8 years. In comparison,

TABLE 6.1 Size and Growth of the Population Reporting Aboriginal Ancestry and Aboriginal Identity, Canada, 1996–2001

	2001	1996	Percentage growth 1996–2001
Total: Aboriginal ancestry[a]	1 319 890	1 101 960	19.8
Total: Aboriginal identity	976 305	799 010	22.2
North American Indian[b]	608 850	529 040	15.1
Métis[b]	292 310	204 115	43.2
Inuit[b]	45 070	40 220	12.1
Multiple and other aboriginal responses[c]	30 080	25 640	17.3

[a] Also known as aboriginal origin.

[b] Includes persons who reported a North American Indian, Métis, or Inuit identity only.

[c] Includes persons who reported more than one aboriginal identity group (North American Indian, Métis, or Inuit) and those who reported being a registered Indian and/or band member without reporting an aboriginal identity.

Source: Adapted from Statistics Canada (2003, January 31, p. 20).

on average, a non-Native male lives for 73 years. Within this same period, aboriginal women increased their life expectancy from 61 years to 71 years, compared with 79.7 years for non-Native females (Indian and Northern Affairs Canada, 1990). Life expectancy continues to improve among the First Nations population. In 2000, it rose to 68.9 years for males and 76.6 years for females, an increase from 1980 of 13.1 percent and 12.6 percent, respectively, according to Health Canada (see figure 6.1). Mortality rates for aboriginal peoples also remained high, which continues to have an adverse impact on their ability to maintain a cross-section that represents all age groups equally within their populations. The reasons for high mortality rates will be discussed later in this chapter.

Aboriginal Youth and Median Age

The 2001 census showed that the median age of the North American Indian population was 23.5 years, compared with 37.7 years in the non-aboriginal population. This means that 50 percent of the North American Indian population in 2001 was under 23.5 years of age. On a province-to-province basis, the median age for Natives in Saskatchewan was 18.4 years, in Manitoba 20.4 years, and in Alberta 21.2 years.

Census figures show that more than one-third of the North American Indian population in Canada was under 14 years of age in 2001, compared with 19 percent of the total non-aboriginal population. When these figures are compared with the median ages documented in the previous paragraph, and when noting that there will be four times more Native youth entering the workforce than are leaving due to retirements, it is clear that employment opportunities will have to be created, training programs established, and other social services made available to help the youth find employment.

North American Indian Seniors

According to Statistics Canada, while the North American Indian population is relatively young, there is a significant increase in those over 65 years of age. The 2001 census enumerated 24 170 North American Indians aged 65 and over, an increase

FIGURE 6.1 Life Expectancy at Birth, First Nations and Canada

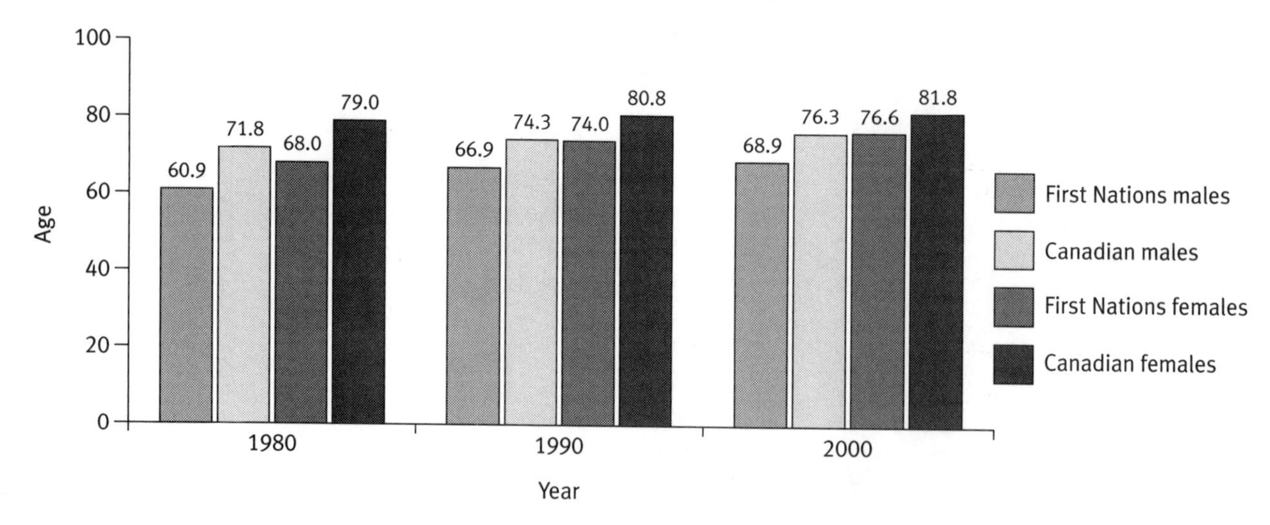

Source: Indian and Northern Affairs Canada (2001).

of 31 percent since 1996. Over half of these people (53 percent) lived on-reserve, a five-year increase of 34 percent. These figures indicate growing pressures on housing, social services, and health care.

Reinstatement of Native Status Through Bill C-31

The biggest factor for the significant population growth of Natives is primarily the result of the reinstatement of Native peoples who had lost their Native status before 1985. After Bill C-31 was passed in 1985 (see appendix 5.3 at the end of chapter 5), these Natives could reapply to have their status returned. Those who were most affected by Bill C-31 were Native women and their children who lost their status when they married non-Native men before 1985.

Those Natives who lost their status through enfranchisement (discussed in chapters 4 and 5) could also regain it after the passage of Bill C-31. Before 1985, if the paternity of children born out of wedlock was identified as non-Native, they were removed from the registry. With the passage of Bill C-31, these children had the right to apply for reinstatement of their Indian status. Between 1955 and 1982, 13 502 adults and children (and their descendants) were enfranchised (Frideres, 1997).

A 1999 court decision giving off-reserve band members a vote in band elections particularly affected reinstated women, many of whom live off-reserve. Bands were given until November 2000 to implement the court decision.

Provincial Distributions of North American Native Populations

Ontario has the highest Native population (21.6 percent) at 131 560 persons, up from 17.7 percent in 1996, followed by British Columbia at 19.4 percent, or 118 295 persons. Nunavut has the smallest population of North American Native people with 95, followed by Prince Edward Island with 1035 persons, or 0.2 percent of the total Native population in Canada of 608 850 persons (see table 6.2).

TABLE 6.2 Population Reporting a North American Indian Identity, Provinces and Territories, 2001

	Number	%
Canada	608 850	100.0
Newfoundland and Labrador	7 040	1.2
Prince Edward Island	1 035	0.2
Nova Scotia	12 920	2.1
New Brunswick	11 490	1.9
Quebec	51 125	8.4
Ontario	131 560	21.6
Manitoba	90 345	14.8
Saskatchewan	83 745	13.8
Alberta	84 990	14.0
British Columbia	118 295	19.4
Yukon Territory	5 600	0.9
Northwest Territories	10 615	1.7
Nunavut	95	0.0

Source: Adapted from Statistics Canada (2003, January 31).

Native Migration to Cities

Increasingly, Natives are leaving the reserves, either for economic reasons or to access social and education services. In 2001, less than half (47 percent) of the North American Indian population lived on reserves, while a total of 151 770 of them lived in one of the 27 major census metropolitan areas. Winnipeg had the largest North American Indian population at 22 955 persons, followed by Vancouver (22 700), Edmonton (18 260), Toronto (13 785), and Saskatoon (11 290), according to Statistics Canada.

These figures mirror the overall aboriginal identity population (see table 6.3). Winnipeg had the highest aboriginal identity (Indian, Métis, Inuit) population at 55 755 persons, an increase of 6.9 percent over the 1996 census, followed by Edmonton (40 930) and Vancouver (36 860). Winnipeg had a significant increase in its aboriginal population of over 10 000 people in the five years between 1996 and 2001. This aboriginal population formed 8 percent of Winnipeg's total population.

Census figures indicate a slow but steady growth among aboriginal people living in Canada's cities. Almost one-half (49 percent) of people who identified themselves as aboriginal lived in urban areas. The on-reserve aboriginal population dropped from 33 percent in 1996 to 31 percent in 2001.

Aboriginal people showed consistently more mobility than did other Canadians. Overall, in the 12 months prior to the 2001 census, held in May 2001, 22 percent of aboriginal people moved their place of residence, compared with 14 percent of non-aboriginals, although approximately 66 percent of those aboriginals who did move did so within their own communities.

GROUP DISCUSSION

Read "Reserves Rack Up $300 Million in Deficits" in appendix 6.1 at the end of this chapter and discuss the following questions:

1. In addition to a lack of federal funding, what are some reasons for reserve deficits?

TABLE 6.3 Population Reporting Aboriginal Identity in Selected Census Metropolitan Areas (CMA) and Census Agglomerations (CA) with an Aboriginal Population of 5000 or More, 1996 and 2001

	2001		1996[a]	
	Number	Percentage of total population in CMA or CA	Number	Percentage of total population in CMA or CA
Winnipeg	55 755	8.4	45 750	6.9
Edmonton	40 930	4.4	32 825	3.8
Vancouver	36 860	1.9	31 140	1.7
Calgary	21 915	2.3	15 200	1.9
Toronto	20 300	0.4	16 100	0.4
Saskatoon	20 275	9.1	16 165	7.5
Regina	15 685	8.3	13 610	7.1
Ottawa-Hull[b]	13 485	1.3	11 500	1.2
Prince Albert	11 640	29.2	10 090	24.9
Montréal	11 085	0.3	9 965	0.3
Victoria	8 695	2.8	6 570	2.2
Thunder Bay	8 200	6.8	7 355	5.9
Prince George	7 980	9.4	5 810	6.7
Greater Sudbury	7 385	4.8	4 815	2.9
Hamilton	7 270	1.1	5 460	0.9
Wood Buffalo	6 220	14.6	5 460	15.1
London	5 640	1.3	4 490	1.1
Sault Ste. Marie	5 610	7.2	3 580	4.3
Kamloops	5 470	6.4	4 425	5.2

[a] In order to facilitate data comparisons, the 1996 CMA and CA data have been adjusted to reflect as closely as possible the 2001 CMA and CA boundaries.

[b] Now known as Ottawa-Gatineau.

Source: Adapted from Statistics Canada (2003, January 31).

2. How will funding deficits affect the delivery of health care, education, and other services to First Nations communities?
3. Why are some First Nations able to keep within their spending limits, while other First Nations are not?
4. What effect does government funding have on the sovereignty of First Nations peoples?

Elementary and Secondary Education

Forty years ago, the majority of Native children attended residential schools set up by the government. Today, they can attend either provincially funded schools or federal schools, at the elementary and secondary levels (Frideres, 1997). Provincial schools are funded by each provincial government. Native cultural or language programs are offered in provincial schools with high Native student enrollment rates. When a Native child attends such an institution, the federal government pays the local school board a per diem fee.

Federal schools consist primarily of band schools and boarding schools. A band school is located on-reserve and the band administers the school, providing a culturally relevant education for its children, within federal government curriculum guidelines. The children often receive their instruction in their Native language, are taught language-specific courses, and receive cultural teachings in addition to the standard curriculum.

Boarding schools are generally for aboriginal children who live in isolated communities and, because of their small populations, have no schools within their vicinity. The children are housed with other families within the community where the school exists. Boarding school students are either integrated into the existing school system off-reserve or receive their education from an off-reserve school created specifically for their benefit. At the elementary level, the majority of Native children attend federal schools as opposed to provincial schools (Frideres, 1997).

Aboriginal-controlled education aims to impart skills to aboriginal children that will enable them to succeed in the outside world, and to immerse Native children in a supportive environment that is culturally relevant in content, style, and outcome. Native people believe that only an educational system that is completely managed and implemented by Native direction will eradicate the injustices of the formerly imposed educational system. Native-run schools have implemented a number of strategies: greater reliance on Native learning and teaching styles, increased exposure to and use of the aboriginal languages, greater awareness and sensitivity of teachers and staff to Native customs and experiences, and the removal of any biased or distorted texts or educational materials (Fleras & Elliott, 1996).

In the years since the creation of band schools, Native student enrollment has increased. For example, in 1991, of the aboriginal people who were 15 years or older, 18 percent had less than grade 9 education compared with the 1981 figure, where 37 percent had less than grade 9. Educational standards are steadily improving for Native peoples. Reasons that contributed to increased Native participation in secondary-level education include the introduction of language and cultural classes into schools with large Native student populations, greater awareness and promotion of education by the bands themselves, and the development of Native-run secondary schools. In the 1996–97 school year, there were 112 060 Native students enrolled in kindergarten, elementary, and secondary schools. The percentage of students remaining in school until grade 12 increased to 71 percent in 1996–97 from just 31 percent in 1981 (Indian and Northern Affairs Canada, 1997).

According to Indian and Northern Affairs Canada, other reasons for Native student retention might be the fact that band-operated schools increased by 54 percent from 1990–91 to 1999–2000, federal funding for postsecondary education rose from $109 million in 1987–88 to $280 million in 2000–1, and aboriginal studies programs have expanded to more than 13 Canadian universities (see figure 6.2).

The figures in the 2001 census of educational characteristics for those claiming aboriginal identity are quite revealing:

Total North American Indian population 15 years of age and older by school attendance	395 325
Not attending school	311 130
Attending school full time	65 715
Attending school part time	18 485

FIGURE 6.2 Educational Attainment in First Nations and Canada, 1996

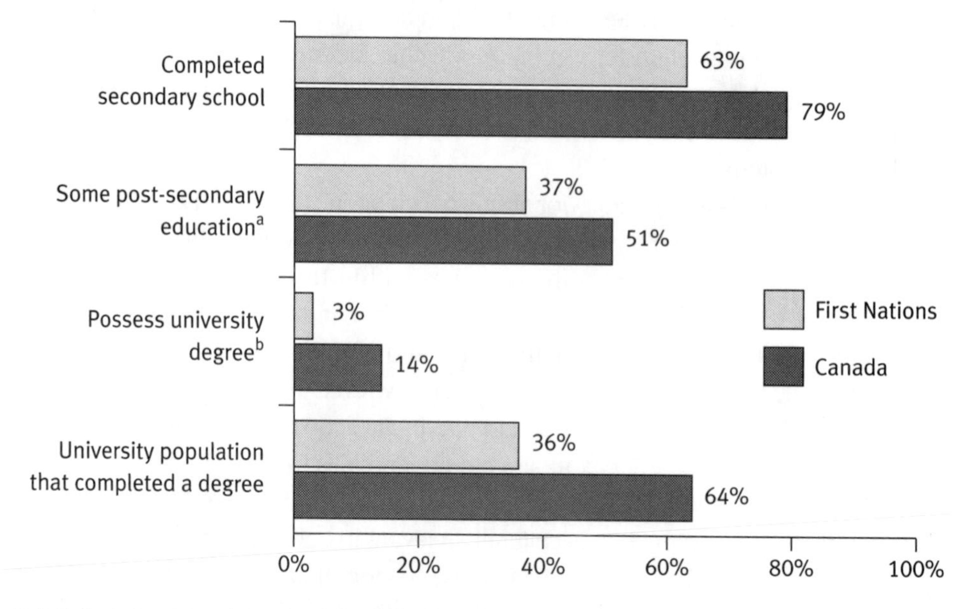

[a] This includes university, trades schools and other non-university postsecondary education.
[b] Population 15 years and older not attending school.
Source: Hull (2000).

Total North American Indian population 15 years of age and older by highest level of schooling	395 325
Less than high school graduation certificate	200 070
High school graduation certificate only	35 470

Postsecondary Education for Natives

Natives recognize the importance of providing postsecondary education for their populations. More and more Native students are enrolling in, attending, and graduating from college and/or university. In 1996, an estimated 27 487 Native students enrolled in postsecondary education compared with 5467 in 1981. In 1995–96, 3929 Native students graduated from either colleges or universities across Canada (Indian and Northern Affairs Canada, 1997).

The following figures from the 2001 census reveal the state of Native postsecondary education:

Total North American Indian population 15 years of age and older by highest level of schooling	395 325
Some postsecondary education	50 355
Trades certificate or diploma	45 425
College certificate or diploma	42 165
University certificate or diploma	5 660
University degree	16 165
Bachelor's degree	12 515
University certificate above bachelor's degree	1 570
Master's degree	3 425
Earned doctorate	280

Total North American Indian population 15 years of age and over by major field of study	395 325
No postsecondary qualifications	285 895
Educational, recreational, and counselling services	13 280
Fine and applied arts	5 330
Humanities and related fields	3 870
Social sciences and related fields	17 430
Commerce, management, and business administration	20 605
Agricultural, biological, nutritional, and food sciences	5 265
Engineering and applied sciences	1 310
Applied science, technology and trades	29 585
Health professions and related technologies	11 410
Mathematics, computer, and physical sciences	970
No specialization	370

Despite these improvements, however, Native enrollment and participation in education continue to lag behind the average Canadian rate. Native students' graduation rates are also behind the national average. Non-Native students are 2.4 times more likely to earn a degree than Native students. Language and cultural differences often account for these discrepancies and have not been adequately addressed. Since 1992, the Ministry of Education and Training through Strategy funding has provided funds to develop and implement initiatives to enhance Native student success at the postsecondary level.

PHYSICAL HEALTH

Compared with the average Canadian, the average Native experiences a lower standard of health. We will examine a number of factors that reflect this reality in the following pages.

Infant and Child Mortality

Statistics Canada reports that in 1999, the First Nations infant mortality rate was 8.0 deaths per 1000 live births, or 1.5 times higher than the Canadian infant mortality rate of 5.5. By contrast, the 1979 First Nations infant mortality rate was 27.6 deaths per 1000 live births, a rate that has been steadily declining. The First Nations and the Canadian population had similar proportions of births with low birth weight in 1999; however, almost twice as many First Nations births were classified as high birth weight in the same year. However, the most recent figures indicate that Native babies still have almost twice the chance of dying as newborns, compared with the rest of the Canadian population. Infant deaths are primarily the result of infectious diseases, respiratory illnesses, sudden infant death syndrome (SIDS), and injuries.

A number of socioeconomic factors – for example, depression, alcoholism, and lack of employment opportunities – and other health factors contribute to this problem. Native living conditions remain below the national average. If a newborn is returned to a reserve, he or she has a greater chance of being raised in a poorly made reserve house, with little or no heat, inferior bathroom facilities (many northern Natives still use outdoor toilets), etc. In addition, many northern Native communities are far from medical facilities. When infants from these reserves become ill, by the time they are taken to the nearest hospital, their situations have become critical.

Another factor contributing to the poor health of some children is the lack of parenting skills of a number of Native mothers and fathers. This can be linked to the residential schools where the grandparents and parents of today as children were not raised in an environment that enabled them to observe parenting skills and behaviours first hand.

The high rate of adolescent pregnancies among Native mothers may also be related to infant ill health and mortality rates. Native mothers on-reserve tend to be younger than the average Canadian mother. Nine percent of Native mothers, as opposed to 1 percent of non-Native mothers, are under the age of 18. The maturity, knowledge, and personal supports that each young mother possesses contribute to her overall ability to raise her child in a healthy and happy environment.

Native communities are working to combat these problems by providing parenting classes and other programs to support parents and their children. For example, in pre-natal classes, mothers-to-be learn about the effects of smoking, alcohol drinking, and caffeine consumption, and how these factors may affect fetal growth and birth weight. In addition, Native health services promote the positive effects of breast feeding. In 1998, a survey conducted for the national Database on Breast-feeding Among Indian and Inuit Women found that 60.7 percent of infants were breast fed at birth, and the rate dropped to 31.1 percent by the time the infants were 6 months old. Breast-feeding rates were the lowest among the mothers younger than 18 (MacMillan, 1996). Further efforts are being made to promote better health and care of Native children of all ages by Native services both on- and off-reserve.

Native children are four times more likely to die from an injury compared with the average Canadian child (63 compared with 15 per 100 000). The potential for more mature Native children dying of their injuries was also higher than the national average. For preschoolers, the rate increased to more than five times the national average (83 compared with 15 per 100 000). Teenagers between the ages of 15 and 19 were three times more likely to die from their injuries when compared with non-Native teenagers (176 compared with 48 per 100 000).

In addition, Native children have an increased risk of contracting an infectious disease, such as bronchitis, pneumonia, and croup, compared with non-Native children. It has also been suggested that the infections that are acquired by Native peoples (both children and adults) tend to occur more frequently and are also more severe in nature (Statistics Canada 1996, *Aboriginal Peoples Survey*, "Health Status"). Although the reasons why Native peoples of all ages tend to have an increased risk for some infectious diseases are unknown, potential factors include nutritional deficiencies, genetics, poverty, overcrowded living conditions, and environmental pollutants such as tobacco and wood smoke.

Adult Mortality and Morbidity

According to Statistics Canada, the crude mortality rate for First Nations in 1999 was 354.2 deaths per 100 000 population. The four leading causes of death were injury and poisoning, circulatory diseases, cancer, and respiratory diseases. For each of the causes of death, the rate has decreased when compared with the 1991 to 1993 period, to 22.4 percent for cancer and 40.9 percent for respiratory diseases such as pneumonia and bronchitis.

The crude mortality rate for First Nations males was 1.3 times higher than the rate for First Nations females in 1999. The rate difference is largely attributable to

FIGURE 6.3 Leading Causes of Death in First Nations, by Sex, 1999

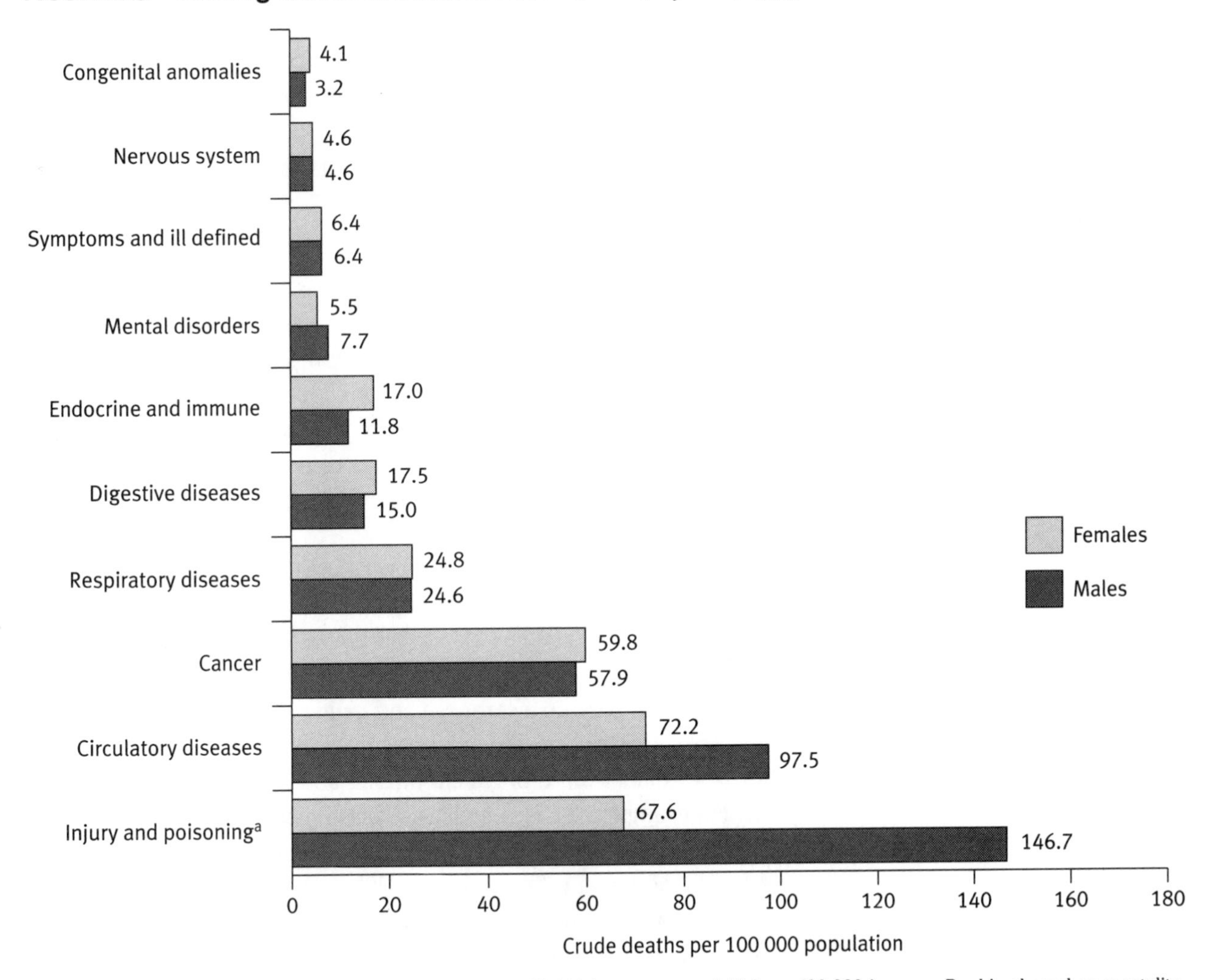

[a] Included in this rate are suicides with a rate of 12.4 per 100 000 for women and 43.3 per 100 000 for men. Ranking based on mortality (deaths per 100 000 population) for First Nations in 1999.

Source: First Nations and Inuit Health Branch, Health Canada, in-house statistics. Reproduced with the permission of the Minister of Public Works and Government Services Canada, 2004.

higher rates among males for injury and poisoning (146.7 deaths among males per 100 000 and 67.6 among females) and to circulatory disease (97.5 deaths per 100 000 among males and 72.2 among females). Age-specific death rates in 1999 were higher in First Nations males than in females for almost all age groups. The largest difference between the sexes occurs in the 5–9 and 20–24 age groups. (See figure 6.3.)

The most common cause of death for First Nations people aged 1 to 44 was injury and poisoning. Among children under 10, deaths were primarily unintentional (accidents). Suicide and self-injury were the leading causes of death for youth and adults up to age 44. For First Nations people aged 45 and older, circulatory diseases were the most common cause of death. These trends parallel the Canadian population as a whole. Motor vehicle collisions were the leading cause of death in all age groups.

In 1999, according to Statistics Canada, First Nations people experienced a disproportionate number of infectious diseases. These include pertussis (3 times higher than the Canadian population as a whole), chlamydia (7 times higher), hepatitis A (5.3 times higher), and shigellosis (almost 20 times higher). The proportion of Canada's total AIDS cases contracted by aboriginal people climbed from 1.0 percent in 1990 to 7.2 percent in 2001, according to Health Canada. Over that same period, the tuberculosis rate among First Nations people remained 8 to 10 times higher than that of the Canadian population.

Dental decay rates for aboriginal children in Ontario are 2 to 5 times higher than rates for non-aboriginal children.

Common Health Problems

Natives have a higher rate of certain types of health problems than the rest of the population. In 1994, the Canadian Medical Association published a paper that revealed the increasing incidence and prevalence of certain types of chronic illness within Native populations. These included diabetes, cardiovascular disease, cancer, and end-stage renal disease. In addition, infectious diseases such as tuberculosis, otitis media, sexually transmitted diseases, and hepatitis have increased (Canadian Medical Association, 1994).

Various groups of aboriginal people are also at a greater than normal risk of developing infectious diseases (such as tuberculosis and AIDS), injuries, respiratory diseases, nutritional problems (such as obesity and diabetes), and substance abuse. As a preventive measure, Native communities and Indian Friendship Centres across Canada are attempting to provide awareness and eating style changes through nutrition programs. Let's now look at some of these diseases.

Various forms of diabetes are prevalent among aboriginal populations at critically high rates. For example, diabetes mellitus affects 6 percent of aboriginal adults, compared with 2 percent of all Canadian adults (MacMillan et al., 1996). See table 6.4 on aboriginal health. Young and Sevenhuysen (1989) evaluated the distribution of diabetes mellitus in Natives across Canada and found that the highest rates of Native diabetes were among Native peoples from the Atlantic region (8.7 percent) and the lowest rates were found among Native peoples in the north (Yukon, Northwest Territories, and British Columbia). It appeared to be lower in Native groups who are continuing to eat a more traditional diet. Native people living in urban areas, women, and particularly Native people living in southern Canada have an increased risk of diabetes (MacMillan et al., 1996). Native diabetes is solidly linked to poor diets; however, this disease (not proven to have existed prior to introduction of European foods) may also be the result of dietary changes — from a diet consisting primarily of meat and vegetables to one that now includes many starches, sugars, and fried foods.

Obesity is another major nutrition-related problem among Canadian Native peoples today. In a study by Young and Sevenhuysen (1989), 704 Cree and Ojibwe adults who lived in northwestern Ontario and northeastern Manitoba were surveyed. Their findings showed that over 90 percent of those surveyed had a body mass index in the overweight or obese range within specific age and gender groups — that is, more Native women between 45 and 54 years old tend to be overweight.

Another nutritional problem is the lack of vitamins and minerals within Native groups. Some of the vitamin and mineral deficiencies include iron (this problem may occur with a low immune system) and a low intake of vitamin D (required for energy) among pregnant women and infants. Native children living in Winnipeg who were originally from Manitoba reserves were found to have iron deficiency anemia. As well, Native children tend to suffer from cavities because of poor dental

TABLE 6.4 Prevalence of Chronic Health Problems Among Native Groups in Canada, 1991

	No. (and %) of population 15 years of age and older with condition									
Condition	North American Indian population on Indian reserves and settlements n = 102 075		North American Indian people off reserves n = 186 295		Métis people n = 84 155		Inuit people n = 20 805		Total[a] n = 388 900	
Diabetes mellitus	8 635	(8.5)	9 790	(5.3)	4 670	(5.5)	405	(1.9)	23 255	(6.0)
High blood pressure	13 110	(12.8)	20 635	(11.1)	9 555	(11.4)	1 995	(9.6)	44 735	(11.5)
Arthritis or rheumatism	14 410	(14.1)	27 870	(15.0)	14 375	(17.1)	2 150	(10.3)	57 995	(14.9)
Heart problem	6 940	(6.8)	11 695	(6.3)	5 905	(7.0)	1 275	(6.1)	25 580	(6.6)
Bronchitis	6 190	(6.1)	17 040	(9.1)	8 875	(10.5)	1 035	(5.0)	32 650	(8.4)
Emphysema shortness of breath	6 785	(6.6)	9 685	(5.2)	4 835	(5.7)	1 120	(5.4)	22 155	(5.7)
Asthma	4 545	(4.5)	11 375	(6.1)	5 755	(6.8)	690	(3.3)	22 135	(5.7)
Tuberculosis	3 445	(3.4)	4 970	(2.7)	2 075	(2.5)	1 350	(6.5)	11 655	(3.0)
Epilepsy or seizure disorder	1 640	(1.6)	2 870	(1.5)	1 030	(1.2)	380	(1.8)	5 910	(1.5)

[a] Totals are less than the sum of the preceding groups because many Native people are included in more than one group.

Source: Adapted from Statistics Canada (1993, p. 4).

care habits and, in some communities, because of the unavailability of fluoride supplementation (unfluoridated water supplies) (MacMillan et al., 1996).

The Native rate of cardiovascular disease (excluding heart problems related to smoking) and some forms of cancers are lower than the national average. For example, both Native men and women were found to have a lower incidence of cancer of the colon, lung, prostate, breast, uterus, lymphoma, and leukemia (MacMillan et al., 1996). However, Natives experienced a higher rate of kidney cancer and Native women had a higher incidence of cancers of the gallbladder, cervix, and kidney. Death due to cervical cancer was five times higher among Native women than non-Natives.

MENTAL HEALTH PROBLEMS

Many social issues that are reported as problems by Native peoples are closely tied to mental health problems. High rates of stress, anomie, low self-esteem, poverty, and so on contribute to problems such as suicide, alcoholism, and other substance abuse.

Suicides

Suicide was among the leading causes of death in First Nations for those aged 10 to 44, according to Health Canada. In 1999, suicide accounted for 38 percent of all deaths in youth (aged 10 to 19) and 23 percent of all deaths in early adults (aged 20 to 44) in First Nations. That year, the First Nations suicide rate was 27.9 deaths per 100 000 population. This rate has not declined from the years 1973–1999. Notably, the 1999 rate was 2.1 times the Canadian population's suicide rate, which was 13.2 deaths per 100 000 population.

In 1999, suicide accounted for approximately 1315.4 potential years of life lost per 100 000 First Nations people. This is greater premature mortality than for all cancers combined and 50 percent more potential years of life lost than for all circulatory diseases.

All First Nations age groups up to 65 years are at increased suicide risk when compared with the Canadian population. First Nations males are at higher risk than females. Using data for the period 1989–1993, the highest First Nations suicide rates were among males aged 15 to 24 and 25 to 34, at approximately five times and four times the Canadian rates. The widest gap with the Canadian rates was seen in females aged 15 to 24 and 25 to 39 – approximately eight and five times the Canadian rates, respectively.

Compared with youths in the general population, suicides of aboriginal youth are more likely to occur in groupings or clusters within a specific time and location. Malchy et al. (1997) found that suicide clusters were similar. Most likely, the youth had attempted suicide previously, had damaged himself or herself physically, was known to someone who had died violently, had recently broken up with someone with whom he or she had a relationship, had a history of moving often and attending more schools, and/or had lived with more parent figures. The study also reported that the choice of method, time, and place of the suicide correlated with previous suicides of youths known to them. Suicide clusters are extremely traumatic and have the potential to be even more so within Native communities because of their small size. Most of the youths know each other and/or may be related. A shared sense of predicament may put aboriginal youths at greater risk of committing suicide; hence, a cluster of suicides may be the result. One suicide often has a profound impact on the community; the effect of two or more is devastating.

Native suicides occur for a number of reasons and are linked very strongly to sociocultural factors. Carson, Butcher, and Coleman (1988, p. 142) identify Native peoples as a high-risk group for suicides because they are from socially disorganized areas. Native peoples are a group undergoing severe societal pressures and find themselves trapped in "a sort of no-man's-land between their past culture and assimilation into the white world." In a conference on suicide held by the Canadian Psychiatric Association Section on Native Mental Health in 1985, a number of issues were linked to Native suicides, including anomie or feelings of powerlessness and hopelessness, breakdown of social roles, norms and responsibilities, community disaster, alcoholism, criminal behaviour, troubled personal relationships, poverty, and low self-esteem (Malchy et al., 1997).

Alcoholism

There is a debate over alcohol misuse among Natives (see appendix 6.3). There are, however, facts that are indisputable. Alcohol and substance abuse is considered a major problem in many aboriginal communities. In 1996–97, according to First Nations and Inuit Health Programs, 46 percent of people in detoxification and treatment facilities in the Regina Health District were of First Nations or Métis descent. Health Canada claims that Native youths are at two to six times greater risk for every alcohol-related problem than youth in the general Canadian population.

Why is there a problem with alcoholism for Native populations? Natives had no access to alcohol until 300 years ago. Their vulnerability to alcoholism may be related to the unavailability of the drug in traditional times. In addition, Adrian, Layne, and Williams (1991) found that factors such as general economic conditions contributed to the levels of alcohol consumption. Sixty percent of the variation in alcohol consumption among non-Native counties was accounted for by such social factors as income, rate of employment, northern isolation, amount of tourism, size of households, and level of industrial activity. Improving the economic situation tended to reduce the amount of alcohol consumption.

Alcoholism or alcohol abuse also leads to other problems including violence, suicides, criminal behaviour, and fetal alcohol syndrome. Fetal alcohol syndrome (FAS) or fetal alcohol effects (FAE) is a major problem in Native communities. According to one study, researchers have found that FAS has reached epidemic proportions in a First Nations reserve in Manitoba. One in 10 children was found to be a product of alcohol teratogenesis. In addition, the researchers estimated that two to three other children out of the 10 demonstrated behavioural and learning difficulties that were caused by exposure to alcohol in utero (Square, 1997). The study recommended that more studies, intervention, and programs were needed to reduce the problems and to identify children who were experiencing academic and behavioural problems as a result of FAS.

The future is not all bleak. Health Canada's National Native Alcohol and Drug Abuse Program (NNADAP) reported in Statistics Canada's Aboriginal Peoples Survey that while in-patient admissions to treatment centres fluctuated between 4500 and 4700 annually through the mid-1990s, and reached a peak of 4987 in 1996–97, the admissions rate dropped 30 percent in 1999–2000. The recidivism rate also dropped 40 percent between 1996–97 and 1999–2000, and the percentage of clients seeking treatment for alcohol abuse had dropped to 43 percent, an 11-year low. These statistics are illustrated in figures 6.4, 6.5, and 6.6.

Other Substance Abuse

Substance abuse, including alcohol, is cited by Native communities across Canada as a major issue. A recent survey found that between 1990 and 1993, more Native youths were using psychoactive substances than their non-Native counterparts. These substances included lysergic acid diethylamide (LSD), marijuana, solvents, and other hallucinogens. Native communities cite inhalants as a cause of major health problems and inhaled intoxicants use is increasingly reported throughout isolated Native communities. The median age of children using solvents is between 9 and 13 years of age (Levinthal, 1999). According to a report on aboriginal health, the median age of children using solvents was 12, and sniffing was reported among Native children as young as 4 years old (MacMillan et al., 1996). Native youths who admitted to using solvents also reported that they came from communities where financial hardship, neglect, family conflict, or child abuse exists (Canadian Medical Association, 1994).

Statistics Canada reports that in 1985–86, use of alcohol and drug treatment centres by aboriginal people in Ontario was six times higher than what would have been predicted based on the number of aboriginal persons in the province or based on equal per-capita use between aboriginal and non-aboriginal people. In the 1991 Aboriginal Peoples Survey, 73 percent of First Nations respondents said that alcohol abuse was a problem in their communities, and 59 percent said that drug use was a problem. In the 1996 Northwest Territories Alcohol and Drug Survey, aboriginal people 15 years and older living in the Northwest Territories were almost three times more likely than non-aboriginal residents to have used marijuana or hashish in the previous year. They were three-and-a-half times more likely to have used LSD, speed, cocaine, crack, or heroin.

FIGURE 6.4 Number of In-Patient Admissions at National Native Alcohol and Drug Abuse Program (NNADAP) Treatment Facilities, 1989–90 to 1999–2000

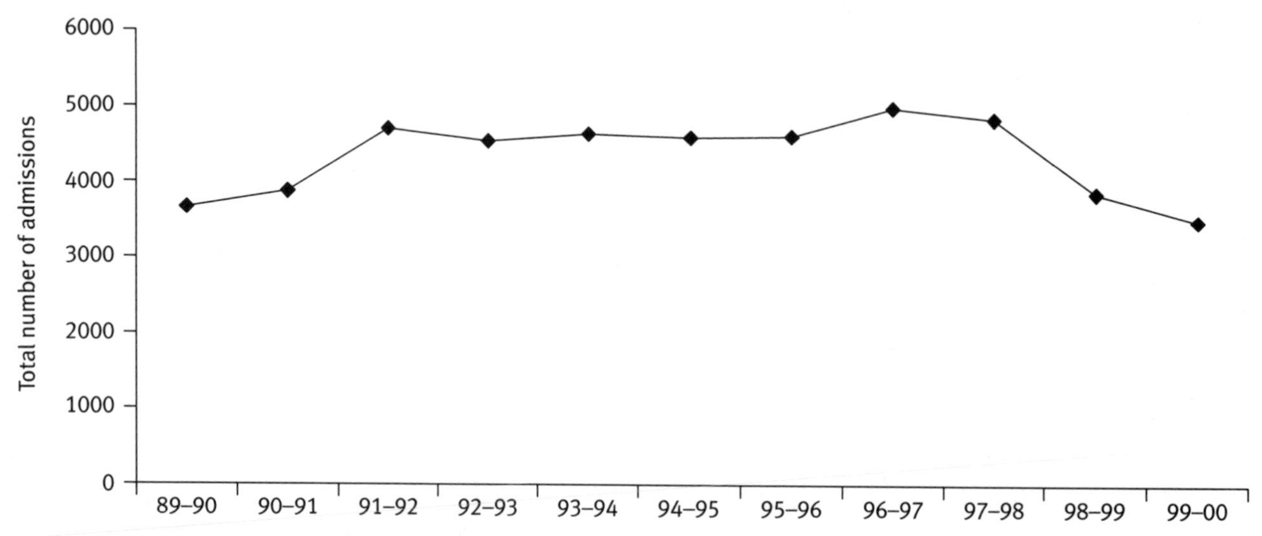

Source: First Nations and Inuit Health Branch, Health Canada, in-house statistics. Reproduced with the permission of the Minister of Public Works and Government Services Canada, 2004.

FIGURE 6.5 Recidivism Rate at National Native Alcohol and Drug Abuse Program (NNADAP) Treatment Facilities, 1990–91 to 1999–2000

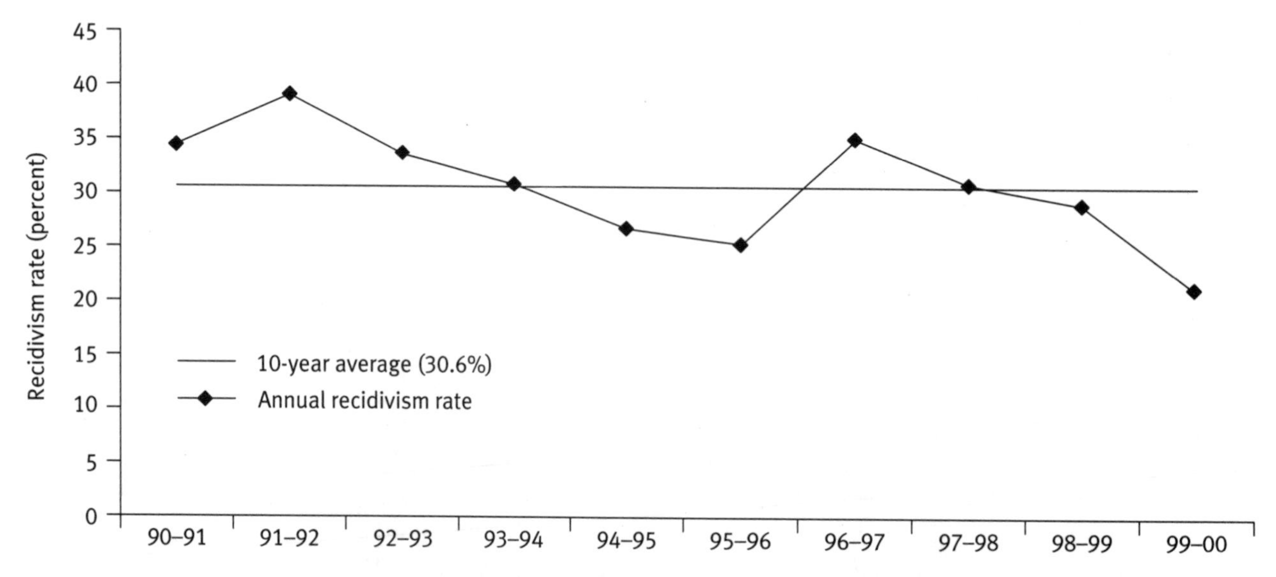

Source: First Nations and Inuit Health Branch, Health Canada, in-house statistics. Reproduced with the permission of the Minister of Public Works and Government Services Canada, 2004.

As well, this population was about 11 times more likely to have ever sniffed solvents or aerosols than the survey's non-aboriginal respondents, and almost 24 times more likely than the general population to have done so. In fact, one in five aboriginal youth reported that they had used solvents. One in three solvent users was under the age of 15. Over half of these youth began using solvents before reaching the age of 11. No progress was reported in reducing drug and alcohol abuse between 1995 and 1997, according to the First Nations and Inuit Regional Survey, 1999.

The percentage of National Native Alcohol and Drug Abuse Program's clients who reported using hallucinogens and other non-narcotic drugs as the primary

FIGURE 6.6 Admissions for Alcohol as the Primary Substance Abused, National Native Alcohol and Drug Abuse Program (NNADAP) Treatment Facilities, 1989–90 to 1999–2000

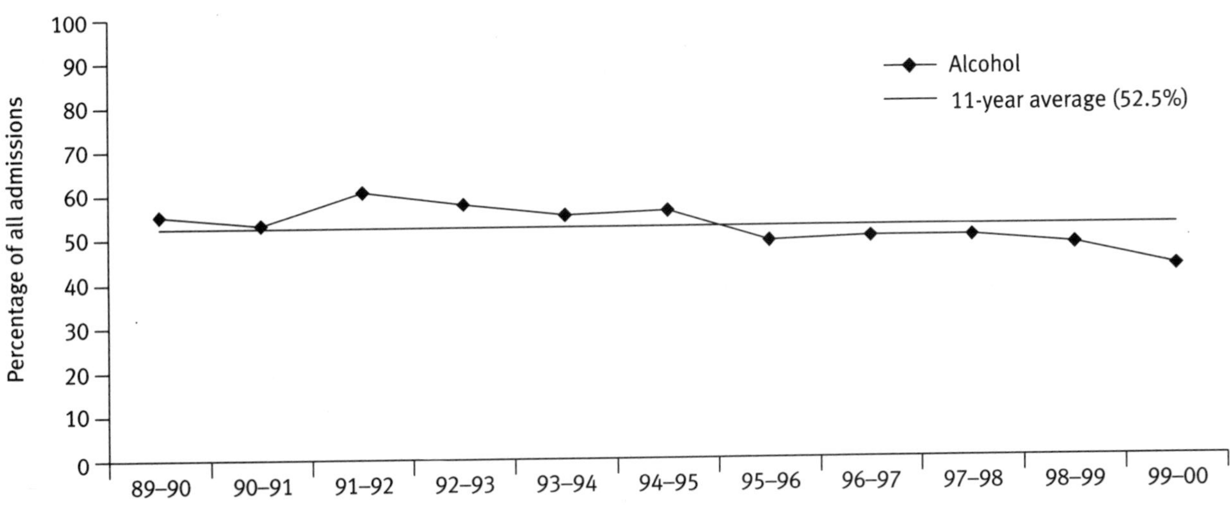

Source: First Nations and Inuit Health Branch, Health Canada, in-house statistics. Reproduced with the permission of the Minister of Public Works and Government Services Canada, 2004.

substance abused has been on an upward trend since the mid-1990s, rising to 10 percent and 14 percent respectively in 1999–2000. Meanwhile, the percentage abusing narcotics has dropped off after reaching 27 percent in 1995–96. However, data from 1999–2000 suggest that narcotic abuse has been rising again in recent years.

Living Conditions

As a result of their poverty, aboriginal peoples generally live in poorer housing and living conditions than non-Natives. Many northern communities still have inadequate water supplies and proper waste disposal. Between the years 1989–90 and 1996–97, the total number of housing units on reserves increased from 60 509 units to 80 443 units. Overcrowded living conditions are known to contribute to escalating tensions and, ultimately, disintegration of relationships and a higher risk of violence. (Note: An indicator for quality of living is one person per room. If there are more people than rooms in a house, the occupants are considered to be living in overcrowded conditions.) Fifteen years ago, one-third of on-reserve houses were overcrowded compared with about 20 percent today (Indian and Northern Affairs Canada, 1997). Despite the increase in the number of Native homes built in the past 15 years, aboriginal peoples, both on-reserve and off-reserve, experience greater overcrowded living conditions compared with the average Canadian (at 1 percent).

Water supplies and sewage disposal in Native communities have improved dramatically. For instance, from 1977 to 1989, only 53 percent of reserve houses had adequate water supplies and 47 percent had adequate sewage disposal. By 1996–97, these services increased to 96 percent of band homes receiving a water supply and 92 percent benefiting from a proper sewage system (Indian and Northern Affairs Canada, 1997). Although "outhouses" can still be found in many northern reserves, the government has assumed responsibility for installing both water and sewage systems in reserves across Canada.

Shelter is a significant issue among First Nations communities, according to Statistics Canada, because only 56.9 percent of homes were considered adequate in 1999–2000. (Adequate shelter is defined as not needing minor or major repairs or replacement.) During those same years, 41.4 percent of the First Nations communities south of 60 degrees latitude reported that at least 90 percent of homes were connected to centralized water treatment plants. Similarly, 33.6 percent of First Nations communities had at least 90 percent of their homes connected to a community sewage disposal system. (See figure 6.7.)

This, of course, isn't saying much. These figures indicate that 43.1 percent of homes were inadequate, that 58.6 percent of homes were not connected to centralized water treatment plants, and that 66.4 percent of homes were not connected to a community sewage system.

While some living conditions have improved, Natives find that their environment is becoming more polluted. For example, Natives who still include traditional foods in their diets have found significant levels of mercury in their circulatory systems due to eating mercury-poisoned fish. In some northern Native communities in Ontario and Quebec, for example, catching and eating the fish within their traditional areas has become greatly reduced because of the fear of mercury poisoning. The Cree from northern Ontario and Quebec were exposed to levels of mercury by eating fish near sites of industrial contamination. Scientists have concluded that these adverse effects to mercury poisoning are only present after a life-long exposure to the substance (Clarkson, 1992). Since mercury poisoning was first brought to the public's attention, mercury levels have decreased in the fish populations and, consequently, the Cree of James Bay have also experienced lower levels of mercury. In other areas and as another issue, polychlorinated biphenyls (PCBs) are commonly detected in northern communities. The breast milk of Inuit women in northern Quebec has been found to contain a total PCB concentration seven times greater than that of non-Native women within southern Quebec (MacMillan et al., 1996). Again, since the publication of these results, these figures have been reduced in recent years. However, Cree and other Native leaders caution that these decreases may not be permanent (industrial activity is ongoing) and, therefore, the issue is not necessarily resolved.

Living Arrangements: Children Under 15

A disturbing trend is seen in statistics in the 2001 census relating to living arrangements for aboriginal children under the age of 15 years. Table 6.5 indicates that only 60.5 percent of aboriginal children in all areas of residence live in a two-parent family, compared with 82.5 percent of non-aboriginal children. This figure increases to 65.0 percent of on-reserve children under 15 living in two-parent families, but the figure still does not come close to the figure for the non-aboriginal population. Further, 35.4 percent of aboriginal children live in single-parent families compared with only 16.9 percent of non-aboriginal children.

These figures do not improve significantly when examining the situations of children under 15 in rural non-reserve areas, urban non-census metropolitan areas, and urban census metropolitan areas. The reasons for the differences between the aboriginal and non-aboriginal statistics are not examined in this book, but they are worthy of future study. Possibly income or health considerations may be behind the reasons why fewer aboriginal children live in two-parent families than do non-aboriginal children. Could there be a higher incidence of marital failure among aboriginals,

FIGURE 6.7 Percentage of On-Reserve Housing Units, Water Delivery Systems, and Sewage Disposal Systems That Are Adequate, First Nations Communities, 1989–90 to 1999–2000

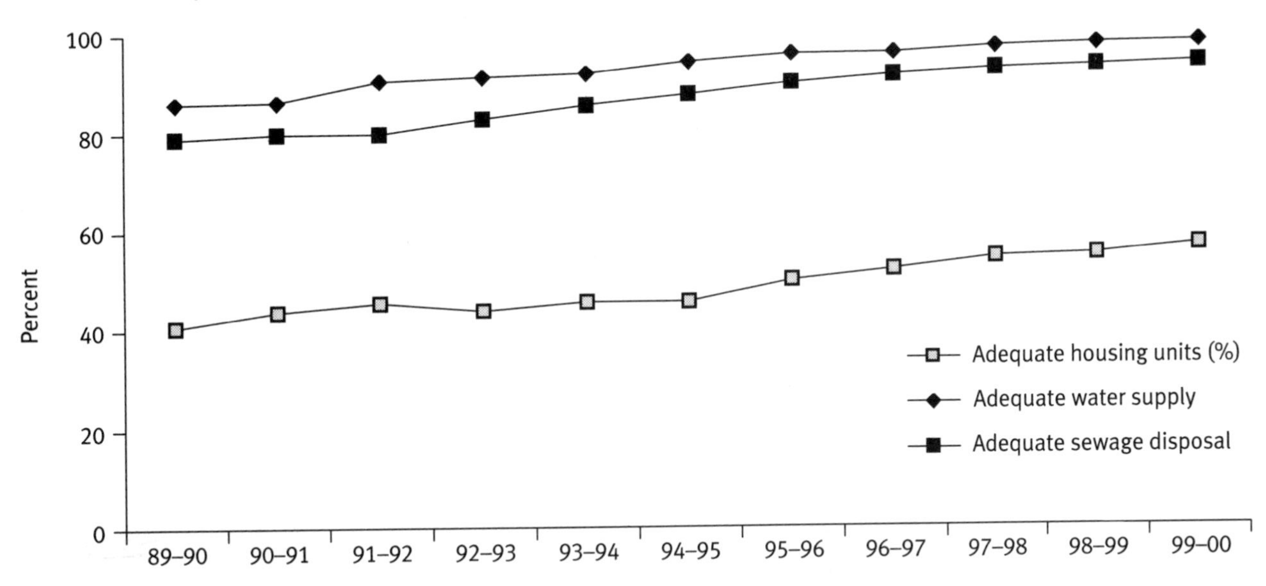

Notes:
1. Adequate housing units is defined as the number of housing units that do not require any minor or major renovations or replacement.
2. Adequate water supply refers to the presence of one of the following water delivery systems: piped, community well, individual well, truck A, truck B, and other. Note: Although adequate water delivery includes truck B water delivery (truck to barrel), the houses have not been plumbed to accept the services and can be considered inadequate.
3. Adequate sewage disposal refers to the presence of one of the following types of sewage disposal systems: piped, community septic field tank, individual septic field tank, septic truck, and other.
4. BC data exclude updates of infrastructure assets since 1987 for some First Nations participating in alternative funding arrangements.
5. 1990–91 data were used for British Columbia in 1991–92.

Source: Indian and Northern Affairs Canada, Information Management Branch, 1989–2000 Capital Asset Management System.

and what are the effects of living in single-parent situations for aboriginal children? How might these figures affect situations such as the need for day care, the incidence of single parents needing social assistance, or mental health issues that may be attributed to these living arrangements? We may be creating problems that don't exist. Whatever the implications of these statistics, further study needs to be initiated.

Administration of Health Services

The federal government assumed jurisdiction for the health of Native peoples after the creation of the *Indian Act* in 1876. Since the 1970s and after the white paper, the government has been slowly transferring the administration of services to the band level. Native peoples within the communities have developed such programs as the NNADAP, the Community Health Worker Program, the Mental Health Worker Program, and Child and Family Services, to name a few. Under these programs, Native peoples have hired their own community members and/or other trained Native professionals to administer and deliver these services. Off-reserve Native populations were often excluded from any such services until the mid-1980s when Indian Friendship Centres began to provide urban Natives with similar health services. As an example, in 1982, the government helped to create the Brighter Futures Program that provides community mental health services in aboriginal communities.

TABLE 6.5 Living Arrangements of Aboriginal and Non-Aboriginal Children Under 15 Years of Age, by Area of Residence, Canada, 2001

	Aboriginal children[a]	Non-aboriginal children
	%	
All areas of residence		
Living with two parents	60.5	82.5
Living with a lone parent	35.4	16.9
Other living arrangements[b]	4.0	0.6
On reserve		
Living with two parents	65.0	–
Living with a lone parent	31.9	–
Other living arrangements[b]	3.2	–
Rural non-reserve		
Living with two parents	71.4	88.5
Living with a lone parent	23.3	10.9
Other living arrangements[b]	5.3	0.7
Urban non-CMA		
Living with two parents	56.9	79.5
Living with a lone parent	39.6	19.9
Other living arrangements[b]	3.5	0.5
Urban CMA		
Living with two parents	49.8	81.4
Living with a lone parent	45.6	18.0
Other living arrangements[b]	4.6	0.6

[a] Those children reported as having an aboriginal identity.
[b] Includes living with other relatives, e.g., an uncle or aunt, or with non-relatives.
– Not applicable

Source: Indian and Northern Affairs Canada (2001).

Despite an increase in the number of health-related services provided to Native communities, aboriginal peoples continue to have less access to health care services compared with other Canadians. Generally, this is a result of such factors as geographic isolation, inadequate allocation of federal funding for aboriginal services, and a lack of personnel trained to meet the needs of Native populations. Since approximately 30 to 50 percent of aboriginal communities are in remote regions, Native health care will continue to experience problems, contributing to an overall lower standard of health for Native peoples. Federal funding for Native health services continues to lag behind the funding given to provincial coffers. In addition, there is a shortage of aboriginal people within the Canadian health care workforce. An increase in the number of Native health care professionals would contribute positively to Native health because of their cultural understanding of Native health issues.

The 1996 report of the Royal Commission on Aboriginal Peoples provided a comprehensive review of a number of issues of Canada's aboriginals. While the commission did not focus specifically on health, it highlighted and confirmed the more serious health issues facing Native peoples today and made some recommendations. The most important recommendation dealt with providing justice and fairness in a renewed relationship between aboriginal and non-aboriginal peoples. It determined that the only way that justice and fairness could occur was to provide Native peoples with a guarantee to practise Native self-determination. If what was said is accurate – that health and economic status go hand in hand – then unless the government settles land claim agreements and provides Natives with greater autonomy over their communities, economic viability, cultural integrity, and improved health for aboriginal peoples will not be achieved. The report also called for a refocus on family supports as opposed to apprehension of Native children by child welfare authorities. As well, it recommended that steps be taken to provide adequate housing, water, and sewage systems within Native communities; the administration of Native education to be totally in the hands of Native peoples; and the creation of aboriginal health centres and healing lodges. These recommendations are based on the premise that, if all of these areas are addressed, then ultimately Native peoples can experience the same quality of life as that experienced by their non-Native neighbours.

SOCIOECONOMIC STATUS

As the 1996 report of the Royal Commission on Aboriginal Peoples mentioned, unfavourable economic, social, and health conditions are inextricably linked to Native peoples' issues and oppression. Poverty has a profoundly debilitating effect on health status. Poverty creates dependency, limits self-expression and self-determination, and contributes to the demoralizing and often passive acceptance of substandard community infrastructures. In this section, we will look at Native employment, income, and social assistance.

Employment

The 1996 labour force participation rate for the total Canadian population (68 percent), according to Statistics Canada, was 1.2 times higher than it was for the First Nations on-reserve population. The gap between the First Nations and Canada was widest among the 15–24 age group, at 30 percentage points. Labour force participation includes both those who are employed and those who are looking for work.

The gap between the employment rates of First Nations people (43 percent) and Canadians (62 percent) was considerably wider, at 19 percentage points, than the gap between labour force participation rates, at 9 percentage points. However, this gap has closed slightly since 1991. The 25–44 age group had the highest employment rate among First Nations people in 1996.

The 1996 First Nations unemployment rate was almost three times higher than the Canadian rate. For all age groups and sexes, the First Nations rates were at least two times higher. The highest unemployment rate was seen in the 15–24 age group, at 41 percent. For both populations, greater educational attainment is correlated with lower unemployment rates. Education may also help to narrow the gap between First Nations and Canadian unemployment levels.

First Nations unemployment data reported by Indian and Northern Affairs Canada for 1997–98 show little change from the 1996 rates; the unemployment rate on First Nations reserves stood at 29 percent, compared with a rate of 10 percent for Canada as a whole. In 2000–1, the employment-to-population ratios of First Nations reserves were substantially higher for postsecondary graduates (64 percent) than for high school graduates (45 percent), according to Indian and Northern Affairs Canada.

The following labour force characteristics are taken from the 2001 census:

Total North American Indian population 15 years of age and over by labour force activity	395 325
In the labour force	226 670
Employed	176 345
Unemployed	50 320
Not in the labour force	168 645
Participation rate	57.3
Employment rate	44.6
Unemployment rate	22.2

Total North American Indian labour force 15 years of age and over by industry	226 665
Industry — not applicable	15 730
All industries	210 930
Agriculture, forestry, fishing, hunting	12 095
Mining and oil and gas extraction	3 735
Utilities	1 605
Construction	16 900
Manufacturing	17 230
Wholesale trade	3 890
Retail trade	17 305
Transportation and warehousing	9 705
Information and cultural industries	2 755
Finance and insurance	2 835
Real estate and rental and leasing	1 930
Professional, scientific, and technical services	4 740
Management of companies and enterprises	55
Administrative and support, waste management, and remediation services	10 165
Educational services	15 680
Health care and social assistance	25 480
Arts, entertainment, and recreation	6 250
Accommodation and food services	15 755
Other services (except public administration)	8 410
Public administration	34 415

Total North American Indian labour force 15 years of age and over by occupation	226 665
Occupation — not applicable	15 730
All occupations	210 935
Management occupations	14 275
Business, finance, and administration	28 315
Natural and applied sciences and related	6 225
Health	6 360
Social science, education, government service, and religion	23 960
Art, culture, recreation, and sport	4 890
Sales and service	59 280
Trades, transport, equipment operators, and related	39 455
Primary industry	16 055
Processing, manufacturing, and utilities	12 120

Total North American Indian experienced labour force by class of worker	210 935
Paid workers	200 210
Employees	197 870
Self-employed (incorporated)	2 335
Self-employed (unincorporated)	10 290
Unpaid family workers	435

Income

Statistics Canada reports that, like unemployment rates, average income for First Nations people is also below that of the Canadian population as a whole, at any age or education level. On reserves, the First Nations income levels in the 1996 census were only half that of Canadians. First Nations income levels are increasing over time, however. Between 1990 and 1995, average individual income among all registered Indians rose from $11 941 to $14 833, according to Indian and Northern Affairs Canada in 2000. For registered Indians on reserves, average individual income over the same period climbed 31.5 percent, compared with a 17.2 percent rise for the Canadian population as a whole. Although education and gender may play a significant role in an individual's labour market participation and income level, many other geographic, social, institutional, and cultural factors are likely to be important, such as regional labour markets, discrimination, and differing social contexts.

Based on the unemployment figures seen in the next section of this book, which shows that approximately 1 in every 5 Natives over 15 years of age was unemployed in 2001, compared with approximately 1 in 14 of the total non-aboriginal Canadian population, income for Natives was considerably below average. The average employment income for Natives was $32 176 according to the 2001 census, compared with $43 486 for the total Canadian non-aboriginal population. One in 15 Native people reported being without income in the census data, compared with 1 in 23 non-aboriginals. In relation to low income statistics, 37.3 percent of North American Indians 15 years and over reported having a low income, compared with only 12.4 percent of the non-aboriginal population. Of unattached individuals over 15 years of age, 59.8 percent of North American Indians reported having a low income, compared with only 37.6 percent of the non-aboriginal population.

The following income-related statistics are taken from the 2001 census:

Total North American Indian population 15 years of age and over by employment income work activity	395 325
Did not work in 2000	59 750
Worked full year full time	90 375
Average employment income	$32 176
Standard of error average employment income	$75
Worked part year or part time	142 290
Average employment income	$12 837
Standard error of average employment income	$38
Total North American Indian population 15 years of age and over by composition of total income in 2000	100.0%
Employment income	72.0%
Government transfer payments	24.3%
Other	3.6%

Total North American Indian population 15 years of age and older by total income groups	395 325
Without income	26 950
With income	368 375
Under $5000	94 595
$5000–$9999	60 485
$10 000–$19 999	93 315
$20 000–$29 999	49 740
$30 000–$39 999	32 440
$40 000–$49 999	17 000
$50 000–$59 999	9 595
$60 000 and over	11 200
Average income	$17 376
Median income	$12 263
Standard error of average income	$26
Total population in private households by economic family status and incidence of low income in 2000	325 450
Number of economic family persons	285 980
Low income	106 785
Other	187 130
Incidence of low income in 2000	37.3%
Number of unattached individuals 15 years and over	39 475
Low income	23 595
Other	15 880
Incidence of low income in 2000	59.8%

GROUP DISCUSSION

1. What strategies could you propose that may economically benefit bands and Native peoples both now and with the increased populations in the near future?
2. What will happen if the present status of Native employment is maintained?

Social Assistance

Not only do aboriginal peoples rely on social assistance more than any other group in Canada, but there is evidence that this reliance is increasing. Government expenditures have doubled over the past two decades (Frideres, 1997). To put this into perspective, however, the expenditure of social assistance on Natives represents about 3 percent of the overall total Canadian social assistance payments. Today, most bands administer the delivery of their own social assistance payments; 78 percent is spent on child and family services and 22 percent is spent on adult care. The funds provide for the basic levels of health, safety, and family unity, as well as for food, clothing and shelter, and counselling to assist them in becoming independent. Despite the high rates of social assistance for Native peoples, figures also indicate that the rate of poverty remains twice as high as that of the general population. Since employment opportunities are not present in many Native communities, social assistance is often offered as an alternative.

Social assistance has created serious problems for Native peoples as a whole. Factors such as a lack of employment opportunities have created a cycle of dependence that is difficult to break. Frideres (1997) cites that many Canadians feel that aboriginal peoples are responsible for their need for social assistance. The possible danger in this assumption is that this draws attention away from more critical issues, and to lay blame on those needing social assistance is to ignore such realities as a lack of education, discrimination, poverty, lack of employment opportunities, and low self-esteem. According to Frideres (1997), these issues prevent aboriginal peoples, as well as other Canadians on social assistance, from fully participating in Canadian society.

The Department of Indian Affairs and Northern Development (DIAND) has been involved in on-reserve social assistance activities to provide individuals and families with the means to meet basic needs of food, clothing, and shelter. DIAND also funds special needs allowances for goods and services that are essential to the physical or social well-being of individuals, and include items such as basic furniture needs and physician-recommended diets. DIAND funds First Nations who in turn deliver programs and services to community members.

DELIVERY OF SERVICES AND PROGRAMS

To understand the programs and services that are provided to address Native concerns, it is important to become familiar with the source of their funding. In general, the majority of Native funding comes from the federal government. To be more specific, four departments, the Department of Indian Affairs and Northern Development (DIAND), Health Canada, Canada Mortgage Housing Corporation (CMHC), and Human Resources Development Canada (HRDC), are collectively responsible for 97 percent of the total federal funding directed at aboriginal peoples. The DIAND's expenditures represent 71 percent of all federal funding directed almost exclusively to Status Indians living on-reserve (see table 6.6). At the present time, and as a result of the **devolution** process, 82 percent of DIAND's funding for programs is administered by the First Nations peoples themselves. The funding from the other departments is directed at the aboriginal populations both on-reserve and off-reserve. The most important aspect to note is that 80 percent of DIAND's programming expenditures are for basic services provided to other Canadians through provincial, municipal, and territorial governments.

devolution
the return of control of programs and services to Native peoples

OFF-RESERVE ABORIGINAL POPULATIONS

The off-reserve aboriginal population needs to be examined separately, since there are numerous issues relating specifically to this group that need to be addressed. According to the 2001 census, 713 000 aboriginal people lived off-reserve, accounting for 70 percent of those persons who identified themselves as aboriginal. This figure includes approximately 46 000 Inuit and 295 000 Métis, leaving the approximate off-reserve First Nations population at 358 000 persons, with approximately 43 percent of these in metropolitan areas.

Consider the Hamilton, Ontario urban area as a typical model. Approximately 1000 aboriginal people have moved into this area since 1996, bringing the total aboriginal population to 7270 persons. According to the article by Cheryl Stepan found in appendix 6.2, this group is characterized by poverty, high unemployment, and low educational achievement.

TABLE 6.6 DIAND's Expenditures on First Nation Communities, 1997–98

Programs/services	Expenditures %	Expenditures $ millions
Schools, infrastructure, housing	23	983
Elementary/secondary education	21	899
Social assistance	16	671
Claims	9	367
Social support services	8	361
Indian government support	8	329
Postsecondary education	6	275
Administration/regional direction/funding services	3	122
Lands and trust services	2	92
Northern affairs	2	88
Economic development	1	57
Self-government	1	39
Total	100	4 283

Source: Indian and Northern Affairs Canada.

Health concerns are one of the most pressing issues among non-reserve aboriginals. Generally, off-reserve aboriginals rated their health status as poorer than that of the general population. For every age group between 25 and 64, the proportion of aboriginal people reporting fair or poor health is about double that of the total population, according to O'Donnell and Tait (2003), in their analysis of the 2001 census as it relates to off-reserve aboriginal people. The health of aboriginal women aged 55–64 is of particular concern, with 40 percent reporting fair or poor health, compared with 19 percent of women in the same age groups in the total Canadian population.

Arthritis, rheumatism, high blood pressure, asthma, and diabetes are the most commonly reported chronic health problems in the aboriginal off-reserve population (see figure 6.8). According to O'Donnell and Tait,

> Among the adult population, 19.3 percent of the non-reserve aboriginal population reported arthritis or rheumatism, nearly twice the proportion of 11 percent among the total Canadian population. Similarly, 12 percent of the aboriginal population reported high blood pressure, compared with 8.7 percent among the total population.

Diabetes is of particular concern, especially among the North American Indian population, where 8.3 percent of the population age 15 and over was diagnosed with diabetes. This figure is somewhat higher than the figure for off-reserve aboriginals, according to Health Canada (see figure 6.9).

In the area of education, 40 percent of the aboriginal people in the Hamilton, Ontario area, according to Stepan (2003), have not completed high school. This compares with 48 percent of the national aboriginal population, as opposed to 26 percent of the total Canadian population. While the figure for the Hamilton area looks marginally brighter, it is an undeniable fact that twice as many off-reserve aboriginals fail to complete secondary school compared with the general Canadian population.

In every category under consideration, off-reserve aboriginal people fared poorly compared with the total Canadian population. Quality of housing, income, health care, and employment rates all fall well below the Canadian average.

FIGURE 6.8 Percentage of Population with Selected Chronic Conditions, Aboriginal Identity Non-Reserve Population, 15 Years and Over, Canada, 2001

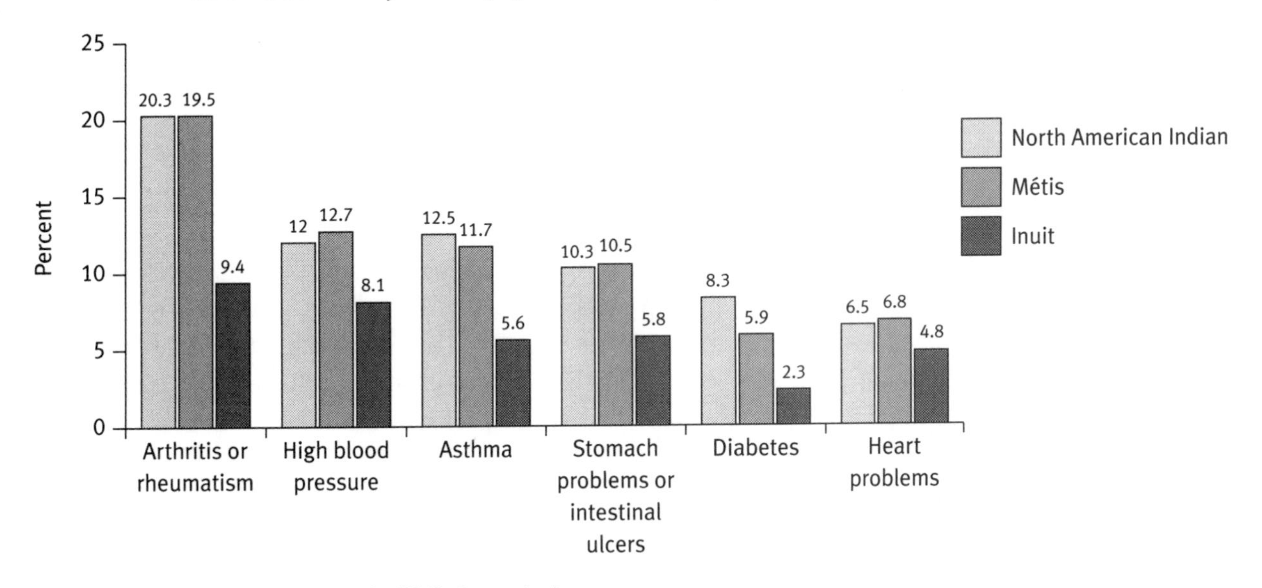

Source: Adapted from Statistics Canada (2003, September).

FIGURE 6.9 Percentage of Population Diagnosed with Diabetes, Canada, 2001

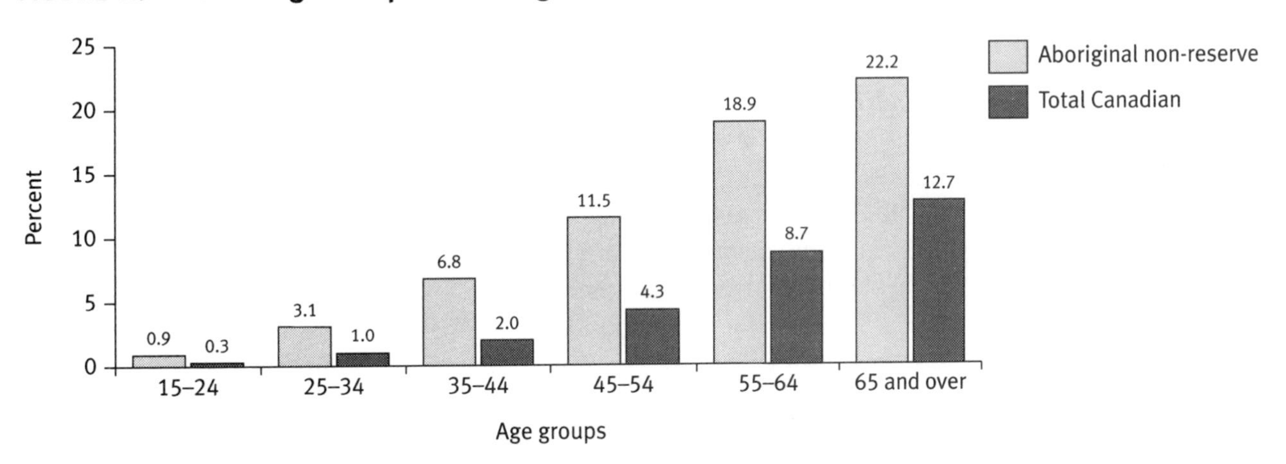

Source: Adapted from Statistics Canada (2003, September) and Statistics Canada, *Canadian Community Health Survey, 2000–01* (2001).

GROUP DISCUSSION

Read the following summary and answer the questions below:

In his book *Surviving as Indians*, Boldt (1993, p. 214) proposes an interesting premise. He believes that Natives have fallen into a complacent mode of thought, which stems from Native survival as distinctive cultures, despite the aggressive attempts of the Canadian government to assimilate Native peoples. He argues that instead of boasting cultural survival, Native cultures are in essence in a state of crisis, "traditional values, norms, customs and social systems have lost their relevance, their legitimacy, and hence their capacity for maintaining social order within their communities." He proposes that for Native cultures to transform into positive forces, they must not become victims of cultural isolation but carry their traditional, fundamental philosophies and principles, and develop a clear vision of what they want to be in the future.

1. Based on everything we have examined thus far, how accurate is Boldt in capturing Native issues? Explain your answers to the group.
2. What strategies would you suggest to reduce the problems Natives are facing so that they can enjoy a quality of life similar to that of other Canadians?

CONCLUSION

Despite the efforts made to improve the aboriginal quality of life, much work still needs to be done. In order to experience the same standard of living enjoyed by most Canadians, Native peoples must become more active in healing themselves and their communities. Native leaders and Native peoples must continue to strive for greater autonomy over services provided to them. Education is perceived by many Natives as one of the integral components in the process toward greater self-determination.

Improving the overall health and prosperity of Canada's Native populations depends heavily upon improving their economic and social conditions through Native self-determination strategies — the ability to identify their own needs, and develop and implement their own strategies. Canadian medical, social, and other professionals must work with Native peoples in order for Native peoples to develop methods of assessing their own needs, and designing and evaluating their own interventions that are meaningful and relevant to each of them as distinct cultures. In addition, aboriginal people need to recognize and develop and use their own professional human resources. This can succeed only if each community adopts a greater sense of responsibility for improving the health and overall status of their community and all First Nations.

To date, the majority of the health, legal, and economic professionals working with aboriginal communities are not Natives. Natives understand that initiatives to attract Native students into these fields are critical. Pre-professional programs that prepare students for these fields are needed. First Nations communities must work cooperatively to accept professionals who are Natives, yet who are not from their own communities. A distrust of a Native by a Native is destructive to all aboriginal peoples and to any initiatives that could otherwise succeed. This is frustrating and potentially might hurt the community and, ultimately, all Natives. Each community must examine its issues and work interdependently to achieve greater health and prosperity for all Native peoples and communities across Canada.

There are a number of professional Native organizations in Canada. They include the Native Physician Association in Canada (NPAC), the Native Psychologists in Canada (NPC), and the Aboriginal Nurses Association of Canada (ANAC). Membership in these organizations has been increasing. Programs such as the pre-nursing program offered at Lakehead University in Thunder Bay, Ontario provide Natives with chances of successfully completing a nursing degree. Native peoples should become more aware and supportive of these organizations (Tookenay, 1996).

Author Vincent Tookenay recommends that Native peoples need to look beyond politics to address the health issues directly. He suggests that Native organizations need to expand their focus and address health issues that are experienced by all aboriginal peoples. In addition, he suggests that the government must establish partnerships with Natives to resolve Native health problems.

WORKSHEET

1a. In every social condition that we examined, Native peoples experience a lower quality of life than that experienced by other Canadians. List four areas in which this occurs; describe them briefly. (4 marks)

1b. Briefly outline or connect some historical events as contributing factors to these issues. (4 marks)

2a. Describe the present federal government's responsibilities to Native peoples. (2 marks)

2b. How has the federal government changed this relationship (if any change has occurred)? Provide examples to support your answers. (2 marks)

3a. If a number of reserves are given the opportunity to build mini-casinos in their communities, what potential benefits do you see for the reserve? To the nearby non-Native communities? Provide support for your arguments. (4 marks)

3b. What potential problems or drawback do you see for the reserves? For the nearby non-Native communities? Provide sound support for your arguments. (4 marks)

TOTAL – 20 MARKS

KEY TERMS

constitution

devolution

APPENDIX 6.1

Reserves Rack Up $300 Million in Deficits, Native Leaders Blame Underfunding

Turtle Island News

OTTAWA (CP) – *First Nations owe more than $300 million and will be sunk deeper into debt by chronic underfunding, say Native leaders.*

Documents released under the *Access to Information Act* show that 245 Native communities across Canada have run up cumulative deficits of $300.3 million. The highest tally is in Manitoba, where 48 bands owe a total of $94.2 million as of [January 2004].

In Atlantic Canada, 20 bands together owe $47.3 million, and 50 in Ontario owe almost $40 million.

Indian Affairs stresses that 70 percent of the country's 614 first Nations have balanced books. Some red ink can be traced to loans for new houses, schools or other big projects, says Dominique LaSalle, director of transfer payments for the department.

But a growing number of First Nations are running deficits because urgent needs routinely outstrip funds, say a British Columbia chief who is working with Ottawa to manage his Penticton Band's debt.

"You have a very difficult choice to make," said Stewart Phillip, also head of the B.C. Union of Indian Chiefs, representing 70 leaders.

"You either meet the need as it arises, and eventually start running a deficit, or you deny the need.

"Unfortunately, that's becoming more and more commonplace, where we're turning band members away."

Ottawa is "painfully aware" of the rising costs linked to a Native population that's growing at twice the rate of non-aboriginals, Phillip said.

"The health costs alone are rising astronomically ... and that's why they're trying to get out from under their fiduciary obligations."

The federal government, under terms of historic agreements, spends more than $6 billion a year for Native programs ranging from education to social assistance to housing.

Funding for Indian Affairs was not curbed even in the mid-1990s when virtually every federal department was cut to pay down a $42 billion deficit.

But funding levels have not been boosted to keep pace with both inflation and population spikes, Phillip says.

"There are thousands of (Native) students who really desperately want to go to school or take training and the money isn't there."

LaSalle, of Indian Affairs, said programs are funded according to formulas based on population. He could not speak to specific shortfalls, but stressed: "Choices are made by the communities."

On the Gull Bay First Nation, about 350 kilometres north of Thunder Bay, Ontario, Chief Wilfred King says many of his 500 residents have no choice but "abject poverty."

"We have an 80 percent unemployment rate and people are living in ... squalor here. There has to be a fundamental shift in policy. I think the federal government owes the First Nations the fiduciary obligation to ensure essential services are there. The manner in which funding arrangements are drawn up has to be changed."

King scoffed at how fast Canada wrote off $750 million in debt owed by Iraq while the most isolated First Nations are denied access to natural resources on their traditional lands. "It's very difficult to reconcile that."

About one-quarter of Canada's 700 First Nations, tribal councils, and Native political groups are under special management because of deficits that exceed 8 percent of their budgets. Of those, about 5 percent have lost control of their finances because of continuing problems.

In Gull Bay, King says an outside manager has been paid almost $500 000 in band funds over the past five years to do little more than write cheques.

Training of reserve staff to help them take back control of their finances has not been offered, King says.

"And we're no further ahead. In fact, we're further in debt."

APPENDIX 6.2

Aboriginals: Now I Know Who I Am

By Cheryl Stepan, *Hamilton Spectator* (October 11, 2003)

More than 7,000 people in the Hamilton area told census takers they are native — a 33 percent jump. The city's native people express pride in their ancestry. But their legacy of struggle continues as almost half of them live in poverty.

The family hid the secret for decades. It was one of those things no one dared talk about, at least not while their mother was alive.

Yet, there was a part of Jean Beauchamp that always knew. There was something special about her, and she could feel it growing up.

So it didn't come as a surprise to her when her aunt called her a few months after her mother died and revealed what her mother never would. Her father was an Indian. That meant she, too, had aboriginal blood in her veins.

"In my heart, I knew. But you didn't talk about things like that," Beauchamp said. Her mother was white, French Canadian and living in Northern Ontario in the '60s, a time she wasn't comfortable publicly acknowledging she was with an aboriginal man.

"It just hurt my mom too much ... because of the stigma of being with an aboriginal. You didn't go out with Indians if you were white."

Beauchamp is part of a tidal wave of people recently discovering and embracing their aboriginal ancestry, including status Indian, Inuit, and Metis — or mixed aboriginal and European — people.

In the Hamilton–Burlington–Grimsby Census Metropolitan Area (CMA) between 1996 to 2001, there was a 33 per cent growth in the aboriginal population.

The 2001 census reports that 7,270 people identified themselves as aboriginal in 2001, up from 5,460. By comparison, the population on Six Nations, Canada's most populous reserve, is around 11,000.

Province-wide, the aboriginal population also increased by 33 per cent, much higher than the growth rate of 6.1 per cent for the entire population ... .

No one can say for sure what's driving the surge in numbers of people who state they are aboriginal because the census doesn't take into account the reasons people claim a certain identity ... .

It's perhaps not surprising that aboriginal people would try to hide behind a white mask [previously]. Decades of oppression and racism, and such government policies as residential schools and adoptions into white families took their toll on a population that was struggling with a changing way of life.

The legacy of that struggle is seen to this day as 48 per cent of aboriginal people in Hamilton live in poverty, according to the Social Planning and Research Council. By rough comparison, slightly more than 16 per cent of the city's overall population are living below the low-income cut-off set by Statistics Canada.

Another factor, according to Sherry Lewis, executive director of Hamilton's Native Women's Centre, a women's shelter, is that aboriginal community leaders are encouraging people to come forward so social and government agencies can get a more accurate picture of the population and its needs.

She said mainstream programs often don't work for aboriginal people because they don't address specific problems – such as residential school syndrome – or take into account aboriginal spiritual and cultural needs.

The 2001 census shows that much of the [aboriginal] community is concentrated in low-income neighbourhoods in the lower city.

The aboriginal population in the CMA has a median income 33 per cent lower than that of the overall population – $16,554 compared to $24,987.

Aboriginals' median income has improved since 1996 when it was just $14,366, but the gap between their income and that of the overall population – which rose too – is not closing.

In 2001, the unemployment rate was 12.3 per cent for aboriginal people, compared to a rate of 5.7 per cent in the overall population.

They also have less formal education – 40 per cent of aboriginal people over age 25 do not have a high school diploma. In the overall population, just 27 per cent of those over 20 years have not graduated.

Aboriginal people also have a disproportionate number of kids in Children's Aid Society custody. Planning and Research Council reports that 43 per cent of children in foster care are aboriginal.

[Note: While the statistics cited in this article apply to the Hamilton, Ontario region, they do not differ significantly from figures in other parts of the province. If the 2001 census shows anything, it shows that aboriginal people across the province have a long way to go to catch up with the economic and social conditions enjoyed by the larger population.]

APPENDIX 6.3

Debate Rages Over Native Alcoholism

By Glen McGregor, *First Nations Drum* (Summer 2001)

Some argue a chief's warning to sober up is welcome recognition of a major problem. Others call it unfair stereotyping.

When Assembly of First Nations Chief Matthew Coon Come warned that native leaders must sober up, he was drawing on a long standing and persistent stereotype of native alcoholism that has never been proven conclusively.

"Our people smoke too much and drink too much," said Mr. Coon Come, Canada's top elected Native. "I think it does not give a good signal if a chief and council and anyone who is in Indian leadership is denying that he has alcohol problems."

To many, Mr. Coon Come's recent [2001] remarks came as a welcome recognition of a health problem endemic to Canada's aboriginal communities.

But to others, it was an endorsement of an unfair stereotype that natives have tried to shake for years.

Had it been anyone but Mr. Coon Come who said it, they suggest, the remarks would be vilified as bigoted and uninformed.

Indeed, former Newfoundland premier Brian Tobin was publicly castigated last year [2000] for saying pretty much the same thing as Mr. Coon Come when he suggested many aboriginal leaders in Labrador are "themselves abusers of alcohol and themselves in need of help."

His remarks set off a rage of controversy, with Phil Fontaine, Mr. Coon Come's predecessor at the AFN, denouncing the comments as "a stereotypical image of our people that's so completely wrong."

Today, the idea that natives are more susceptible to the mind-bending effects of alcohol remains so tenacious that even some natives believe it.

In her book *Firewater Myths* [1976], anthropologist Joy Leland reported that many American Indians believe they have a physiological weakness to the effects of alcohol and that alcoholism is "in the blood."

Ms. Leland concluded that young natives used the hereditary explanation as an excuse for their own abuse of alcohol, even though studies show aboriginals do not metabolize alcohol much differently than people of other races.

In Canada, social-scientific data suggest that aboriginal communities are hit harder by substance abuse than non-aboriginal communities. But the data is far from conclusive.

In a major study of existing research, Health Canada admitted it is difficult to measure alcohol and drug abuse on reserves because of poor response rates and cultural differences that complicate surveys. This makes direct comparison to non-aboriginal populations difficult.

Instead, epidemiologists who study native alcoholism rely on data that show why natives get sick or die.

Injury and poisoning are leading causes of mortality and morbidity in aboriginal communities, both of which are consistent with alcohol abuse.

Few would argue, however, that alcohol is not a problem in Canada's aboriginal communities.

A 1984 survey of First Nations communities in Manitoba found that 86 per cent rated alcohol as either a "serious problem" or "major problem."

A study in Ontario the following year found that alcohol consumption was as much as 35 per cent higher in counties that have native reserves than those who don't.

But other data assembled by Health Canada show that a lower proportion of aborginals drink daily (two per cent versus three per cent of non-natives) and fewer drink weekly (35 per cent versus 46 per cent) than non-aboriginals. Also, almost twice as many aboriginals count themselves as teetotallers. About 15 per cent of aboriginals say they abstain from drinking, compared with eight per cent of other Canadians.

"There are indications that drinking is more tenacious among young people on reserves," said Gary Roberts of the Canadian Centre on Substance Abuse. "But there's not a lot of good information."

He says figures show that aboriginal youth are between twice and six times as likely to have alcohol problems as non-natives of the same age.

Mr. Roberts says another test of drinking problems, the rate of fetal alcohol syndrome, has also been tested in aboriginal communities, but it is difficult to compare to non-native rates because of a lack of data.

The perception of high rates of native alcoholism is partly grounded in reality, but has been embellished by non-aboriginals who have limited exposure to reserves.

Non-natives are likely to form their opinion on native drinking from the people they encounter on city streets, he said. "It comes from people's perceptions, noticing that particularly off reserves in Western Canada you will find individuals of aboriginal descent living on the street."

Off-reserve natives are believed to have a much higher rate of alcohol and drug dependency, but again, there is little reliable information to back up this theory. Data collection in urban centres has been even less rigorous than on the reserves.

Mr. Roberts said there is nothing but anecdotal evidence to support Mr. Coon Come's assertion that there is an alcohol problem among the aboriginal political leadership.

"But if it does occur, it is going to limit their effectiveness to become active on the alcohol abuse problems in their communities," he said.

CHAPTER 7

Natives and Current Judicial Issues

Chapter Objectives

After completing this chapter, you should be able to:

- Outline the traditional forms of social control used by Native peoples in pre-contact times, and in earlier periods of European contact.
- Cite current Native adult and Native youth incarceration rates compared with those of the general Canadian public.
- List the major concerns and issues identified by aboriginal peoples that have conflicted with the Canadian judicial system.
- Explain the negative impact of judiciary discretion on Natives as a minority culture.
- Describe the existing Native programs and their effectiveness within the present judicial system.
- Outline what Native diversionary programs exist.

INTRODUCTION

They say that
The wheels of "Justice,"
They grind slowly.

Yes we know.
But they grind
And they grind
And they grind

And they grind.
It seems like they grind
Forever ...

Art Solomon, Anishnaabe Elder (1990).

Native peoples have a general mistrust of the Canadian judicial system, based on past inequities and negative experiences. Native peoples are the most overrepresented population within the Canadian prisons and penitentiaries. Although only 2.8 percent of the general adult population are aboriginal, Natives accounted for 18 percent of the prison population in 2001. They were younger on average than non-aboriginal inmates, according to Statistics Canada, had less education, and were more likely to have been unemployed. They were also considered at higher risk to re-offend, and they had a higher set of needs than non-aboriginal inmates, including substance abuse, employment, personal needs, and family/marital needs.

NATIVES' TRADITIONAL PRACTICES OF SOCIAL CONTROL

Before we study the conditions of Native peoples in today's Canadian judicial system, it is important to review the systems of social control that traditional Native societies used to resolve their conflicts.

Prior to European contact, First Nations peoples were self-governing. Administering justice to community members evolved over time into intricate methods of regulating areas of social interaction where conflict was likely to occur. Contrary to many non-Native written accounts, the Native peoples of northern North America were not lawless. Unique to each Native nation, Native cultures used distinct methods of law, which we will refer to as social control, that were reflective of their customary values, practices, and traditions. The Native systems of social control were responsible for providing parameters within three basic areas of communal living: regulations regarding property (interference or damage to personal possessions), interpersonal dynamics (conflicts both physical and verbal), and international or intertribal affairs (disputes between tribes or with other tribal cultures).

Historically, no Native culture within the northern part of the Northern Hemisphere used holding cells for punishment. They did not practise methods of incarceration. How Native social control worked must be considered from the perspective of their lives, prior to European contact. As discussed in chapter 2, each member of the community had a strong interdependence on their families and the community. Each person — young and old — played a significant role in the survival and maintenance of the community. The primary goal of resolving any communal or individual dispute was to mediate the case to everyone's satisfaction, and to do this promptly. Native communities came face to face to resolve problems (where the offender was made to understand the consequences of his or her inappropriate behaviour). Each party was involved until, ideally, a fair and satisfactory settlement of the issues was reached. Aboriginal traditional dispute mechanisms that focused primarily on sustaining the health of the community and its individuals, rather than a preoccupation with reforming or punishing the offender (RCAP, 1996b; Frideres, 1997), confirm that according to traditional Native ways, when a crime was committed, atonement and community stability were priorities. Criminal behaviour was seen as a community responsibility. In contrast, Canadian law enforcement today focuses on the protection of society from its individuals.

When one member of the community committed an inappropriate act, the community showed disapproval by collectively shunning, ridiculing (Silverman & Nielsen, 1992), or admonishing the individual. In extreme or chronic cases, the communities would banish the individual for a specific period of time or permanently. In a harsh climate, this was equal to the death penalty, because the individual relied heavily on the community for survival; community approval was extremely important to his or her well-being. Consequently, using incarceration as a deterrent was not necessary. As an example, stealing was rare because the accumulation of personal possessions was not a Native held value (see also chapter 4). However, when the property of an individual was destroyed or damaged, if the offending person did not immediately respond with retribution, the families would intervene to try to resolve the issue. If this was unsuccessful, the community members would apply collective disapproval tactics – that is, shunning, taunts, berating, etc. – to influence the individual to change his or her behaviour. The offending person would invariably resolve the issue to avoid or terminate further community disapproval. Community approval was vital for survival of the whole community, and individual acceptance of the community norms required complete acquiescence.

Traditional dispute resolution techniques were also unique to each Native culture. The Dene Nations' form of social control was based loosely on a structured three-tier system. First, when someone had conflict with another community member or another individual, they would attempt to resolve the conflict between themselves. If unable to come to an agreement, they would approach an older person or elder to mediate the situation. If the situation became heated to a point that the community was being affected, the community would deal with the situation. In such an instance, community members would form a public opinion and force the individual whom the community believed to be in the wrong to take measures to deal with the offence. How was this accomplished? In most Native cultures, the fact that the entire community disapproved of the matter was often enough to cause the offending party to deal with the issue. Furthermore, pressure was placed on the offending person to make some kind of restitution or to opt for self-banishment for a period of time (Morrison, 1997).

The Ojibwe of the Woodland cultures lived in a harsh terrain and cold climate. Their very survival often depended upon the maintenance of a balance between communal needs and obtaining the resources required for survival. Cooperative interpersonal relationships were vital to their continued existence; hence, individual behaviour, especially the regulation of aggression, was carefully regulated and monitored. The ability to minimize and control aggressive tendencies within the community was, in part, a result of the Ojibwe beliefs in the spirit world and the potential to offend supernatural forces. Personal conflicts and confrontations were scrupulously avoided for fear of offending the spirit of some deceased person or a spirit from their environment. In addition, community members feared bad medicine that could be placed on an offending person by a medicine man. Personal or community misfortune, disease, or even death could be the result of someone's inappropriate actions. Abuse of the system of borrowing or lending possessions (each individual had very few personal possessions) rarely occurred because of fear of revenge by the spirit world. Thus, this explains, in part, how Ojibwe communities could exist without the presence of an enforcement body, courts, or prisons (see Kuyek, 1991).

In their book *Aboriginal Peoples and Canadian Criminal Justice*, Robert Silverman and Marianne Nielsen (1992) relate the consequences of misdemeanours by community members during the annual tribal hunts of the Plains Cree and Plains Ojibwe hunters. During the hunt that took place in late summer or early fall, several hunters would be assigned duties to keep order during the march, watch for enemies, and ensure that the younger hunters would not rush ahead and frighten the herd. If anyone was caught firing too early, they were punished by having their belongings seized, their tipi cover slashed, and/or by being flogged. If the person submitted to these consequences without rebellion, his belongings were usually returned. With a repeat offence, the offender could be banished or killed.

GROUP DISCUSSION

Read the following scenario:

Serina is living in her own home with her three children. Much to her chagrin, her next door neighbour often has loud parties late at night. Both she and her children have been awakened by the noise on countless occasions. One night, Serina is awakened by loud talking and music coming from her neighbour's backyard. Her youngest begins to cry loudly and cannot be consoled. The weather has been stiflingly hot, the youngest child is teething, and Serina is suddenly very angry. She immediately marches over to the neighbour's place and has a loud argument with the male of the household, who promptly pushes Serina. She falls heavily to the ground and breaks her arm.

1. Based on the information that we have just completed reading, describe the kind of response that would have been made under traditional Native law.
2. Describe the kind of response that would have been made by all parties under the laws in Canada today.

EARLY JUDICIAL CONFLICTS BETWEEN NATIVES AND NON-NATIVE LAWS

As we noted earlier, Native clashes with European governments and, later, the Canadian government and their laws are not new. From the beginning of Native–non-Native relationships, with the imposition of every new law, Native peoples struggled and protested against inequities and interference with their own forms of laws and justice. An example of non-Native law infringing on traditional Native governments and their practices exists in what led to the Métis rebellion headed by Louis Riel. The rebellion was a struggle to defend Native lands from government encroachment. The government was involved in massive land acquisitions at the time to build the nation. The imposition of non-Native laws in this case meant that Riel was hanged for treason along with eight Cree chiefs. The Métis and Indians felt that they had been defending their lands and their laws.

Another example of historical Native–Canadian government conflict was between the Native peoples of the north Pacific coast and the Canadian government with regard to the potlatch. The potlatch is a ceremony that serves many purposes: to receive one's name, to mourn the death of a chief or feast the successor, to recognize a change in one's status, and to save face, etc. The potlatch was also seen as a means of improving one's status within the community — the more one gave away, the greater the person's status in the eyes of the community members. During the potlatch feast, gifts would be given, history would be recounted and/or re-enacted, etc. The Pacific coast peoples used elaborate masks and solid plates of copper as part of their potlatch ceremonies.

From the beginning, Europeans disapproved of and misunderstood the potlatch ceremony. William Duncan, an influential lay missionary of the church Missionary Society, wrote, "I hear that instances are numerous where persons have been hoarding up property for ten, fifteen or twenty years, at the same time almost starving themselves and wanting for clothing, have given it all away to make a show for a few hours and be thought of consequence." In 1872, the Department of Indian Affairs reported that "the Chiefs still employ practices to maintain as large a share of influence as possible. ... The Superintendent of Indian Affairs of British Columbia considers that these usages have an injurious tendency and encourage idleness." Another comment condemning the potlatch, and which also showed their misunderstanding, was in a report to the Canadian government in 1884 by Roman Catholic and Methodist missionaries: "During the whole winter, schools are deserted by all those children whose parents attend the dance ... when the winter is over they have squandered all their summer earnings and are compelled to leave their homes and roam about in their canoes in search of food, and thus neglect cultivating their lands and sending their children to school. ... Church and school cannot flourish where potlaching holds sway" (Kuyek, 1991). As a result, Sir John A. Macdonald introduced an amendment to the *Indian Act* in 1884 that banned the potlatch. The law was not repealed until 1951.

GROUP DISCUSSION

Re-read the quotations in the last paragraph. What comments indicate that these non-Natives were voicing concerns that were culturally biased?

Despite the introduction of legislation outlawing the potlatch, west coast Natives continued their traditional practices. As a result, a number of Native peoples were convicted of committing an illegal act. In the 1920s, a number of west coast Natives were charged, and the items (including ceremonial masks, copper plates, and blankets) involved in the potlatch were seized. One Native spent as much time as six months in jail for his role in the potlatch ceremony. The contraband was sold, and the ceremonial masks and copper plates ended up in private and public collections across North America. The potlatch law was controversial, however, and was overturned by the 1951 revisions to the *Indian Act*. Unfortunately, by this time, many of these Native communities were dealing with the resistance of younger generations to the potlatch practice, a ceremony with which they had little or no experience as a result of the Canadian law. Today, the potlatch is regaining a resurgence as west coast Native groups once again practise traditional ceremonies.

CONFLICTS WITH THE JUDICIAL SYSTEM

In the book *Bridging the Cultural Divide*, produced by the Royal Commission on Aboriginal Peoples (1996a, p. 21), Native issues are explained in this manner:

> From economic and social disempowerment to problems in the criminal justice system, Aboriginal peoples' issues are seemingly indivisible – one crosses over to another in an interconnected and almost continuous fashion. Alcoholism in Aboriginal communities is connected to unemployment. Unemployment is connected to

the denial of hunting, trapping and gathering practices. The loss of hunting and trapping is connected to dispossession of land and the impact of major development projects. Dispossession of land is in turn connected to loss of cultural and spiritual identity and is a manifestation of bureaucratic control over all aspects of life. This oppressive web can be seen as some of the dis-empowerment of communities and individual Aboriginal citizens.

Therefore, Native experience with judicial and other social, economic, political, and spiritual issues are all interwoven. The justice system, many argue, has failed aboriginal peoples and, with the *Indian Act*, justice has also been denied to them. Many of these events were discussed in chapter 5. In the following section, Native judicial conflicts will be studied from the following perspectives: systemic issues, community disputes, and disputes over Native rights (which include land, fishing, and hunting).

Systemic Issues

According to Statistics Canada, aboriginal people are more likely than are non-aboriginals to have some form of contact with police for what could be considered serious reasons. Aboriginals are more likely to come into contact with the police as victims of crime (17 percent versus 13 percent), as witnesses to a crime (11 percent versus 6 percent), and by being arrested (4 percent versus 1 percent).

Aboriginal people are less satisfied with the police than are non-aboriginals, although both groups seem positive toward the job the courts are doing and feel that the prison system and the parole system are doing a good job at supervising and controlling prisoners.

Statistics show an overrepresentation in sentenced custody admissions, as aboriginal youth admissions accounted for nearly one-quarter of total admissions to sentenced custody (see figure 7.1).

By the same token, aboriginal adults are overrepresented in prisons, probation, and conditional sentences. It has been mentioned that aboriginal people represent nearly 3 percent of the adult population of Canada, but account for nearly 18 percent of admissions to custody (see figure 7.2).

It can be seen that there is considerable variation across the country with respect to the presence of aboriginal people in the general adult and adult inmate populations. The western provinces and the territories are home to the largest proportion of aboriginal people in the general adult populations, but have the greatest disproportionate representation of adult admissions to custody. Aboriginal adult inmates are more likely to be incarcerated for crimes against the person than are non-aboriginals, and are considered at higher risk to re-offend.

The disproportionately high rate of Native incarceration and Native conflicts with the law first came to the attention of the Canadian public after a number of studies were released in the early 1960s. In 1965, a national survey undertaken by the Department of Indian Affairs confirmed the high rates of Native incarceration, and listed the types of offences and the number of problems experienced by the Native peoples who were processed through the system. Ten years later, the Law Reform Commission of Canada researched the same issue and reported not only findings that were similar to the earlier report but confirmed the lack of improvements to the conditions during this time. A number of conferences and reports validated

FIGURE 7.1 Aboriginal Youth Overrepresented in Admissions to Sentenced Custody[a]

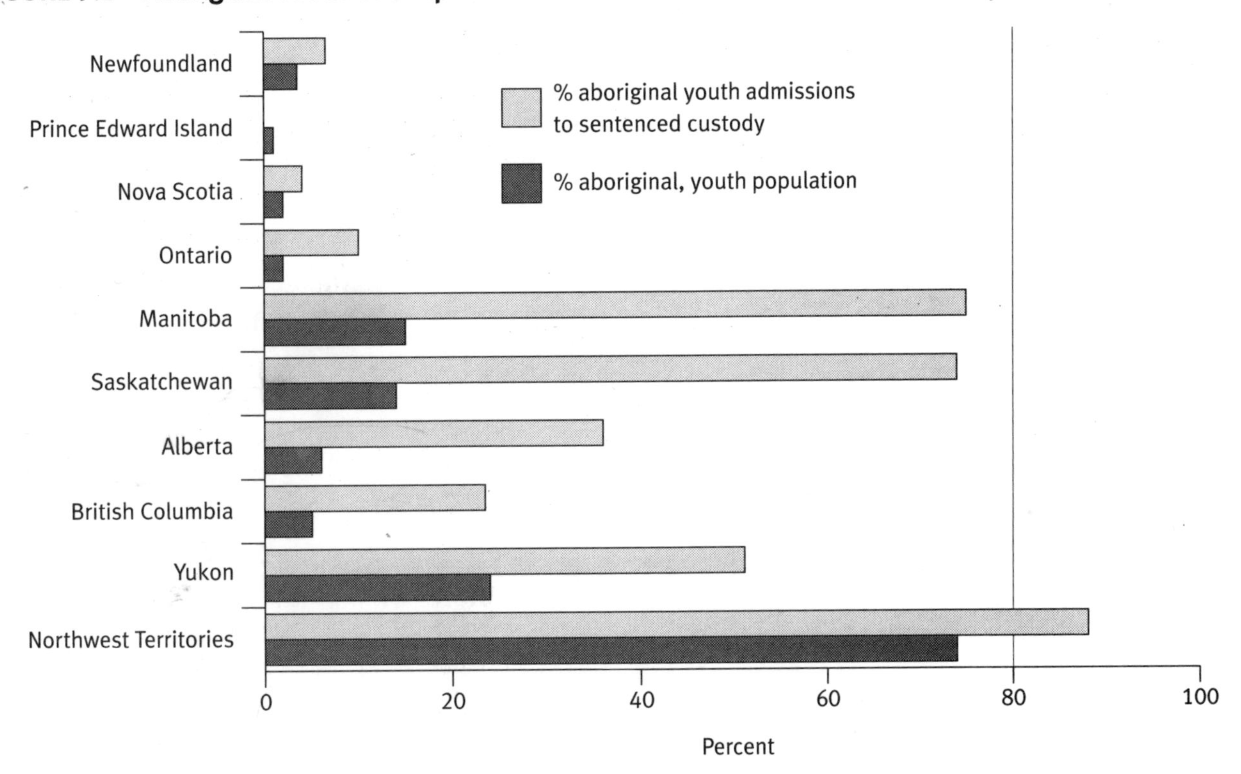

[a] New Brunswick and Quebec were unable to report sentenced custody admissions by aboriginal status. Figure excludes unknown numbers.

Source: Adapted from Statistics Canada (2001, June 14).

the findings — the Aboriginal People and the Criminal Justice System conference, Edmonton (1975), and the national survey published by the Métis and Non-Status Indian Crime and Justice Report (1975) (Laurentian University, Department of Native Studies, 1995).

What did these reports reveal? They cited a number of serious problems relating to aboriginal peoples:

- Aboriginal peoples are overrepresented in admissions to custody, especially in the western provinces.
- Native peoples experience more incarceration due to unpaid fines than non-aboriginal people (possibly as a result of poverty of Native peoples as a whole).
- Provincial offences for aboriginal peoples are predominantly related to liquor offences.
- The types of offences differ between aboriginal peoples and other offenders; however, the lengths of sentences do not differ.
- Fewer Natives are granted parole.
- A greater number of Status Indians come into conflict with the judicial system as opposed to Métis and other non-Status aboriginal peoples.
- Aboriginal peoples who are incarcerated tend to be unemployed and have lower educational achievement levels.

FIGURE 7.2 Aboriginal Adults Overrepresented in Admissions to Custody

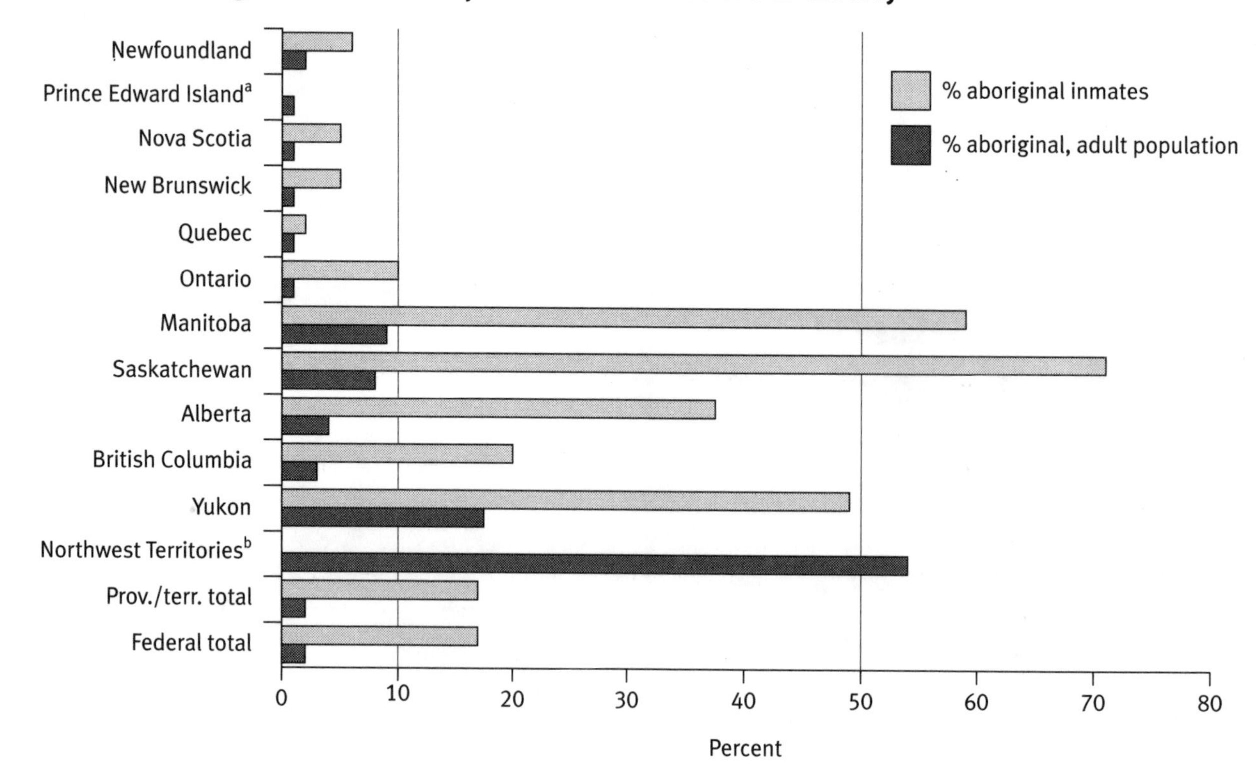

[a] Amount too small to be expressed for % aboriginal inmates.
[b] Figures not available for % aboriginal inmates.
Source: Adapted from Statistics Canada (2001, June 14).

- The high incarceration rates are influenced by systemic problems, discrimination, a general lack of cultural awareness by the judicial system personnel (police, lawyers, Crown attorneys, justices of the peace, judges, prison personnel, etc.), and cultural differences.

Today, these problems remain and the rate of severity within these issues has risen. Today's problems include the following:

- The percentage of Native peoples in jail far exceeds the national average; the rate has steadily increased.
- The rate for a person to be incarcerated more than once is higher among Natives than among the general public.
- A greater percentage of Natives are in provincial jail than in federal penitentiaries; in some cases, up to 95 percent of inmates are Native, especially in the prairie provinces. In Ontario, the figures tend to vary according to the jail or penitentiary.
- More Native women than men are in provincial jails. In Saskatchewan, Native women are eight times more likely to be arrested than non-Native women.
- In 1983, 70.9 percent of Natives expected to be incarcerated in a provincial jail by the age of 25 (compared with 8 percent for other Canadians).

- Native youth are overrepresented in the criminal justice system as juvenile delinquents; more Native juveniles come from troubled families than non-Native juveniles.
- Native offenders are less likely to receive parole, temporary passes, and opportunities to enter half-way houses.
- Native incarceration rates are higher compared with the rest of the Canadian population.
- The judicial system remains dominated by non-Native staff who make discretionary decisions with little or no Native cultural sensitivity or awareness.
- The current laws and judicial procedures are contrary to traditional Native forms of social control.

Based on their experiences with this system, the animosity and suspicion that Native peoples have toward the criminal justice system have become ingrained. Many Natives argue that they have unique cultural and spiritual needs that have remained unmet by the current judicial body. But changes in both the court and correctional institutions have been established, which may lead to greater sensitivity and declining aboriginal involvement on the "wrong" side of the criminal justice system.

Community Disputes

Disputes within the communities involve a number of specific issues that fall under two basic categories: family violence and community violence (social, spiritual, economic, and political). It is from this context that we will examine community issues.

FAMILY VIOLENCE

As we have mentioned in earlier chapters, the traditional Native concept of a family consists of both the nuclear family and extended family members — grandparents, aunts, uncles, cousins, and non-blood relations. The importance of the traditional concept of community was considered a vital link to the health of the community. Both of these structures, which are critical to the maintenance of health within aboriginal communities, have been damaged, resulting in many societal problems.

No other social problem has been so debilitating within Native communities as that of family violence. Poverty, the lack of employment opportunities, low education attainment, poor housing, and other social issues lead to family violence. The situation remains critical in many reserves and in enclaves of Native populations within urban centres. Many Natives contend that underlying all of the issues is the fact that the basic needs of aboriginal peoples remain unmet. The problem of Native family violence must be understood from this context.

The Royal Commission on Aboriginal Peoples (RCAP) confirmed the existence of a number of key family violence issues. First, for many Native children, family violence is a fact of life. The RCAP (1993) cites that many of the reports of abuse, alcoholism, and violence are first-hand experiences and that few children have grown up unaffected by these problems — Status Indians, non-Status Indians, Métis, and Inuit alike. The RCAP report (1996c) cites a 1989 study by the Ontario Native Women's Association in which 80 percent of respondents (out of 104) revealed that they had personally experienced family violence.

Many aboriginal women and their children bear the brunt of most of the violence: "spousal assault is an immense and usually hidden problem ... [the] women do not seek medical attention for injuries inflicted by their spouses, unless they absolutely have to" (RCAP, 1996b). In 1993, a study from Lethbridge, Alberta found that, out of 61 Native women, 91 percent reported personal experience with family violence. These abuses ranged from psychological abuse (blaming — 88 percent, swearing — 82 percent) to being slapped (77 percent), hit (64 percent), and punched (54 percent). Sixteen percent reported that they had been touched against their will and forced into sex with their partners. Similar findings were found in other provinces. The Ontario Native Women's Association reported in 1993 that in Ontario, 8 out of 10 aboriginal women had experienced violence; 87 percent had been physically injured and 57 percent had been sexually abused (Ponting, 1997). In yet another study examined by the RCAP (1996c), 62 percent of Native women who were murdered were murdered by their husbands. Wife assaults in Canadian society in general are reported to be one in eight; but one in three aboriginal women is a victim of wife abuse. Wife abuse problems tend to be higher on-reserve than off-reserve. Bleak reserve conditions correspond with the frequency of wife abuse that occurs.

Native women are also more likely to physically abuse their children. As a result of marital abuse, some aboriginal women respond with violence, ending up without their families and/or children, and/or in prison.

Recent data from Statistics Canada indicate that aboriginal people are more likely to be victims of spousal violence. Approximately 20 percent of aboriginal people who reported having a current or ex-spouse with whom they had contact in the last five years, reported being assaulted by their spouse, as compared with 7 percent of non-aboriginals. While there were no statistically significant differences between aboriginal and non-aboriginal male spouses, there were large variations for females. Approximately 25 percent of aboriginal women reported having been assaulted by a current or ex-spouse in the five years previous to the year that statistics were gathered, as compared with 8 percent of non-aboriginal women.

While family violence is a pervasive social problem that cuts across all demographic areas in Canada, the impact of the problem, as mentioned in chapter 6, is felt more heavily within Native communities. Most Native communities are small. The effect of family violence often is felt outside the home, affecting extended family members (who may be part of the problem) and other community members. Family violence is a problem that affects the majority of Native communities.

COMMUNITY VIOLENCE

Community violence is also a problem. This type of violence is a result of political, ethnic, economical, and spiritual differences. As pointed out, the communities were traditionally egalitarian societies that were bound together through the clan system, cultural similarities, and out of necessity (survival in a demanding environment). At present, many bands are organized into competing clans, classes, reserves, and other interest groups. Unresolved issues have resulted in physical violence. Aboriginal self-government is seen as a means to resolve and find solutions to problems, such as economic underdevelopment and violence. However, present community problems may be further exacerbated by the political elite of Native communities who have monopolies on power in such things as housing allotments, employment opportunities, and band membership decisions. Exclusionary hiring and other political practices occur as a result of this nepotism. Native communities are seeing the emergence of a social class system with a distinct gap between the "haves" and the "have-nots" (Ponting, 1997). Charges of unethical practices have been made by numerous bands throughout Canada as a recurring problem.

Religious struggles have also erupted between traditional practices and European-introduced religions. European religions have in the past and, to some extent in the present, influenced or acted as centres of power within Native communities; in some situations, they have been responsible for abuses of their power. Within the recent past, different religious denominations exerted such a strong influence within certain Native communities that all other religious groups were banned from entering or providing religious ceremonies within these communities. Author J.R. Ponting (1997) argues that church authority also imposed guidelines that were outside the boundaries of moral and ethically appropriate behaviour. In a report included in the 1993 Royal Commission on Aboriginal Peoples, Ponting reported that "Christian churches ... have a role in promoting the silence about sexual abuse and sexual assault ... there was little discussion about sexual abuse because people were taught ... that anything sexual was dirty. The effects of this silence are still being felt today."

Traditional spiritual abuse is also cited as a concern. As more elders are holding positions of honour with the communities, they may also be guilty of exercising their own forms of abuse. They are held in places of honour for their "spiritual" or "medicine" gifts. Their words are taken as spiritual teachings and elders are often given places of unconditional honour. To confront an elder whose behaviour is sexually inappropriate, for example, is difficult because of their position and influence within the communities. In more subtle ways, the elders may be using their powers for personal gain, at the expense of their community members. These abuses may enter the realm of criminal behaviour and, as such, community members must be aware of these dangers.

Other groups that are vulnerable to abuse are the elderly and the mentally or physically impaired. At another time, the elders were held in high regard as important and integral links to the cultural teachings and ways of living. Today, Native elderly suffer from neglect and abuse at the hands of their family and community members. Another area of concern is financial exploitation of the elderly, perpetuated by either family members or other community members. There is a significant incidence of incest and sexual abuse involving the mentally or physically handicapped.

Substance abuse is a serious condition that is strongly linked to family violence. However, while violence often occurs in proportion to the amount of substances being abused, other addictions need to be addressed as an equal contributor to family violence. Alcohol was found to be present in most cases involving domestic disputes, suicides, and other violent acts.

Gambling addictions have wreaked as much damage as substance addiction. The potential for child abuse and neglect and financially induced discord also occur with this addiction, which is seen by some as the newest addiction problem within Native communities. A study of Native gambling in Alberta suggested that the prevalence of gambling problems among Natives is twice that of the general population (Nechi Training and Research and Health Promotions Institute, 1994). Gambling addictions added to the poverty of Native peoples and the accompanying problems (child neglect, family violence, violence in general, etc.). Gambling addictions have the

FIGURE 7.3 Aboriginal People More Likely To Be Victims of Violent Crime[a]

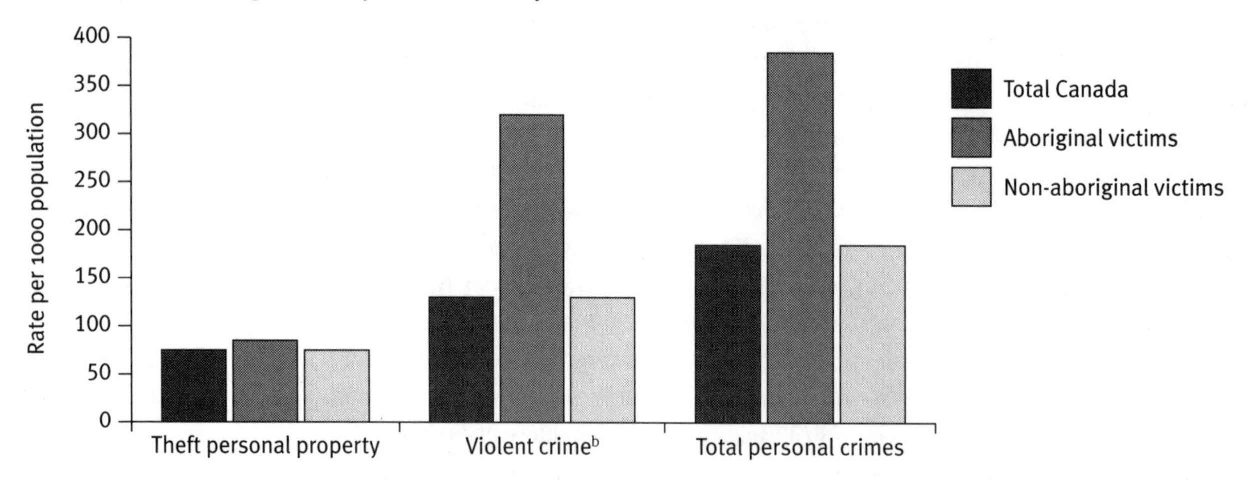

[a] Includes incidents of spousal physical and sexual assault.
[b] Includes sexual assault, assault, and robbery.
Source: Adapted from Statistics Canada (2001, June 14).

potential to cause havoc in families and communities already experiencing radical social problems. In the coming years, the societal effects of casino developments on reserve lands will be interesting to examine.

In general, aboriginal people tended to feel safe within their communities. Although they were more likely to be victims of violent crime than in other parts of Canada (see figure 7.3), aboriginals felt that their communities were safer than non-aboriginal communities, according to the Statistics Canada General Social Survey in 1999.

Native Rights Disputes

Native disputes are not all criminal in nature. As discussed in chapter 5, the Canadian government and Native peoples have had other legal battles mainly connected to the land, its resources, and/or its use. As Oren Lyons, a Six Nations Iroquois Confederacy spokesperson and faith keeper for the Onondaga nation, said, "Land is the issue, land has always been the issue" (Morrison, 1997). Aboriginal self-determination is the heart of aboriginal peoples' demands for their own judicial systems, their rights to the land, and their right to self-government.

To give First Nations greater autonomy over services and initiatives that address and combat Native criminal activities, the Canadian government has begun to transfer more of the financial and administrative power for Native services and expenditures into the hands of the First Nations governments. The changes were not made quickly but after years of lobbying and protests from Native communities and political organizations. To put this into perspective, towns and municipalities receive 100 percent of their money to run the services within their jurisdiction. As of 1998, the bands began to administer more of their affairs and the percentage given as transfer payments was approximately 90 percent of the Department of Indian Affairs and Northern Development's (DIAND) operating budget.

Gaining control over expenditures and administration has been a definite sign of progress; however, First Nations must still follow guidelines and policies set by the government with regard to the format and criteria of their services. If the bands do not follow these parameters, they are not eligible to receive the funding. Again, most of the policies have been created by the DIAND and the Canadian government and so the bands must still live within guidelines and protocols that may not always be culturally sensitive. A reform called Alternative Financing Arrangements was developed to enable bands to spend money on their own priorities during the course of a five-year funding agreement.

As discussed in chapter 5, in the minds of many aboriginal peoples, the right to govern themselves has never disappeared or was never given up. Because Native peoples are requesting self-government, in 1995 the federal government developed a self-government policy. This policy sets parameters to negotiate some degree of aboriginal jurisdiction. Each interested First Nation must negotiate as an individual nation. Only the provincial governments will bear responsibility for Métis and off-reserve aboriginal peoples. Finally, the federal policy requires that the *Canadian Charter of Rights and Freedoms* must apply to the aboriginal-based governments. Native nations will have the opportunity to create their own legislation with the powers of a contemporary public administration; they will be able to create their own constitution and pass their own laws. The First Nations who are involved in self-government have the right to operate outside the *Indian Act* if they so choose. At present, a growing number of First Nations have entered into self-government negotiations with the federal government. However, the process is new and some First Nations appear to be waiting to see the outcome on those already in process before proceeding with applications of their own.

Various battles have been brought into the court system and have been won, including

- *Hamlet of Baker Lake v. Minister of Indian Affairs and Northern Development*, [1979] 1 FC 487. At issue, the validity of aboriginal title, which existed before colonization, and its survival afterward.
- *Guerin v. The Queen* (1984), 13 DLR (4th) 321. At issue, the government's fiduciary responsibility toward the Musqueam band, and the fact that the government did not always act in the best interests of the Natives.

While a few battles have been won, others have been lost:

- The Sarnia, Ontario Chippewas lost an Ontario Court of Appeal ruling in 2000 to regain 1030 hectares of city land improperly surrendered nearly 150 years ago.
- The Squamish Nation of British Columbia reached an out-of-court settlement in a 1977 case filed against the federal government to be compensated for lands expropriated and sold. The settlement was far less than the Squamish were seeking.

The Nunavut agreement was signed in 1993 by the Inuit of the Central Arctic, Baffin, and Keewatin regions of northern Canada. Over 20 years in the making, the agreement will provide the aboriginal peoples with 2 million square kilometres in the central and eastern Arctic with direct Inuit ownership to 350 000 square kilometres. In addition, there is a cash settlement of $1.4 billion to be paid out over 14 years and a $13 million training trust fund. In terms of self-government, the Inuit will have control over a full range of provincial-type responsibilities (Smart & Coyle,

1997). The claim is in response to Inuit demands for a separate territory that reflects their values and perspectives. In the coming years the new government will be interesting to observe as it assumes control over all legal responsibilities and begins to function as a government with its own legislative assembly.

The relationship between the Canadian government and Native populations, especially where land is concerned, has not always been amiable. Tensions have arisen even today. At times, Native–Canadian government relationships have become extremely tense around the land issue. The Oka crisis was one such case.

LAND DISPUTE AT OKA

One of the more tense disputes occurred at the beginning of the 1990s when privately held lands, which had historically belonged to the Mohawk, were sold to expand a golf course. The Mohawks looked at these lands as common lands, used for recreational and other community purposes and with access to a Mohawk cemetery. In 1987, Le Club de golf d'Oka Inc. sought to have its lease renewed for a nine-hole golf course. The Kanesatake Band Council sought to block this proposal and claimed the land as its own. Friction developed, and the municipality of Oka obtained an injunction ordering the Mohawks to "abstain from interfering, disturbing, intimidating, or threatening municipal employees" (Frideres, 1997). When Le Club de golf d'Oka Inc. submitted a proposal to the municipality of Oka to expand its golf course from 9 to 18 holes, the municipality approved and sold the land for $70 000 on the condition that the land be used for the golf course expansion. As a result, in 1989, 300 Mohawks instigated a peaceful march through the streets of the town of Oka, asserting their ownership of the land and their wish that the land be maintained as a recreational site. Interspersed with this incident were other conflicts, band council tensions, and unsatisfactory negotiation processes for land unification for the Native community of Kanesatake. Subsequently, the band government was in a state of turmoil and the land agreement developed was rejected by the First Nation of Kanesatake. In retaliation, a small group of Mohawks took up arms and set up a number of barricades. Tensions escalated and gunfire was exchanged between the Quebec police and armed Mohawks behind the barricades. A police officer was killed. Consequently, the Canadian armed forces became involved and 2500 armed forces moved in. The blockades were eventually removed by the army and the main instigators of the armed siege were arrested. The dispute between the government and the Mohawk people has never been completely resolved.

One of the results of the Oka crisis was the formation in 1991 of the Royal Commission on Aboriginal Peoples (RCAP). The Mulroney government established the commission to report on the situation of aboriginal peoples in Canada. Released two years later than planned, in 1996, many of the commission's recommendations were ignored and few recommendations have been implemented as of 2004. The five-volume RCAP report was the most expensive royal commission report in Canadian history at $58 million.

Oka was not the last violent confrontation over either land rights or harvesting rights. Three further disputes captured national attention. In 1995, a group of Natives at Gustafsen Lake, British Columbia refused to leave a publicly owned ranch, claiming that the land was unceded and was used for sacred ceremonies. After an occupation of about four months and a shootout with police, Native protesters were convinced to surrender and face police charges.

Ipperwash, Ontario saw the death of a Native protester at the hands of the Ontario Provincial Police in 1995 (see appendix 7.1). The Stoney Point reserve had been appropriated from the Kettle and Stoney Point First Nation in 1942 for use as a military base. The land was to be returned after the war, but it was not, although compensation was paid. In 1993, a group of Chippewa set up camp in the territory. The military, who had been called in, withdrew from the territory in 1995 in the face of rising violence. An agreement was worked out with the federal government for the transfer of the land.

Nearby Ipperwash Provincial Park was occupied by the Chippewas. The park contained a burial ground and part of the reserve. During attempts by the Ontario Provincial Police to clear out the protesters, one of the Natives, Dudley George, was killed. In 2004, the family of the victim and First Nations activists were still calling for a public inquiry into the shooting.

Violence continued to characterize some protests. The Burnt Church band reacted when non-Natives destroyed Native lobster traps in Miramichi Bay, New Brunswick. The non-Natives feared a threat to lobster stocks in the area. The band agreed to stop fishing in 2000, but the matter of who regulates the fishery, the band or the government, remains unanswered. In 2003, Natives, primarily from the Six Nations near Brantford, Ontario, occupied land in Hamilton, Ontario that was intended to be used as an expressway. The Natives claimed that part of the land was sacred and contained Native burial sites. Protesters were removed by police, and an agreement for compensation was worked out between the Hamilton city council and the elected council of the Six Nations, although the hereditary council did not accept the agreement.

HUNTING AND FISHING DISPUTES

Hunting and fishing disputes have become more prevalent in recent years. Historically, hunting and fishing were primary sources of food for Native peoples in Canada. Community solidarity, social organization, and culture were strengthened by the necessity of food gathering, and the need to pull together for the survival of the group enhanced and promoted community involvement.

Why are hunting and fishing rights so important today to Native people? The introduction of new foods and technology lessened the importance of game and fish. However, for many Native peoples, hunting and fishing practices continue to play an important role in food gathering, especially for Native communities in the north.

Hunting and fishing rights hold symbolic importance to Native peoples both as a legal right and as a mark of cultural distinctiveness. Treaties were signed in good faith with the promise that they would not be abrogated. As an example, a report of the commissioners at the signing of Treaty 8 reported:

> Our chief difficulty was the apprehension [of the Indians] that the hunting and fishing privileges were to be curtailed. The provision in the treaty under which ammunition and twine is to be furnished went far in the direction of quieting the fears of the Indians, for they admitted that it would be unreasonable to furnish the means of hunting and fishing if laws were to be enacted which would make hunting and fishing so restricted as to render it impossible to make a livelihood by such pursuits. But over and above the provision, we had to solemnly assure them that only such laws as to hunting and fishing as were in the interest of the Indians and were found necessary in order to protect the fish and fur-bearing animals would

> be made, and that they would be as free to hunt and fish after the treaty as they would be if they never entered into it. (Morse, 1985, p. 359)

The right of Indians to hunt and fish for food on unoccupied Crown lands has always been recognized by Canada. These pursuits have been recognized by the *Royal Proclamation of 1763*, and various other legislation and treaties, as a basic component of aboriginal rights. For example, the *Royal Proclamation of 1763* promised that "[Indian lands] should not be molested or disturbed in the possession of such parts of our Dominions and Territories as, not having been ceded to or purchased by us are reserved to them or any of them as their hunting grounds." The Robinson–Huron treaties signed in 1854 promised and agreed "to allow the said Chiefs and their tribes the full and free privilege to hunt over the territory now ceded by them and to fish in the waters thereof as they have heretofore been in the habit of doing."

While these federal Acts and treaties recognize Native rights, a number of provincial statutes outline specific hunting and fishing restrictions. For example, the *Migratory Birds Convention Act* of 1916 states, "there shall be established the following close seasons during which no hunting shall be done except for scientific or propagating purposes. ... Eskimos [Inuit] and Indians may take in any season auks, auklets, guillemots, murres and puffens and their eggs for food and their skins for clothing, but the birds and eggs so taken shall not be sold or offered for sale ... [and] shall not take such birds or the eggs in a birds sanctuary."

For a long time, this legislation was not enforced for Natives. In a precedent-setting case, in May 1968, a Native man from the Northwest Territories killed a female mallard duck and was charged with breaking this law. He was charged for hunting out of season. The Native man was a member of an Indian band under Treaty 11. In convicting the Indian despite the treaty defence, the court concluded that even though the federal government had made a treaty promise with the Indians, the federal government had breached its promise by enacting the legislation that banned the killing of birds out of season (Smart & Coyle, 1997). The government is taking the stand that they are honouring treaties but also that any law passed by the provincial or federal governments supersedes these promises.

Aboriginal rights to fish and hunt continue to be fought for in court cases across Canada. In most situations, the court makes decisions based on whether the Native groups had practised hunting and fishing traditionally. For example, aboriginal fishing rights were recognized in 1990 with the British Columbia Shuswap Indians, citing that they had the right to hunt for food in their people's traditional hunting grounds (Smart & Coyle, 1997). Whether these rights prevail against federal or provincial legislation is questionable and appears to depend upon the judge's decision in each situation.

At least two court cases have been brought before the judiciary, and many more are likely to follow:

- *R v. Sparrow*, [1990] 1 SCR 1075. At issue was whether aboriginal harvesting rights took precedence over later restrictive legislation. The Supreme Court of Canada overturned the conviction and ordered a new trial. The new trial never took place because the Crown withdrew the charges.
- *R v. Adams*, [1996] 3 SCR 101. At issue was whether aboriginal harvesting rights took precedence over later laws. The Supreme Court of Canada

> allowed Adams's appeal. It was the court's view that the Mohawks of the Akwesasne Reserve have an aboriginal right to fish for food in Lake St. Francis, a right protected under s. 35(1) of the *Constitution Act, 1982*.

Although both cases were decided in favour of the Natives, these decisions do not apply to other cases on similar issues. Future cases will be decided on their individual merits.

GROUP DISCUSSION

After reading the sections on Native protests over aboriginal land rights and harvesting rights, read appendix 7.1.

1. Discuss whether you feel that Natives have the right to take violent action in order to achieve their goals.
2. Do some research on the Ipperwash crisis of 1995. Attempt to find articles that look at both sides of the issue. Discuss your opinions on which side was in the right. Discuss your opinions on the reaction of the Ontario Provincial Police at Ipperwash.

CRIMINAL MATTERS

It may seem that we have refocused on judicial matters. The issues that we have just completed discussing, however, have sometimes become criminal matters. From this perspective, it is important to understand why Native peoples have had so many problems with the judicial system in Canada.

Aboriginal peoples are overrepresented within the judicial system as offenders, but are dramatically underrepresented within the same system as staff. For example, less than 1 percent of the police force (including city, regional, and provincial and the RCMP) is aboriginal (Frideres, 1997). In provincial jails, only 2.7 percent of the employees are Native and, at the federal level, aboriginal employees comprise only 4 percent of Correctional Service Canada (Frideres, 1997). Despite the development of an aboriginal justice of the peace program a few years ago, the number of aboriginal justices of the peace and judges is dismally low. Despite an increase in the number of Native cultural awareness activities provided to judicial staff in recent years, court personnel know surprising little about Native cultures or Native peoples. The courts are well versed at dealing with written facts presented in court, but are little equipped to deal effectively with social facts, such as cultural differences and socioeconomic conditions.

The people who make decisions for Native offenders in the judicial system are predominantly non-Natives who have limited understanding of the cultural differences that exist. This is a key contributing factor to high Native incarceration rates. For example, reports by the Aboriginal Justice Inquiry of Manitoba (1989–90) and the Grand Council of the Crees (1991) concluded that overpolicing contributed greatly to the higher aboriginal crime rates. They found that police often used race as an indicator for their patrols, for arrests, detentions, etc. As an example, police in cities tend to patrol bars and streets frequented by aboriginal peoples, as opposed to private clubs whose main clientele are white business people. The report was also careful to point out that the findings did not suggest that police racism existed but rather that the police patrolled areas where they felt there would be more crime and, with a higher police presence, it meant that more criminal activity would be detected.

Another example cited was the fact that police rarely arrest whites for being intoxicated in a public place. In comparison, Native peoples are often charged with intoxication. Add a little resentment from the offenders, and they are also charged with obstruction of justice, resisting arrest, assaulting a peace officer, etc.

According to the 1991 Grand Council of the Crees study, police are also cited as providing greater law enforcement attention and less peace-keeping and other services to aboriginal communities. Pauktuutit, the Inuit Women's Association of Canada, in its report in 1995, *Inuit Women and Justice*, also confirmed problems with underpolicing in Labrador. They cite that the RCMP are not supportive of the women who are victims of family and other types of violence (Pauktuutit, 1995). The overall concern of Natives is that they are faced with overpolicing for minor or petty offences such as drinking violations and are underprotected from more serious offences such as assaults and other violent crimes (particularly family violence).

discretion
involves the choices that judges, justices of the peace, police, and Crown attorneys may make in their judicial capacity within the confines of the law

Specific professionals within the judicial system also have the right to use **discretion**, to be practised within legal parameters. However, Natives argue that discretion used without cultural sensitivity also lends itself to the high rate of Native participation within the legal system as offenders. For example, it is difficult to determine whether Native peoples are treated differently by the police. However, evidence suggests that aboriginal peoples are more likely to receive a formal charge than non-aboriginal peoples in a similar situation. In a study done in 1990, Yerxa found that nearly 80 percent of the native men he surveyed had been arrested at some time in their lives. As mentioned earlier, upon reaching court, it was found that Native peoples are less likely to receive bail, are more likely to be placed in jail, and are less likely to be placed on probation (Frideres, 1997).

systemic discrimination
laws and policies with discriminatory effects but without prejudicial intent

Native offenders also face **systemic discrimination**. As evidence, the report cites cases such as Donald Marshall, Jr. and Betty Osborne, whose status as Natives influenced the courts' finding of guilt, and subsequent incarceration, or, conversely, the findings of non-guilt for crimes perpetuated by non-Natives on aboriginal peoples.

GROUP DISCUSSION

Read the brief summaries of the Donald Marshall and Betty Osborne cases in appendix 7.2 at the end of this chapter.

1. What suggests that these cases were related to systemic discrimination?
2. What could be done to eliminate systemic discrimination within the judicial system?

Many Natives believe that the quality of justice obtained by Native peoples has been poor and is related to discrimination and irrelevance of current legislation and the judicial system to the Native culture. Native peoples claim that the Canadian legal system of justice does not reflect the perceptions of what a justice system means to many First Nations peoples. According to *For Seven Generations: An Information Legacy of the Royal Commission on Aboriginal Peoples* (DIAND, 1997),

FIGURE 7.4 Zone of Conflict in the Justice Arena

Aboriginal response to the law	Expectation of legal system
• Regular teaching of community values by elders and others who are respected in the community	• Everyone under obligation to obey set laws as determined by superior state authorities
• Warning and counselling of particular offenders by leaders or by councils representing the community as a whole	• Society reserves the right to protect itself from an individual who threatens to harm its members or its property
• Mediation and negotiation by elders, community members, and clan leaders, aimed at resolving disputes and reconciling offenders with the victims of the misconduct	• Retributive punishment: justice requires that a man should suffer because of and in proportion to his moral wrongdoing; punishment is set by legislation; judgment is imposed
• Payment of compensation by the offenders (or their clan) to their victims or victims' kin, even in cases as serious as murder	• The perpetrator is the object of sentencing; retributive incarceration and rehabilitation are means to deter and punish offenders
• In court, a front that appears silent, uncommunicative, unresponsive, and withdrawn — based on non-interference and learn-by-observation preference of behaviour and on desire to maintain personal dignity and integrity	• Expected behaviour in court: defendant must give appearance of being willing to confront his/her situation and voice admittance to error and show remorse and willingness to change; must express desired motivation for change
• Reluctance to testify for or against others or him/herself, based on a general avoidance of confrontation and imposition of opinion or testimony	• Obligated to testify and defend oneself in order to get at the facts based on an adversarial mode of dealing with legal challenges
• Often pleads guilty on the basis of honesty or non-confrontational acquiescence	• Expected to plead not guilty on the basis that one is innocent until proven guilty

Source: Dumont (1993, p. 42).

it was found that the judicial system, the courts, police, corrections centres, and other services connected with the administration of justice are elements that continue to be foreign to Native peoples. In essence, the system has rejected Native peoples, and in turn, Native peoples have rejected the non-Native justice system — at great cost to themselves. To further illustrate that Natives and mainstream Canadians have different perceptions of justice, see figure 7.4.

DISCUSSION NOTE

Figure 7.4 displays an obvious weakness in its failure to recognize the existence of differences among Native cultures. However, it does provide a means to better understand the existence of alternative perceptions of Native peoples to the concepts of law and social order.

GROUP DISCUSSION

1. Contrast the differences cited between the Canadian legal system and aboriginal perceptions with regard to justice.

2. Discuss the potential to develop a program, service, or a revision within the current judicial system based on the traditional Native system of conflict resolution.

ALTERNATIVE JUDICIAL METHODS AND PREVENTION SERVICES

The Royal Commission on Aboriginal Peoples (1996c) summarized its findings by saying that, in order for the system to meet the needs of Native peoples, elements of their cultures and traditions must be included in the current judicial system. Further recommendations included providing more funds for aboriginal court workers, more paralegal programs, and more aboriginal-focused information kits; establishing aboriginal law student programs; hiring more aboriginal court staff; and appointing more aboriginal justices of the peace and judges.

Let's look at some different services that are intended to provide more accessibility and further supports for Native peoples within the judicial system.

Aboriginal Policing

Aboriginal policing was initially developed in the early 1970s to supplement, not supplant, federal police force activities. However, an autonomous aboriginal police force was developed and, within the past few years, Native police officers have replaced most of the Royal Canadian Mounted Police and Ontario Provincial Police on reserves. Community-based policing involves a more holistic approach to policing where the duties, responsibilities, and activities of the Native police become part of other public and social institutions. Native representation in the general policing population remains very small, however. For example, only 2.5 percent of the RCMP employees are aboriginal (Frideres, 1997). See appendix 7.3 for information on the Native constables initiative.

Native Court Workers

Native court workers are workers of aboriginal descent who are available to help an aboriginal defendant in a number of ways, which include ensuring the defendant has legal counsel, interpreting the court process to the defendant, providing the defendant with advice to appeal to have their cases postponed for a variety of reasons, writing pre-sentence reports, and providing interpreting services in the defendants' Native language. The Native court worker may also access jails to provide support to the Native jail inmates. Because they are in court on a regular basis, court workers have the best opportunity to locate clients for diversion or other programs.

Native Legal Clinics

Community legal clinics provide legal advice and representation at no cost to people who cannot afford a lawyer. This is a service that is provided to all eligible Canadians. However, a number of Native legal clinics provide legal advice and services to a largely Native clientele.

Aboriginal Justices of the Peace

The Aboriginal Justices of the Peace Program was developed to train, recruit, and appoint Native justices of the peace during the early 1990s. A number of Native justices of the peace are located in areas with high populations of Native peoples in reserve and in urban settings. The justice of the peace must apply federal and provincial laws but can bring a Native understanding and perspective to the legal process. Ideally, the Native justice of the peace can lead to an interpretation of the law that will improve the quality of the justice received by Native peoples, especially in the use of discretionary practices. For example, aboriginal justices of the peace may have greater sensitivity in providing a balance between protection and safety of the community, and the right of the individual to avoid pre-trial detention, unless it is clearly warranted (RCAP, 1996a).

Alternative Criminal Justice Projects

Native alternative criminal justice projects are composed of community sentencing panels or sentencing circles, which comprise community members (often a tribunal of elders or people chosen by the community). The Crown reviews the file and discusses whether the case is appropriate for **diversion** with a First Nations coordinator. Some factors that will determine whether the case is appropriate for a diversionary process include the consent of the accused person, the gravity of the offence, a previous criminal record of the accused, and the nature of the previous criminal record. Criminal proceedings are stayed if the diversionary process is selected. However, the case can go back to court if the individual does not comply with the sentence handed down by the Native Diversionary Committee.

diversion
the removal of a case from the court system to be addressed by a panel of Native elders and community members who then decide its outcome

Within the diversionary process, there are no judges, prosecutors, or defence councillors. Lawyers may or may not be present and are only used for advice. The defence lawyer does not speak on behalf of the defendant. In some communities, the proceedings are conducted in the First Nations person's language of the accused. The community panel will listen to the information presented to them for the case and make decisions by consensus. The following sentences may be given: community service — for example, chopping wood, shovelling snow for seniors, and cleaning up the community; counselling — for example, healing circles, AA meetings, and treatment centres; fines; and restitution. However, the diversionary committee cannot impose a jail sentence. If the person complies with the panel's decision, the court will drop the charges in provincial court. However, if the person fails to comply, the provincial process can be resumed. Decisions made by the community are generally culturally relevant and provide Native peoples with a vehicle for greater self-determination. In addition, these decisions help community members develop the ability to handle problems and assume responsibility for their community members.

This diversionary system has been widely used in the United States for many years, but has only been implemented in Canada within the past 10 years. The sentencing circles enable the communities to take responsibility for the crimes committed by their members. Those who are opposed to the circles cite potential problems as a result of who may become a member of the sentencing circle (conflict of interest because of a connection between circle member and plaintiff). Sentencing circles

FIGURE 7.5 Aboriginal Youth Overrepresented in Alternative Measures[a]

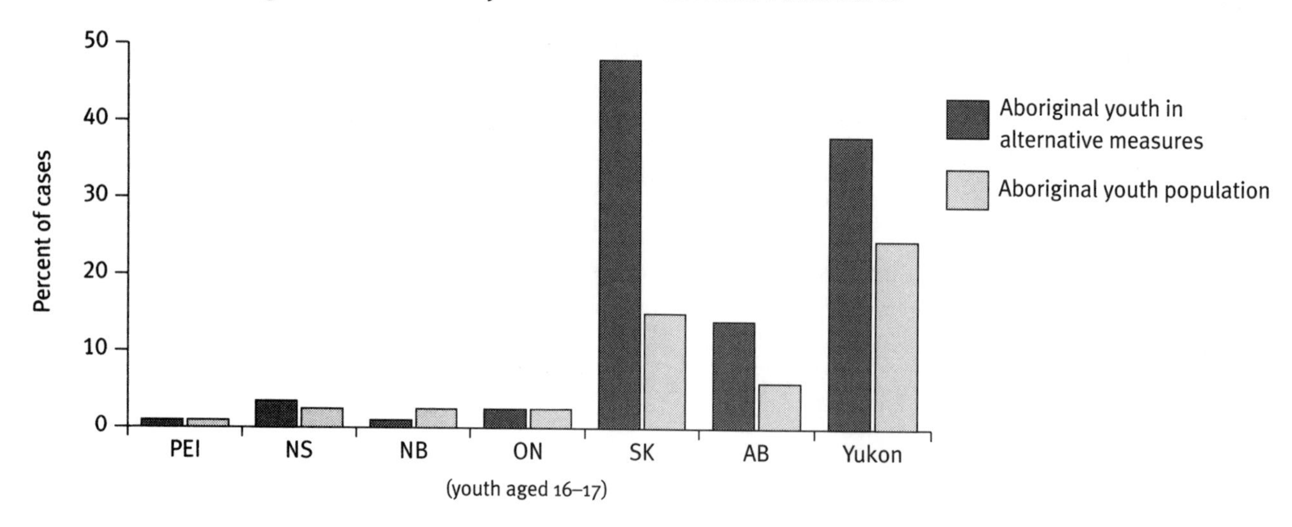

[a] Data unavailable for Newfoundland, Quebec, Ontario (youth aged 12–15), Manitoba, British Columbia, and the Northwest Territories. Unknown aboriginal status: Prince Edward Island (0%); Nova Scotia (19%); New Brunswick (11%); Ontario (youth aged 16–17) (0%); Saskatchewan (18%); Alberta (44%); Yukon (0%).

Source: Adapted from Statistics Canada (2001, June 14).

are relatively new and their value or success has yet to be determined. Also, there have been no uniform guidelines given to state what type of action will be taken toward the person charged with the crime or how the sentence will be enforced (Frideres, 1997).

The *Youth Criminal Justice Act* (2002), which replaced the *Young Offenders Act*, is modelled in part on the Native healing circle concept. The Act provides for extrajudicial sanctions for first-time offenders charged with non-violent crimes. Extrajudicial sanctions are usually community-based programs. Instead of appearing in court, an offender may appear before a committee of citizen volunteers to discuss the offence and to be sanctioned for the offence. Parents, guardians, and victims may also be involved, but the youth does not need a lawyer unless he or she specifically requests one. Sanctions include restitution, community service, anger management program, or some similar sanction agreed upon by all parties involved, including the victim. In every case, a letter of apology must be written to the victim. If the sanctions are completed during the prescribed period of time, the youth will not have a criminal record.

The Department of Justice has developed the Youth Justice Renewal Initiative to provide assistance to aboriginal communities in dealing with young offenders. The legislation, which uses restorative justice concepts that promote community healing and culturally relevant approaches to youth crime, acknowledges the traditional aboriginal approach to justice. Aboriginal communities have also been funded to develop their capacity to participate in options contained in the *Youth Criminal Justice Act*.

Already alternative measures programs are becoming overburdened. In 1998–99, according to Statistics Canada, while representing 4 percent of the youth population, aboriginal youth accounted for 15 percent of alternative measures cases, up from 12 percent in 1997–98 (see figure 7.5).

Solutions

The federal government, through Correctional Service Canada and the Department of Justice, has recognized that aboriginal-specific and culturally appropriate programs are required to address the needs of aboriginal offenders. Specifically,

- The solicitor general released the Federal Task Force Report on Aboriginal Peoples in Federal Corrections in 1989.
- The *Corrections and Conditional Release Act* provided for aboriginal-specific provisions in 1995.
- These developments provided structure to the development of a specific policy on aboriginal programming in Correctional Service Canada.
- A National Strategy on Aboriginal Corrections was developed by Correctional Service Canada in 1997 to provide some concentrated focus on aboriginal programs, aboriginal community developments, aboriginal employment/recruitment, and partnerships on aboriginal issues.
- Correctional Service Canada has the following aboriginal-specific services, programs, and initiatives targeted toward the safe and successful reintegration of aboriginal offenders:
    - ❑ Aboriginal treatment and healing programs;
    - ❑ Aboriginal-specific health strategies;
    - ❑ Research projects on aboriginal reintegration;
    - ❑ Aboriginal healing lodges (8 across Canada);
    - ❑ Halfway houses for aboriginal offenders (24 across Canada);
    - ❑ Agreements with aboriginal communities to offer services to aboriginal offenders;
    - ❑ A national employment/recruitment strategy;
    - ❑ Elders working in institutions and in the community;
    - ❑ Aboriginal liaison services in federal institutions;
    - ❑ Support to Native brotherhood and sisterhood groups;
    - ❑ Aboriginal offender employment and job placement;
    - ❑ An aboriginal gangs reintegration project.

Results of these programs are beginning to appear. According to Correctional Service Canada, there has been some measurable progress in aboriginal federal corrections in the past few years and some of the early results are very encouraging. For example, in 1998 the Research Branch determined that aboriginal healing lodges were reporting a re-offence rate of 6 percent for aboriginal offenders completing their sentence at a healing lodge, compared with a national rate of 11 percent. As well, the proportion of aboriginal offenders serving their sentences in the community has increased from 28.5 percent in 1998 to 33.3 percent in 2000.

CONCLUSION

Native peoples have placed an emphasis on the healing required by their communities. From this perspective, the bands have made concentrated efforts to assume control over the services that are provided to them. At this point, bands have now become more autonomous in their decision making and administration of education, health, community and economic development, etc. However, many of the initiatives are considered preventive in nature. For true changes to come, First Nations, Métis, and Inuit people are beginning to recognize the need for further control over their moneys, for more Native-specific services, particularly in the realm of professional services, and over their governments. The bands are recognizing that the healing of their communities cannot happen overnight, and that it has to be a just, inclusive, and sustainable process. It should not just address one issue facing Native peoples but work as a net cast widely to address all needs, at all stages and conditions, and with all age, gender, and Native cultural groups. Hence, Native communities are continuing to demand the right to be more self-determining and self-governing. To this end, aboriginal peoples are reaching into the principles of sovereignty to create new relationships with the existing governments of Canada and the provinces.

GROUP DISCUSSION

Reread the address by Chief Dan George on p. v of this book. In writing this address, Chief Dan George was really giving the Native version of the history of Canada. Consider the following:

1. When he talks about forgetting the past and getting on with the future, what suggestions would you make that could provide Native peoples with a positive vision of the future?
2. What kind of future do you foresee for Native peoples within the country of Canada? Is positive change possible, spearheaded by Native peoples themselves and by the Canadian government with its laws? Provide your own thoughts on this matter.

WORKSHEET

1. Discuss four reasons why Native peoples might question the fairness of the Canadian judicial system. (4 marks)
2. Explain the significance of the potlatch to Native peoples and identify the reasons why the Europeans disapproved of the ceremony. (2 marks)
3. Identify the key issues on which Native peoples can base their claim for legal right to self-government. (4 marks)
4. List six critical social issues that are having a negative effect on Native communities. (3 marks)
5. What conclusions can be drawn from the results of the Aboriginal People and the Criminal Justice System Conference, Edmonton (1975) and the

National Survey published by the Métis and Non-Status Indian Crime and Justice Report (1975)? (2 marks)

6. Describe the fundamental differences between the traditional Native justice system and the justice system in Canada today. (3 marks)
7. Identify four different services that are intended to provide more accessibility and further supports for Native peoples within the judicial system. (2 marks)

TOTAL — 20 MARKS

KEY TERMS

discretion

diversion

systemic discrimination

APPENDIX 7.1

Previously Secret Ipperwash Wiretaps, Film Damning for OPP

The Toronto Star

Native protester Anthony (Dudley) George didn't appear to know he was dying when he was cut down by two bullets from an Ontario Provincial Police sniper, according to a conversation recorded in a previously secret police wiretap.

"He got knocked down but he got back up," said native protester David George, who was near Dudley George the night of September 5, 1995, when he was shot at Ipperwash Provincial Park. "He didn't even know."

The comments were recorded hours after the shooting by an OPP wiretap in a maintenance building at Ipperwash Provincial Park. The OPP admitted this summer in court that it had no warrant to make the wiretap or tape.

The tape, obtained by CBC News through access to information, captures remarks and video of David George telling of his feelings of shock and disbelief after the shooting.

"We had sticks and rocks," he said in a conversation with his girlfriend, which was secretly recorded by police. "They had guns, shields and clubs. ... They opened up on us. I can't believe it ... . We weren't shooting at them. We had sticks and rocks ... I'm willing to take a lie detector and I'm sure everybody else here is." David George said that he was convinced that police had to know the protesters were unarmed.

Lawyer Jeff House, who represented several of the Stoney Point natives involved in the confrontation, said he would have liked to have seen the videotape and heard the wiretapped conversations when he was representing native people charged with assaulting police and mischief after the confrontation.

House said he could have used comments by two OPP officers who posed as journalists and filmed natives the day before the OPP marched on the park.

In that conversation, one officer asks, "Is there still a lot of press down there?"

"No, there's no one down there. Just a big, fat [expletive deleted] Indian," says the other.

Later on, one officer says, "We had this plan, you know? We thought if we could get five or six cases of Labatts 50 we could bait them and we'd have this big net and a pit."

"Creative thinking," says another. "Works in the south with watermelon." OPP Superintendent Bill Crate said yesterday that the OPP has impersonated journalists "on very rare occasions."

The OPP says the two officers have already been disciplined — one underwent native sensitivity training, the other was working on a contract that was not renewed.

Source: *Hamilton Spectator* (2004, Jaunary 22), p. A11. Reprinted with the permission of Torstar Syndication Services.

APPENDIX 7.2

Case of Donald Marshall, Jr.

The following account is a real-life example of blatant miscarriage of Canadian justice, with strong racial overtones.

On May 28, 1971, 17-year-old Donald Marshall and a friend, Sandy Seale, decided to ask for money from two men who were leaving a tavern in Sydney, Nova Scotia. After a confrontation and a scuffle, one of the men stabbed Seale and slashed Marshall. Seale died from his injuries.

Despite having no physical evidence to connect Marshall to the stabbing, the police promptly made him their chief suspect. Their case was influenced by three other teenage witnesses who agreed to testify against Marshall. None of the witnesses had seen the stabbing but after being questioned by the police, two of them agreed to testify that they had seen Marshall stab his friend. The prosecutor refused to allow the defence lawyer to see the original statement taken from the three witnesses, who contradicted their final statements to the police. In addition, one of the witnesses told both the Crown and defence lawyers that he had never seen Marshall stab Seale, but was told he could be charged with perjury if he changed his testimony. He decided to continue to testify that he had seen Marshall stab the victim.

Ten days later, a man went to the police and told them that he had been one of the men approached by the two boys on the night of the murder. He related how he had washed blood from the knife used, at his home. He gave a description of the killer, which did not match Marshall's description. However, the police did not question Marshall again, or search for the knife in the home of the man who had been accused by the witness and by Marshall. They closed their books on the case.

Outcome

Marshall spent 11 years in jail until an acquaintance of his overheard the real murderer boast of the stabbing. He told Marshall to contact a lawyer and the case was re-opened. The previous witnesses admitted to giving false evidence and the court acquitted Marshall of the murder. However, they said that Marshall was convicted largely because of his evasive statements in this trial. This statement exonerated the police and the judicial system from any blame on the grounds that the credibility of the criminal justice system would otherwise have been damaged.

Case of Betty Osborne

In a logging town in northern Manitoba, in November 1971, four young non-Native men were drinking heavily and driving around a town called The Pas. They were looking for a compliant young Indian girl with whom to have sex — Natives were thought to be "easy." They spotted Helen Betty Osborne walking by herself and tried to persuade her to join them. When she refused, they grabbed her and forced her to get into their vehicle. As they drove, they ripped off Betty's clothes while she tried to resist them. One of the men held her while another man sexually assaulted her. The other two men watched the assault while they continued to drink.

Osborne's naked body was discovered the next day in a secluded bush. She had been stabbed 56 times in her chest and back with a screwdriver and her skull had been cracked by the same screwdriver.

The young men talked about the murder to a number of townfolk over the next few years, even to a local sheriff. However, no one came forward with this information or contacted the police. By the time the police found clues pointing to the four men, they could not prove their guilt unless witnesses would come forward to identify the killers. No one did.

It wasn't until 1985 that the case was re-opened when the police placed an ad in the local paper, asking people for information on the murder of Betty Osborne. Among the responses was one from a woman who had heard one of the men bragging about the murder at a party back in 1972. It took 14 years for this woman to come forward.

Outcome

At the trial in the 1980s, only three of the four men were charged and tried before an all-white jury (20 prospective Native jurors were rejected by the lawyers). Only one of the men was convicted of the murder. The other man responsible for the actual rape and killing was given complete immunity from all charges related to the crime.

APPENDIX 7.3

First Nations Policing in Ontario

By R.C. George

The following article by Ron George, an Inspector and Aboriginal Liaison Officer for the Ontario Provincial Police, describes the basic purpose and role of First Nations Policing in Ontario.

History of First Nations Policing Agreements

In response to a need for an improved policing service to First Nations communities, an Ontario task force on policing was established in 1972. Subsequent to a comprehensive review, a federal–provincial–First Nations tripartite policing agreement was reached in 1975. The agreement specifically delegated the responsibility of the administration of that agreement, then known as the Indian Constable Program, to the Ontario Provincial Police. The First Nations and Municipal Policing Bureau (FNMPB) of the OPP currently manage this responsibility.

Self-government initiatives of the 1980's, bolstered by the *Constitution Act of 1982*, led to the Ontario First Nations Policing Agreement (OFNPA) of 1991. This tripartite arrangement embodies the agreed upon terms negotiated by representatives of the Provincial Territorial Organizations (PTO) and the independent Indian Bands that represent First Nations in Ontario with the Federal and Provincial governments. In addition to the many terms of the agreement, a provision was established whereby the participating 87 First Nations communities could negotiate a transfer of policing responsibilities to autonomous First Nation police services.

Since 1991, fifty-five First Nation communities have negotiated and implemented a total of seven self-policing arrangements. These arrangements include the Anishnabek, Nishnawbe-Aski, and United Chiefs and Council of Manitoulin (UCCM) regional police services, and single community police services in Akwesasne, Lac Seul, Six Nations and Wikwemikong ... .

The benefits of the Ontario First Nations Policing Agreement have been enormous; however, not all has gone well. Currently, there does not exist a signed document that reflects the contemporary wishes of all parties. The last signed agreement expired on March 31, 1996. Negotiations have subsequently been slow and frustrating for all parties. First Nations' negotiators maintain their request for governments to provide additional funding to enhance the overall program and increase the First Nation Constable complement appropriately. As an interim measure they have asked for an overall complement increase of 19 officers. To date, the parties have developed a framework for a future agreement; however, final seal and approval may not be realized for some time.

First Nations Constables

The Ontario Police Services Act provides that the Commissioner of the Ontario Provincial Police can appoint First Nations Constables (FNC) for the purpose of servicing First Nations communities. Currently, there are approximately 310 FNC's in the province of Ontario, 83 of whom continue to be administered by the First Nations and ɔal Policing Bureau of the OPP pursuant to the terms of the Ontario First Nations Agreement. The majority of officers are administered by and are account- he terms of the seven self-policing agreements mentioned earlier.

ions Policing Section

nistrative First Nations Policing Section (FNPS) operates within the organ- ɔarameters of the First Nations and Municipal Policing Bureau of the OPP eadquarters in Orillia, Ontario. In partnership with First Nations commu- consistent with their aspirations, negotiated policing agreements and the First Nations Policing Section is committed to facilitating a smooth transition of services to self-policing. The section consists of one Inspector (manager) and four sergeants ... .

The Future

In summary, times are changing and efforts on the part of the OPP to improve service delivery to Aboriginal people will reflect a commitment to stay current with the rapidly developing issues. The initiatives undertaken by the OPP ... are but a small attempt to improve understanding in this area. The question is, does education improve the relationship between service provider and recipient? Furthermore, does an agent of service delivery who lacks understanding of a racial group more often exhibit racist behaviour toward that group? If the answers to these questions are yes, then the opposite is also true, that when knowledge increases, the number of incidents characterized by racism will diminish. Accordingly, the pursuit of education and the resulting elements of understanding and improved service delivery to the Ontario Aboriginal community is a reasonable goal for all police service organizations.

Source: *Forum on Corrections Research, 12* (2000, January), http://www.csc-scc.gc.ca/text/pblct/forum/v12n1/index_e.shtml.

Bibliography

PREFACE TO THE SECOND EDITION

Baxter, P. (2004). A portrait of Canadian diversity. Unpublished manuscript. Georgian College, Barrie, ON.

Maynard, J. (1996). *Through Indian eyes: The untold story of native American peoples.* Pleasantville, NY: Reader's Digest.

INTRODUCTION

Curley, L. (2003, Spring). Cultures and subcultures. Instructor's notes for Diversity Awareness course. Hamilton, ON: Mohawk College.

Curtis, J.E., & Lambert, R.D. (1997). Culture. In B. Sheafor et al. (Eds.), *Basic communication and helping skills.* Toronto: Allyn & Bacon.

Harpur, T. (2004, January 4). Symbols are all about reality. *Sunday Star*, p. B7. Copyright: Tom Harpur. Reprinted with the permission of Torstar Syndication Services.

Longman dictionary of contemporary English. (1987). Harlow, UK: Longman.

Price, R.T. (1991). *Legacy: Indian treaty relationships.* Calgary: School of Native Studies, University of Alberta.

CHAPTER 1: Origins of Native Peoples

America's ancestors? Scientists uncover 30,000-year-old site in Siberia. (2004, January 2). *Hamilton Spectator*, p. B7.

Beck, P.V., Walters, A.L., & Francisco, N. (1992). *The sacred: Ways of knowledge, sources of life.* Arizona: Navaho Community College Press.

Bishop, J.E. (1993). Strands of time. *The Wall Street Journal.*

Brizinski, P. (1993). *Knots in a string: An introduction to native studies in Canada* (2nd ed.). Saskatoon: University of Saskatchewan.

Canadian Geographic. (1992, September/October).

Discover Magazine. (1993, October). Vol. 14, no. 11.

Dumont, J. (1976, February). Journey through daylight-land: Through Ojibwa eyes. *Laurentian University Review, 8*, 31–43.

Ellis, C.D. (Ed.). (1995). *Cree legends and narratives from the west coast of James Bay.* Winnipeg: University of Manitoba Press.

Goodman, J. (1981). *American genesis*. New York: Summit Books.

Intertribal Association Chattanooga (CITA). (1998, January 29). DNA and native American origins. http://www.chattanooga.net/cita/mtdna.html.

Longboat, H. (2000, January). Personal interview.

Magocsi, P.R. (2002). *Aboriginal people of Canada: A short introduction*. Toronto: University of Toronto Press.

Miller, J.R. (2002). Introduction. In P.R. Magocsi (Ed.), *Aboriginal people of Canada: A short introduction* (pp. 9–11). Toronto: University of Toronto Press.

Morrison, R.B., & Wilson, C.R. (Eds.). (1988). *Native peoples: The Canadian experience*. Toronto: McClelland & Stewart.

National Park Service. (1995, December 22). Introduction to Beringia. *Bering Land Bridge National Preserve*. http://www.nps.gov/bela/html/history.htm.

Sault Star. (1996, August 17). Sault Ste. Marie, ON.

Webster's encyclopedic unabridged dictionary of the English language. (n.d.). New York: Crown.

CHAPTER 2: Native Cultures Prior to European Contact

Berry, J.W. (1999). Aboriginal cultural identity. *Canadian Journal of Native Studies, 19*, 1–36.

Ceram, C.W. (1971). *The first American: A story of American archeology*. New York: Mentor.

Crowe, K.J. (1991). *A history of the original peoples of northern Canada*. Kingston, ON: McGill-Queen's University Press.

Dickason, O.P. (2002). *Canada's First Nations: A history of founding peoples from earliest times* (3rd ed.). Toronto: Oxford University Press.

Fiedel, S.J. (1987). *Prehistory of the Americas*. Cambridge, UK: Cambridge University Press.

Francis, D. (1992). *The imaginary Indian: The image of the Indian in Canadian culture*. Vancouver: Arsenal.

Harris, R.C. (Ed.). (1987). *Historical atlas of Canada: Vol. 1. From the beginning to 1800*. Toronto: University of Toronto Press.

Indian Act. (1985). RSC 1985, c. I-5, as amended.

Jenness, D. (1932). *The Indians of Canada*. Ottawa: National Museums of Canada.

McMillan, A.D. (1995). *Native peoples and cultures of Canada*. Vancouver: Douglas & McIntrye.

Magocsi, P.R. (Ed.). (2002). *Aboriginal peoples of Canada: A short introduction*. Toronto: University of Toronto Press.

Miller, J.R. (2002). Introduction. In P.R. Magocsi (Ed.), *Aboriginal peoples of Canada: A short introduction* (pp. 11–14). Toronto: University of Toronto Press.

Morrison, R.B., & Wilson, C.R. (Eds.). (1986). *Native peoples: The Canadian experience*. Toronto: McClelland & Stewart.

Native people. (1988). In *The Canadian encyclopedia: Vol. 3*. Edmonton: Hurtig Publishers.

O'Donnell, V., & Tait, H. (2003). Aboriginal peoples survey 2001 — Initial findings: Well-being of the non-reserve aboriginal population. Statistics Canada. Housing, Family and Social Statistics Division. Catalogue no. 89–589–XIE. Ottawa: Minister of Industry.

Ontario. Ministry of Education. Independent Learning Centre. The meaning of culture. In *Peoples of native ancestry*, Lesson 2 (pp. 17, 18–19). Toronto: Queen's Printer.

Restoule, J.P. (2000). Aboriginal identity: The need for historical and contextual perspectives. *Canadian Journal of Native Education, 24*, 102–112.

Rogers, E.S., & Smith, D.B. (1994). *Aboriginal Ontario: Historical perspectives on the First Nations*. Toronto: Dundurn Press.

Statistics Canada. (1998, January 13). Aboriginal data. *The daily*. Catalogue no. 11-001. http://www.statcan.ca/Daily/English/980113/d980113.htm.

Statistics Canada. (2003, January 31). *Aboriginal peoples of Canada: A demographic profile, 2001 census (analysis series, 2001 census)*. Cataloque no. 96F0030.

Young, N. (2004, January 18). Book review. Mark Abley, Spoken here: Travels among threatened languages. *Sunday Star*, pp. D12–D13.

CHAPTER 3: Impact of Colonization on Natives

Barraclough, G. (Ed.). (1978). *The Times atlas of world history*. Toronto: Fitzhenry & Whiteside.

Benton-Benai, E. (1998). *The Mishomis book*. Hayward, WI: Indian Country Communications.

Crowe, K.J. (1992). *The history of the original peoples of northern Canada*. Kingston, ON: McGill-Queen's University Press.

Deagan, K.A. (1992, January). Europe's first foothold in the new world: La Isabela. *National Geographic, 181*, 40–52.

Frideres, J.S. (1993). *Native peoples in Canada: Contemporary conflicts* (4th ed.). Scarborough, ON: Prentice-Hall.

Indian Act, 1876. (1876). SC 1876, c. 18.

Indian and Northern Affairs Canada & Health Canada's Medical Services Branch. (1998, February). *1997 Royal Commission Report on Aboriginal Peoples*. http://www.inac.gc.ca/strength/path.html.

Jenness, D. (1932). *The Indians of Canada*. Ottawa: National Museums of Canada.

Judge, J. (1986, November). Where Columbus found the new world. *National Geographic, 170*, 567–599.

Miller, J.R. (2002). Aboriginals: Introduction. In P.R. Magocsi (Ed.), *Aboriginal peoples of Canada: A short introduction*. Toronto: University of Toronto Press.

Morse, B.W. (1985). *Aboriginal peoples and the law: Indian, Métis and Inuit rights in Canada*. Don Mills, ON: Carleton University Press.

National Post. (1998, October 27). http://www.nationalpost.com/news.asp.

Ontario. Ministry of Education. Independent Learning Centre. Early contacts. In *Peoples of native ancestry*, Lesson 6 (pp. 4–7). Toronto: Queen's Printer.

Ontario. (2001). *History*. http://www.gov.on.ca/MBS/english/about/history.html.

Sewell, C.F. (2001). Decolonization through harmonization. *Canadian Journal of Native Education, 25*, 99–104.

Surties, R.J. (1971). *The original people*. Toronto: Holt.

Tanner, H.H., & Pinther, M. (1987). *Atlas of Great Lakes history*. Norman, OK: University of Oklahoma Press.

Waldman, C. (n.d.). *Atlas of the North American Indian*.

Wotherspoon, T., & Satzewich, V. (1993). *First Nations: Race, class, and gender relations*. Scarborough, ON: Nelson.

CHAPTER 4: Treaty Making: Loss of Native Lands and Autonomy

Assembly of First Nations. Bill C-6 – The Specific Claims Resolution Act. http://www.afn.ca/Legislation%20Info/billc6.htm.

Assembly of First Nations. Bill C-7: First Nations Governance Act. http://www.afn.ca/Legislation%20Info/bill_c.htm.

Baxter, P. (2004). A portrait of Canadian diversity. Unpublished manuscript. Georgian College, Barrie, ON.

Bell, S. (1998, December 18). Nisga'a chief offer limited citizenship to defuse non-native resentment. *National Post*.

Bill C-6. (2002). *An Act to establish the Canadian Centre for the Independent Resolution of First Nations Specific Claims to provide for the filing, negotiation, and resolution of specific claims and to make related amendments to other Acts*. Passed as the *Specific Claims Resolution Act*, SC 2003, c. 23.

Boldt, M. (1993). *Surviving as Indians: The challenge of self-government*. Toronto: University of Toronto Press.

Constitution Act, 1982. (1982). RSC 1985, app. II, no. 44.

Cote, A. (2000 July). Temagami First Nation and Teme-Augama Anishnabai re-enter into land claim negotiations with Ontario. *Anishinabeck News*. http://www.anishinabek.ca/.

Dowd, A. (2002, April 3). Vote on Indian treaties sparks anger in Canada. Reuters. Forest Conservation Portal. http://forests.org/articles/reader.asp?linkid=9591.

Energy, Mines and Resources Canada. (1991). Canada/Indian treaties. In *The national atlas of Canada* (5th ed.). Ottawa: Geographical Services Division.

Frideres, J.S. (1997). *Native peoples in Canada: Contemporary conflicts* (5th ed.). Scarborough, ON: Prentice-Hall.

Indian and Northern Affairs Canada. Historic treaty information. http://www.ainc-inac.gc.ca/pr/trts/hti/site/maindex_e.html.

Indian and Northern Affairs Canada. Specific claims status. http://www.ainc-inac.gc.ca/ps/clm/csm_e.html.

Indian and Northern Affairs Canada. Status of claims in Ontario. http://www.ainc-inac.gc.ca/ps/clm/onm_e.pdf.

Indian and Northern Affairs Canada. Treaties with aboriginal people in Canada. http://www.ainc-inac.gc.ca/pr/info/is30_e.html.

Indian and Northern Affairs Canada. (1871). *Treaty 1*. Ottawa: Indian and Northern Affairs Canada.

Morse, B.W. (1985). *Aboriginal peoples and the law: Indian, Métis and Inuit rights in Canada*. Don Mills, ON: Carleton University Press.

Obonsawin, R. Sovereignty or colonialism – The path is ours to choose. *Anasazi, 8*, 1–2.

Ontario. Archives of Ontario. (2002). Aboriginal lands and treaties in southern Ontario. http://www.archives.gov.on.ca/english/aborige/appmap2.htm.

Ontario. Ontario Native Affairs Secretariat. (2002). Milestone reached in Temagami land claim settlement. http://www.nativeaffairs.jus.gov.on.ca/english/news_181202.htm.

Price, R.T. (1992). *Indian treaty relationships*. Edmonton: Plains Publishing.

Rogers, E.S., & Smith, D.B. (1994). *Aboriginal Ontario: Historical perspectives on the First Nations*. Toronto: Dundurn Press.

Royal Proclamation of 1763. (1763). RSC 1970, app. II, no. 1.

University of Alberta. Law Library home page. http://www.library.ualberta.ca/aboutus/law/index.cfm.

Tecumseh, Shawnee Chief. (circa 1795). http://www.afn.ca/About%20AFN/description_of_the_assembly_of_f.htm.

CHAPTER 5: Native Assimilation Laws and Practices — Prior to and Within the Indian Act

Aboriginal Canada Portal. National aboriginal organizations. http://www.aboriginalcanada.gc.ca/abdt/interface/interface2.nsf/engdoc/1.html.

Assembly of First Nations. (1999). http://www.afn.ca/.

Assembly of First Nations. Bill C-7 — First Nations Governance Act. http://www.afn.ca/Legislation%20Info/bill_c.htm.

Baxter, P. (2004). A portrait of Canadian diversity. Unpublished manuscript. Georgian College, Barrie, ON.

Bell, S. (1998, October 28). Residential schools "cruel": United Church apologizes. *National Post* [Final edition], p. A10.

Boldt, M. (1993). *Surviving as Indians: The challenge of self-government*. Toronto: University of Toronto Press.

British North America Act. (1867). 30 & 31 Vict. c. 3 (UK).

Brucyhac, J. (1991, October). Otstungo: A Mohawk village in 1491. *National Geographic*.

Christmas, B. (2003, July 28). Out of the past: First Nations need to rebuild both their economies and their identities. *Time*, p. 39.

Cockerill, J., & Gibbins, R. (1998). Reluctant citizens? First Nations in the Canadian federal state. In J. Ponting (Ed.), *First Nations in Canada: Perspectives on opportunity, empowerment, and self-determination*. Toronto: McGraw-Hill Ryerson.

Council Fires. (1994, January). [Newsletter of the North Shore Tribal Council.]

Constitution Act, 1982. (1982). RSC 1985, app. II, no. 44, s. 35.

Dickason, O.P. (2002). *Canada's First Nations: A history of founding peoples from earliest times*. Toronto: Oxford University Press.

Francis, D., & Morantz, T. (1983). *Partners in fur: A history of the fur trade in eastern James Bay*. Kingston, ON: McGill-Queen's University Press.

Frideres, J.S. (1997). *Native peoples in Canada: Contemporary conflicts* (5th ed.). Scarborough, ON: Prentice-Hall.

Gradual Civilization Act. (1857). 20 Vict., c. 26 (UK).

Graveline, F.J. (2002). Teaching tradition teaches us. *Canadian Journal of Native Education*, *26*, 11–29.

Hall, A.J., & Madison, J. (1987, September). Architect of the constitution. *National Geographic*, *172*, 340–373.

Imai, S., Logan, K., & Stein, G. (1993). *Aboriginal law handbook*. Scarborough, ON: Thomson Canada.

Indian Act. (1985). RSC 1985, c. I-5.

Indian and Northern Affairs Canada. (1997, November). Aboriginal self-government. http://www.ainc-inac.gc.ca/.

Indian and Northern Affairs Canada & Health Canada's Medical Services Branch. (1998, February). 1997 Royal Commission report on aboriginal peoples. http://www.inac.gc.ca/strength/path.html.

Jenness, D. (1932). *The Indians of Canada*. Ottawa: National Museums of Canada.

Joe, R. (1998, June 24). The poetry of Rita Joe. In *MIKE'S Mi'kmaq Place*. http://fox.nstn.ca/~mtsack/more.html.

Leslie, J. & Maguire, R. (1978). *Historical development of the Indian Act* (2nd ed.). Ottawa: Department of Indian Affairs and Northern Development, Treaties and Historical Research Centre.

Macdonald, J.A. (1879, May 1). *House of Commons Debates*, p. 66.

Meissner, D. (1998, November 10). Nisga'a approve and mark treaty. *National Post*. http://www.canada.com/national/nationalpost/index.html.

Miller, J.R. (2002). Introduction. In P.R. Magosci (Ed.), *Aboriginal people of Canada: A short introduction*. Toronto: University of Toronto Press.

O'Callaghan. (1856–1857). Treaties and Historical Research Centre. Sault College Library, Sault Ste. Marie, ON.

Ojibwe history. http://www.dickshovel.com/ojib.html.

Ponting, J.R. (1997). *First Nations in Canada: Perspectives on opportunity, empowerment, and self-determination*. Toronto: McGraw-Hill Ryerson.

Quebec Act. (1774). 14 Geo. III, c. 83 (UK).

Ryan, J. (1996). Restructuring First Nations' education: Trust, respect and governance. *Journal of Canadian Studies, 31*, 115–132.

Supply and Services Canada. (1991). *Indian Act past and present: A manual on registration and entitlement legislation*. Ottawa: Queen's Printer.

Trevithick, S.R. (1998). Native residential schooling in Canada: A review of the literature. *Canadian Journal of Native Studies, 17*, 49–86.

Wikwemikong First Nation Land Claims Office. (1994). Point Grondine video footage plus Albert Peltier's explanation of the issues. Office copy.

Wotherspoon, T., & Satzewich, V. (1993). *First nations: Race, class and gender relations*. Scarborough, ON: Nelson.

CHAPTER 6: Natives and Socioeconomic Issues

Aboriginal Youth Network. Addictions. http://www.ayn.ca/health/en/addictions/addiction_alcohol.asp.

Adrian, M., Layne, N., & Williams, R.T. (1991). Estimating the effect of native Indian population on county alcohol consumption: The example of Ontario. *International Journal of Addiction, 25*, 731–765.

Boldt, M. (1993). *Surviving as Indians: The challenge of self-government*. Toronto: University of Toronto Press.

Canadian Medical Association (CMA). http://www.cma.ca/.

Canadian Medical Association (CMA). (1994). *Bridging the gap: promotion of health and healing for aboriginal peoples in Canada*. Ottawa: CMA.

Canadian Medical Association (CMA). (1996). *Canadian Medical Association News, 6*(1).

Canadian Psychiatric Association Section on Native Mental Health. (1985, October). *Suicide in the North American Indian: Causes and prevention*. Shannonville, ON.

Carson, C.C., Butcher, J.N., & Coleman, J.C. (1988). *Abnormal psychology and modern life* (8th ed.). Glenview, IL: Scott Foresman.

Clarkson, L. (1992). *Our responsibility to the seventh generation: Indigenous people and sustainable development*. Winnipeg: International Institute for Sustainable Development.

Correctional Service Canada. Aboriginal Initiatives Branch. Aboriginal offenders: Overview. http://www.csc-scc.gc.ca/text/prgrm/correction/asissues/know/7_e.shtml.

Correctional Service Canada. Aboriginal Initiatives Branch. Facts and figures: Aboriginal offender statistics. http://www.csc-scc.gc.ca/text/prgrm/correction/abissues/know/4_e.shtml.

First Nations and Inuit Health Branch, Health Canada. (2004). In-house statistics. Ottawa: Public Works and Government Services Canada..

Fleras, J., & Elliott, J.L. (1996). *Unequal relations: An introduction to race, ethnic and aboriginal dynamics in Canada*. Scarborough, ON: Prentice-Hall.

Frideres, J.S. (1997). *Aboriginal peoples in Canada: Contemporary conflicts* (5th ed.). Scarborough, ON: Prentice-Hall.

Hull, J. (2000). *Aboriginal postsecondary education and labour market outcomes: Canada 1996*. Ottawa: Indian and Northern Affairs Canada.

Indian and Northern Affairs Canada. Social assistance program. http://www.ainc.inac.gc.ca/ps/soci_e.html.

Indian and Northern Affairs Canada. (1990). *Highlights of aboriginal conditions*. Ottawa: Supply and Services Canada.

Indian and Northern Affairs Canada. (1997). *Basic departmental data 1997*. http://www.ainc-inac.gc.ca/.

Indian and Northern Affairs Canada. (2001). *Basic departmental data 2001*. Catalogue no. R12-7/2000E. http://www.ainc-inac.gc.ca/.

Levinthal, C.F. (1999). *Drugs, behavior, and modern society*. Needham Heights, MA: Allyn & Bacon.

MacMillan, H.L., et al. (1996). Aboriginal health. *Canadian Medical Association Journal, 155*, 1569–1598.

McGregor, G. (2001). Debate rages over native alcoholism. *First Nations Drum*. http://www.firstnationsdrum.com/Sum2001/Cult-debate.htm.

Malchy, V., et al. (1997). Suicide among Manitoba's aboriginal people: 1988 to 1994. *Canadian Medical Association Journal, 157*, 1133–1138.

O'Donnell, V., & Tait, H. (2003). Aboriginal peoples survey 2001 — Initial findings: Well-being of non-reserve aboriginal population. Statistics Canada. Housing, Family and Social Statistics Division. Catalogue. no. 89-589-XIE (pp. 13–15). Ottawa: Industry Canada.

Postl, B. (1997). It's time for action. *Canadian Medical Association Journal, 157*, 1665–1666.

Reserves rack up $300 million in deficits, native leaders blame underfunding. (2004, February 18). *Turtle Island News*, p. 1.

Royal Commission on Aboriginal Peoples (RCAP). (1996). *Report*. Ottawa: Supply and Services Canada.

Royal Commission on Aboriginal Peoples (RCAP). Indian Affairs web page. Social development: health and social indicators. http://www.inac.gc.ca/strength/socio.html.

Square, D. (1997). Fetal alcohol syndrome epidemic on Manitoba reserve. *Canadian Medical Association Journal, 157*, 59–60.

Statistics Canada. Female inmates, aboriginal inmates, and inmates serving life sentences: A one day snapshot (Juristat). http://www.statcan.ca/english/IPS/Data85-002-XIE1999005.htm.

Statistics Canada. Selected educational characteristics. http://www12.statcan.ca/english/census01/products/standard/themes/RetrieveProductTabl.html.

Statistics Canada. Selected income characteristics. http://www12.statcan.ca/english/census01/products/standard/themes/RetrieveProductTabl.html.

Statistics Canada. Selected labour force characteristics. http://www12.statcan.ca/english/census01/products/standard/themes/RetrieveProductTabl.html.

Statistics Canada (1991, 1993, 1996). *The daily*. Catalogue no. 11-001. http://www.statcan.ca/Daily/English/980113/d980113.html.

Statistics Canada. (1991). *Aboriginal peoples survey*. Ottawa: Supply and Services Canada.

Statistics Canada. (1996). *Aboriginal peoples survey*. Health status. Ottawa: Supply and Services Canada.

Statistics Canada. (1996). *Aboriginal peoples survey*. Mortality statistics. Ottawa: Supply and Services Canada.

Statistics Canada. (1996). *Aboriginal peoples survey*. Substance abuse. Ottawa: Supply and Services Canada.

Statistics Canada. (2001). *Aboriginal peoples of Canada: A demographic profile*. Catalogue no. 96F0030XIE2001007. Ottawa: Supply and Services Canada.

Statistics Canada. (2001). *Aboriginal peoples survey*. Ottawa: Supply and Services Canada.

Statistics Canada. (2001). *Canadian community health survey, 2000–01*. Ottawa: Supply and Services Canada.

Statistics Canada. (2003, January 31). *Aboriginal peoples of Canada: A demographic profile, 2001 census (analysis series, 2001 census)*. Catalogue no. 96F0030.

Statistics Canada. (2003, September). *Aboriginal peoples survey 2001 — Initial findings: Well-being of the non-reserve aboriginal population, 2001*. Catalogue no. 89-589.

Stepan, C. (2003, October 11). Aboriginals: Now I know who I am. *Hamilton Spectator*, p. F5.

Tookenay, V.F. (1996). Improving the health status of aboriginal people in Canada: New directions, new responsibilities. *Canadian Medical Association Journal, 155*, 1581–1583.

Young, T.K., & Sevenhuysen, G. (1989). Obesity in northern Canadian Indians: Patterns, determinants, and consequences. *Canadian Mental Health Association Journal, 49*, 786–793.

CHAPTER 7: Natives and Current Judicial Issues

Aboriginal Justice Inquiry of Manitoba. (1989–1990).

Asbury, K. (1996). Fact sheet on the disappropriate imprisonment of native people in Ontario. Toronto: Ontario Native Council on Justice.

Canadian Charter of Rights and Freedoms. (1982). Part I of the *Constitution Act, 1982*, RSC 1985, app. II, no. 44.

Canadian Criminal Justice Association. (2000, May 15). Aboriginal peoples and the criminal justice system. A special issue of the *Bulletin*. Ottawa. http://www.ccja-acjp.ca/en/aborit.html.

Correctional Service Canada. Aboriginal Initiatives Branch. Facts and figures. http://www.css-scc.gc.ca/text/prgrm/correctional/abissues/know_e.shtml.

Correctional Service Canada. Aboriginal Initiatives Branch. Facts and figures: Aboriginal offenders overview. http://www.csc-scc.gc.ca/text/prgrm/corectional/abissues/know/7_e.shtml.

Correctional Service Canada. Aboriginal Initiatives Branch. Facts and figures: Aboriginal offender statistics. http://www.csc-scc.gc.ca/text/prgrm/correctional/abissues/know/4_e.shtml.

Department of Indian Affairs. (1872).

Department of Indian Affairs and Northern Development (DIAND). (1997). *For seven generations: An information legacy of the Royal Commission on Aboriginal Peoples.* Ottawa: Libraxus. http://www.libraxus.com/RCAP/.

Department of Justice Canada. Aboriginal communities. http://www.justice.gc.ca/en/ps/yj/partner/aborig.html.

Department of Justice Canada. Canada's Youth Criminal Justice Act. http://canada.justice.gc.ca/en/dept/pub/ycja/youth.html.

Dickason, O.P. (2002). *Canada's First Nations: A history of founding peoples from earliest times* (3rd ed.). Toronto: Oxford University Press.

Dumont, J. (1993). Justice and aboriginal peoples. *Aboriginal peoples and the justice system: Report on the Round Table on Aboriginal Justice Issues by the Royal Commission on Aboriginal Peoples.* Ottawa: Supply and Services Canada.

Frideres, J.S. (1997). *Native peoples in Canada: Contemporary conflicts* (5th ed.). Scarborough, ON: Prentice-Hall.

George, R.C. (2000, January). First Nations policing in Ontario. *Forum on Corrections Research, 12.* http://www.csc-scc.gc.ca/text/pblct/forum/v12n1/index_e.shtml.

Grand Council of the Crees. (1991).

Indian and Northern Affairs Canada. Justice. http://www.ainc-inac.gc.ca/ps/jus_e.html.

John Howard Society. (2003, March). *Youth criminal justice manual.* Hamilton, ON.

Kuyek, J. (1991). *Substance abuse: Legal and ethical considerations.* Sudbury, ON: Cambrian College.

Laurentian University. Department of Native Studies. (1995). *Aboriginal people and the criminal justice system.* Sudbury, ON: Laurentian University Press.

Law Reform Commission of Canada. (1991). *Aboriginal peoples and criminal justice.* Ottawa: Minister of Justice.

Morrison, A.P. (1997). *Justice for natives: Searching for common ground.* Montreal: Aboriginal Law Association of McGill University.

Morse, B.W. (1985). *Aboriginal peoples and the law: Indian, Métis and Inuit rights in Canada.* Don Mills, ON: Carleton University Press.

Nechi Training and Research and Health Promotions Institute. (1994). *Spirit of bingoland: A study of problem gambling among Alberta native people.* Edmonton: Alberta Alcohol and Drug Abuse Commission.

Pauktuutit, The Inuit Women's Association of Canada. (1995). Appendix: Violence against women and children: the concerns of Labrador women. In *Inuit women and justice: Progress report no. 1.* Ottawa.

Ponting, J.R. (1997). *First Nations in Canada: Perspectives on opportunity, empowerment, and self-determination.* Toronto: McGraw-Hill Ryerson.

Previously secret Ipperwash wiretaps, film damning for OPP. (2004, January 22). *Hamilton Spectator*, p. A11.

Royal Commission on Aboriginal Peoples (RCAP). (1993). *Violence against aboriginal women*. Ottawa: Supply and Services Canada.

Royal Commission on Aboriginal Peoples (RCAP). (1996a). *Bridging the cultural divide*. Ottawa: Supply and Services Canada.

Royal Commission on Aboriginal Peoples (RCAP). (1996b). *Public hearings*. Hay River, NWT, 93-06-17: 110. Ottawa: Supply and Services Canada.

Royal Commission on Aboriginal Peoples (RCAP). (1996c). *Report*. Ottawa: Supply and Services Canada.

Silverman, R.A., & Neilsen, M.O. (1992). *Aboriginal peoples and Canadian criminal justice*. Toronto: Harcourt Brace.

Smart, S.B., & Coyle, M. (1997). *Aboriginal issues today: A legal and business guide*. Toronto: International Self-Counsel Press.

Solomon, A. (1990). The wheels of injustice. *Songs for the people: Teachings on the natural way*. Toronto: W.C. Press.

Statistics Canada. Female inmates, aboriginal inmates, and inmates serving life sentences: A one-day snapshot (Juristat). http://www.statcan.ca/english/IPS/Data/85-002-XIE1999005.htm.

Statistics Canada. (2001, June 14). *Aboriginal people in Canada (Canadian Centre for Justice Statistics series)*, 1999 ed. Catalogue no. 85F0033.

Wotherspoon, T., & Satzewich, V. (1993). *First Nations: Race, class, and gender relations*. Scarborough, ON: Nelson.

Yerxa, J. (1990). *Report on the survey of the First Nations of Alberta*. Edmonton: John Yerxa Research Inc.

Glossary of Terms

A

aboriginal rights
special rights, such as the right to hunt and fish, held by aboriginal people

aboriginal
original people of an area; may include First Nations, Métis, and Inuit

acculturation
the merging of cultures as a result of prolonged contact with each other; in essence, the cultures develop cultural modifications

administration
the execution of public affairs as distinguished from policy making

annuities
yearly amounts of goods or moneys received by the Natives based on specific treaty agreements

assimilation
an act, process, or instance of absorbing a population or a cultural group into another's distinctive cultural traditions

autonomy
self-government; independence

B

Bill C-31
1985 amendment to the *Indian Act* that allowed for reinstatement of status to Natives who had lost it for a variety of reasons

British North America Act
a statute enacted on March 29, 1867 by the British Parliament providing for the confederation of Canada

C

clan
a group of people who share a common ancestor

constitution
the core system of rules and principles by which a nation or group is governed

cultural genocide
deliberate and systematic destruction of the culture, traditions, language, and ways of being of a specific cultural group

culture
abstract values, beliefs, and perceptions of the world that are shared by a society and reflected in the behaviour of the people in a society

D

denomination
a religious organization

devolution
the return of control of programs and services to Native peoples

discretion
involves the choices that judges, justices of the peace, police, and Crown attorneys may make in their judicial capacity within the confines of the law

diversion
the removal of a case from the court system to be addressed by a panel of Native elders and community members who then decide its outcome

E

egalitarian society
the belief in human equality, especially with respect to social, political, and economic rights and privileges

enfranchisement
loss of Native status through the *Indian Act* of 1876

extinguish
to end something permanently by process or agreement

F

fast
from a traditional Native perspective, to fast is to abstain from food and, in some cultural practices, water; the intent of a fast is to purify one's self to connect with the spiritual world

fiduciary responsibility
legal duty to act in the best interest of another person; usually seen in the relationship between guardian and ward

First Nations
refers to Indians as opposed to other aboriginal groups such as Inuit or Métis

H

holistic
balance in all aspects of life — emotional, physical, mental, and spiritual

I

Indian Act
the principal federal statute dealing with Indian status, local government, and the management of reserve lands and common moneys

indigenous
living or occurring naturally in a region; similar to aboriginal, but can be applied to non-native groups

interdependence
being influenced or determined by another

L

Lands for Life
land-use planning undertaken by the Ontario government for Crown lands; Crown lands are currently used by Natives as part of their treaty rights relating to hunting and fishing

language
the words, their pronunciations, and the methods of combining them used and understood by a community

legislation
laws passed by the federal and provincial governments; a way of defining the powers of an institution

linguistics
the study of general categories of human speech

M

Meech Lake accord
the 1987 agreement between the provinces and the federal government regarding amendments to the Canadian Constitution

N

Native
a term for First Nations peoples

O

oral tradition
information that is passed from one person to another by word of mouth

origins
the place or source from which things come; their beginning

P

paternalism
a system under which an authority undertakes to supply the needs and/or regulate the conduct of those under its control in matters affecting them as individuals, as well as in their relations to authority and to each other

policy
a plan of action that has been chosen and that guides or influences future decisions

R

reserve
the land base with which Indian status is integrally connected that was set aside for Indians and held in trust by the government through the Department of Indian Affairs

royal commission
an official inquiry appointed by Parliament to investigate matters of public concern

S

Seven Grandfathers
traditional Native teachings describing the qualities of wisdom, love, respect, bravery, honesty, humility, and truth by which a person's life should be guided

sovereignty
self-government

spiritual
for Natives, to be spiritual is to respect and believe that all things in the world are alive and have a role in the land or "Mother Earth"

subculture
a group that has the general characteristics of a culture but also has distinctive features in their values, norms, and lifestyles

systemic discrimination
laws and policies with discriminatory effects but without prejudicial intent

T

treaty
"an international agreement between States in written form and governed by the international law, whether embodied in a single instrument or in two or more related instruments and whatever its particular dimension" (Morse, 1985)

U

usufructuary right
the right to use and benefit from the land, based on its traditional use and occupancy

Index

D

E

F

G

M

N

O

P

T

U

V

W

Y